WHAT ARE YOU DOING?

1/6/82

What Are You Doing?

HOW PEOPLE ARE HELPED
THROUGH REALITY THERAPY

Cases edited by Naomi Glasser

HARPER & ROW, PUBLISHERS, New York

Cambridge, Hagerstown, Philadelphia, San Francisco,
London, Mexico City, São Paulo, Sydney

1817

FIRST EDITION

Designer: Lydia Link

Library of Congress Cataloging in Publication Data
Main entry under title:
What are you doing?
1. Reality therapy—Case studies. I. Glasser,
Naomi.
RC489.R37W33   616.89′14   80–7586
ISBN 0–06–011646–3

---

80 81 82 83 84 10 9 8 7 6 5 4 3 2 1

TO
Zita Gluskin
AND
Joan Miller

Contents

viii / *Contents*

Preface

In 1962 William Glasser gave his first public speech on reality therapy. It was not easy for him to give a name to the principles of therapy he had been developing with G. L. Harrington, M.D., and putting into practice, but if he was going to talk about it, he needed to name it, and reality therapy it became.

By 1979 reality therapy had been applied to entire programs in agencies and institutions and had become the basis for educational programs in many schools and even a number of school districts. Thousands of people throughout the United States and Canada were studying it in courses leading to certification as reality therapists, and four hundred people, many in private practice, had already been certified.

In the early days, just after *Reality Therapy* had been published and the interest had become instantly evident, I sometimes wondered if the therapy was so connected with William Glasser, the man, that it would last only as long as he did. I no longer believe this is a possibility. Professional people working in a diversity of situations, coming from all kinds of backgrounds, with personalities as different as the cases they treat and styles that are distinctly individual, all use reality therapy for the same reason. It works.

The case histories are all by therapists who have been trained, tested, and granted a certificate by the Institute for Reality Therapy based in West Los Angeles. I selected the cases to show as many different kinds of problems as possible, but some were selected for other reasons. Two marital counseling cases, for example, appear similar—they both involve childless couples in their late twenties—but the therapists have such different personalities and styles I felt it was important to include both. But whether the case history is about a mute boy, a seriously delinquent and depressed youth in a treatment center, or a middle-aged alcoholic, what it has in common with the others are the steps and principles of reality therapy, which are explained in Chapter 4, by William Glasser. I hope that as you read the cases you will be able to follow the reality therapists as they use these steps and learn how people can look at what they are doing and find more satisfying ways to live.

NAOMI GLASSER

Introduction

This book is an attempt to fill the gap that often exists between theory and practice. It is one thing to know reality therapy, and another to read detailed accounts of people who have been greatly helped by a variety of reality therapists. From my experience it would seem that this illustrative book would particularly fill the needs of huge numbers of people contemplating therapy, and even some in therapy, who have no specific idea of what therapy is all about. Here is a chance for them to learn how people like themselves have gone to a therapist and received help.

The cases are so varied that anyone seeking help should be able to identify with at least one, if not more than one, client in this book. There is nothing abstract or difficult to understand—what happens is clear cut and easily applicable to anyone. By reading all the cases, you can get a clear understanding of the principles even if the problems do not directly correspond with your own. In most instances, these are principles that anyone can use regardless of what therapy one becomes involved with.

Another valuable role this book can play is in assisting people who have close relatives and friends who need help. Knowing what successful help is, you can aid people you care about in getting successful help and also, perhaps more important, support them while they are in the process. The role that supportive people can play will be made clear in reading many of these cases. Especially important is that they learn to use the question, "What are you doing?" instead of the usual, not too helpful remark, "How are you feeling?" Here, over and over, it's the doing that counts. When that begins to happen the feelings take care of themselves.

This book can also serve as a teaching aid in every area of the helping professions and in the direct training of counselors and therapists. Here are actual cases that can be studied, discussed, and criticized. Students can role-play the clients and learn how they might duplicate the work of the therapists, experts all, and in so doing discover how difficult the simple and clear-cut steps are to apply in practice. Teachers who teach therapy and counseling can use this book to support their theoretical presentations, to point out to students that here is a theory that is backed up in practice—and that, most of all, it is a theory that can be taught, in a large variety of situations. Finally, like those who contemplate therapy, and can identify with one or more clients, those who are learning will be able to identify with at least several of the therapists, some of whom work in public agencies.

Besides these considerations, there is the fact that the people of this book, both clients and therapists, are interesting people whom you might wish to meet. What they have accomplished is, in some instances, so dramatic as to be almost beyond belief, and even the less dramatic cases have the human appeal that is always associated with learning about people who have struggled successfully against the odds. I still never fail to learn and be encouraged by seeing people succeed—and I think it will be hard for anyone to read this book and not experience that same warm feeling.

WILLIAM GLASSER, M.D.

WHAT ARE YOU DOING?

1

Jennifer Joins the Club

A Fifteen-Year-Old Girl Gives Up Self-Destructive Behavior

Ann Lutter

As a reality therapist, I was strongly interested in making friends this first session, yet I, Ann Lutter, was on the stand as much as my client, Jennifer Wykes. It was all part of the agreement Jenny had made with her father: she would agree to go away to school as well as to see a therapist, and he would agree to "renegotiate" at Thanksgiving time. If she was still unhappy at Mendon Academy— the school that had been chosen, in Vermont—by Thanksgiving, she could return home. As a further part of the compromise, Mr. Wykes was permitting her to choose her own therapist—although the choice was only between the school counselor and me. In this first session, then, she was feeling me out as much as I was her, so I decided to start out on good, solid ground—something safe, something neutral. Vermont.

"Is this your first time in Vermont, Jenny?"

"Yeah."

"Do you like it?"

"No."

Ah well, I thought to myself, at least I won't have to worry about getting a word in edgewise. "Do you have any interests? What do you like to do?"

"Get high and make love."

"Anything else you like to do?"

"No."

"I can understand that—whatever you do really keeps you hopping."

Jenny's refusal to open up did not surprise me, since her father's phone call had prepared me beforehand. ". . my ex-wife is trying to get Jennifer committed to a correctional center for juveniles. Apparently she found some writings in Jennifer's room and is using them as evidence. Jennifer's behavior is certainly destructive—very destructive, and especially to herself—but committing her is not going to help.

"That's why I'm calling you. Jennifer's been seeing a psychoanalyst for six years now. Six years, three times a week, and it's done absolutely nothing for her. I think it's time to try something else."

He had read William Glasser's *Reality Therapy*,[1] and after calling Dr. Glasser, had been referred to me.

Because he was disillusioned with psychoanalysis and to put his daughter in a new environment, Mr. Wykes was sending Jenny to Mendon in Vermont. His great hope was to separate her from what he termed "the East Coast Manson crowd" with whom she had been spending all her time. Most of them quite a bit older than Jenny, this crowd would pass the day in Central Park, where they experimented with a wide range of drugs—LSD, pot, amphetamines, barbiturates, and possibly others. Jenny was becoming more and more a part of the group, and when she began to talk of one of them as her lover, Mr. Wykes decided something had to be done.

"For one thing," he explained, "he's twenty-four years old. You have to remember that Jennifer's only fifteen, which means she's still highly impressionable. I'm sending her to Vermont just so she can escape that kind of influence, so she'll have time out to think."

It seemed a difficult situation for him. He was divorced, and Jenny lived with her mother, not him. In addition, his business required a fair amount of traveling, so he could hardly stay on top of the situation as much as he wished.

As the interview progressed, it became obvious that Jenny didn't like the idea of leaving her friends for a strange new school in New England. This provided Jenny with yet another reason for rebelling against her parents' wishes.

"I see by your boots you're into horses. You must like riding."

"Yeah, but I'm not going to ride at Mendon."

[1] New York: Harper & Row, 1965.

It seemed Jenny had been sent West that past summer to a riding camp—against her will. Naturally, she hated the whole experience, and her refusal to ride this fall was simply an act of defiance. She'd "show them."

When I asked her about her one sister, who was three years older, I discovered that she was "square" and "as much of a fuck-up as everyone else." "To be square," I learned later, meant sleeping with only one person and limiting oneself to one drug—perhaps even something as staid and conventional as pot or hash, as she put it.

Jenny viewed the others in her family in just as demeaning a way. As far as she was concerned, her whole life was glutted with people she hated. Nobody had any insight—her father, her mother, her step-mother; they were all just "fuck-ups." Only she and her friends knew and understood the proper way to live, only they were sensitive toward others. Consequently, I was going to have to deal not only with a certain amount of stubbornness on Jenny's part but with a rather limited, egocentric attitude as well.

In fact, this same attitude permeated the way in which she dealt with her very own peer group. One of the reasons why she "knew" Mendon would be awful was the fact that the students would all be about the same age as she. Jenny's friends in New York were up to nine years older, and so anyone her own age seemed immature beyond comparison. "I can only relate to Dave and his friends," she would say. "Everybody else is fucked up. That scene is too fucking intense."

"Does your family think you're fucked up?"

"Of course, why would I be here?"

"Are you?"

"No."

When the session had ended, I asked her what her choice in therapists would be. She answered, "You." And that was that.

Naturally, the first few sessions were spent working toward the same goal—namely, making friends. Making friends and sharing. For, as we worked our way further into her ideas, we also worked our way into each other's private lives.

"I hate my mother," she would say. "I never want to see her again." In reacting to such a statement, I never passed judgment. Opinions would only have destroyed the rapport we were building. Given her strong and stubborn nature, opinions would only have driven her further in the opposite direction. As it was, I chose to share similar experiences in my own past.

"Look, Jenny, I can understand what you're feeling. For over twenty years I hated my own mother. She was alcoholic, and sometimes she turned that house into an absolute hell for me. I hated her for that. And I did everything in my power to make life miserable for her. But I was the one who lost out on that deal, not her. Here I was staying up late at night, thinking of ways to get back at her, while she was safe in bed, sleeping like a baby. It wasn't getting me anywhere. All I'm saying, Jenny, is that it took me twenty years to learn to let her live her own—what I would call—fucked-up life. Now I don't let her bother and upset mine, but if only I had learned that twenty years ago."

By opening up, I not only established a greater trust between us, I encouraged Jenny to begin sharing with me.

Nevertheless, for a large part of those first few sessions, Jenny spent her time whining and complaining. Everyone, but absolutely everyone, was a member of the "Fucked-Up Club," and as far as she was concerned, her parents were up to date on their dues.

Her mother didn't trust her at all. If Jenny came home twenty minutes late, her mother was already on the phone to the police. And yet, there had been a time when Jenny did confide in her mother—or, in any case, had tried. Apparently, as her friends began to experiment with sex and various drugs, Jenny would talk about such things with her mother from time to time. Gradually gaining more confidence, Jenny no longer talked about those topics in the abstract but would relate stories of acquaintances or friends who were experimenting. And eventually she confided in her mother as a true friend would—she began to share with her mother her own experiences with drugs and sex. That was when "the fucking shit hit the fan."

"I trusted her, but she turned right around and used it against me. Tell me that isn't fucking intense—I trust her and she takes advantage of it. I hate her."

As a result of this, Jenny spent long nights awake at Mendon, thinking of ways to get back at her mother. She wanted very much to hurt her. There was something else, too. Apparently some of her mother's lovers had tried to seduce Jenny while her mother was occupied with something in another part of the house, and when Jenny reported such happenings, her mother refused to believe them.

As for her father, Jenny hated him, too, but for a different reason. Though it did not come out until a year later, she had never forgiven him for leaving. Getting a divorce was his sin, and she wasn't going to allow herself to forget that.

Quite early on, then, it became clear that Jenny was not going to cooperate with her parents' wishes. She felt if she were to survive, she couldn't. Jenny had learned that if she wanted to see Dave, she had to lie in order to see him, or she'd be grounded; truth had its price in Jenny's household, and it didn't seem worth paying. She was giving up horses at Mendon to spite her parents. And although she was an accomplished violinist, Jenny was also avoiding that instrument at all costs. To Jenny there was little difference between the violin and the Black Plague, between riding horses and catching the flu.

What's more, the atmosphere at Mendon itself promised to challenge us. Since it was primarily designed for students like Jenny, Mendon was comprised entirely of students who had left or been expelled from a previous school for personal reasons. Therefore, the temptations the school offered its students could easily shock the naïve outsider. Students "had a line" on virtually everything at Mendon: LSD, pot, soapers, black angels, crystal meth—the list went on and on. The security was quite loose. No one inspected the rooms or the frequent packages arriving from outside sources. Gangbangs with friends and hallmates were not uncommon, and the full gamut of sexual experiences was available to Jenny. Finally, it seemed to me the students could do pretty much what they wanted. If they were caught smoking pot or guilty of "cohab" (cohabitation), they were assigned to "Sinner's Squad," and they'd simply have to paint for the day or help around the grounds for a few hours. Considering the atmosphere, therefore, one might understand why a night of getting stoned and "making love" would seem more appealing than doing a close reading of Milton's *Paradise Lost*.

Needless to say, living in this kind of environment, Jenny found plenty of subjects to discuss in the sessions, and gradually, as the sessions progressed, she came to trust me. Numerous situations arose to test that trust she had tentatively placed in me, but one in particular confirmed me in her eyes.

Each year Mendon takes the students who wish to go on a departmental trip to one of several foreign countries. Jenny's inclusion in the group was in doubt, however, thanks to a false rumor circulated by one of her less enthusiastic fans at the school. The administration caught wind of it and immediately telephoned me, asking whether or not she actually *was* pregnant; she certainly wouldn't be joining them if that were the case. I answered quite simply, "Who knows? I doubt it. I have more faith in Jenny than that. Frankly, she's done and seen far too much at her age to slip up in such a careless, stupid way." As it turned out, Jenny decided not to go after all, but my handling of the situation helped confirm her trust in me and paved the way for more meaningful interaction between us.

Nevertheless, trust and friendship are only two of many factors to stress in reality therapy. In addition, I absolutely never passed judgment on Jenny's behavior or opinions. To have criticized her actions would only have imitated her mother's approach to dealing with Jenny's behavior, and Jenny would have cut me off as quickly as she had cut off her mother.

Instead, I accepted her values and her analysis of the situation and proceeded from there. Applying her attitudes, and not mine, we then sought practical, realistic solutions to the problem.

"I hate my mother. She's a fucking bitch. A real fuck-up. She's always calling me up, nagging me: 'Why don't you write me? Why don't you do this? Why don't you do that?' I can't stand it when she calls."

"Maybe there's a middle-of-the-road solution. How can you compromise with her?"

"You mean give in."

"No, I'm not asking you to give in—just to find a happy medium."

"Like what?"

"Well, is it worthwhile not writing your mother and then getting all those hassling phone calls? How is that working out for you?"

"They bug the shit out of me. I don't want her calling me."

"Would writing a note once in a while help? Would the phone calls stop then?"

"Maybe."

Of course, getting Jenny to compromise with her mother was only half the battle. Her mother had to change her attitude as well.

"Quite frankly, Ann, I don't think it's asking too much for my own daughter to write me a letter once a week. Really, I don't."

"But it is! At this stage, it *is* asking too much of your daughter. For the moment, I think you should be content with a quick note every couple of weeks—perhaps once a month. Later on, that may well change. But you can't expect to push her into writing a letter once a week now. She'll turn away from you even more than she has."

As a result they compromised, and Jenny was sending cards to her mother every couple of weeks. At first, she was extremely wily about the whole affair, choosing cards that already had something printed on the inside; all Jenny had to do was sign it, address it, and send it. But the practice helped—her mother was happier.

As we talked, Jenny began to realize that she did indeed have choices in every situation, and that she had to be ready to accept the concomitant consequences of each choice. Obsessed with her parents' shortcomings, for example, Jenny would bemoan "the complete control" they exercised over her life. I devoted a fair amount of time, therefore, to pointing out the fact that her life functioned the way it did precisely because she chose it to. In addition, I wanted her to view her actions in a new and larger context. Jenny needed to realize that her actions affected others around her; they didn't exist in a vacuum.

"Your mother's values are very different from yours, aren't they?"

"You're not kidding. She's really screwed up."

"Well, if you're going to run into one another, you'll have to learn how to resolve those differences. You can't just ignore one another. Find a happy medium where you're both as satisfied as possible."

"Impossible. You can't deal with people like that. I'm just going to run away. Screw them both."

"Well, that's one possibility. Let's think about that for a minute. You need a plan to run away. What will you need?"

"Money, food, places to stay. I've got all those. I have friends who live all across the country on the way out West. I could stay with them, and they could lend me the necessary money, too."

"Okay, good. Now what are the advantages and disadvantages to running away? What will improve by your running away, and what will you have to give up?"

"The only problem is that I'd have to give up school. I mean, I do want an education. I want to finish school."

She would decide that for now it wasn't worth it, and full circle we would come, back to the original subject.

"What can you do to compromise with your parents? Take sex, for example. What are your values on sex?"

"Me, I'm more liberal than them. They're all hung up on sex. They tell me it's wrong to sleep with someone unless you're married."

"Have you ever slept with someone you had just met?"

"Of course! It's no big deal."

"I'm not saying it is. To you it's not, but to your parents it is. How can you both possibly compromise on that?"

"You mean getting to know someone better before sleeping with them?"

"That's one possibility, anyway. Have you ever had a relationship where you interacted without sex or drugs?"

"No."

Clearly, Jenny's self-worth was extremely low at this time, and her relationships with males reflected this feeling. She slept with anyone who wished to; maybe then, she hoped, they would accept her.

Other times, we discussed the misplaced values of society itself. Many were the sessions that dealt with the double standards of society. While smoking pot was illegal and therefore, by implication, immoral, drinking alcohol was legal and supposedly moral. Jenny also had to deal with her mother's sermons on "those male lovers of yours," while at the same time her mother was seeing various lovers of her own. The most obvious double standard of all, however, was her mother's penchant for certain pills—it was difficult for Jenny to recognize the difference between her mother's pill popping and her own. Yet her mother berated her constantly for experimenting with drugs.

Such were the problems that Jenny and I faced together. I would always raise the choices inherent: either accept the values of society or make society accept yours. Jenny would at least start to recognize the practical difficulty of converting society's views to her own.

In dealing with her parents, we made some headway as well. Each time she complained of their being "fucked up," I'd say, "That may well be true, but is telling them so helping you out?"

Likewise, when she complained about the school's punishing her for something, I simply pointed out her role in the situation:

"They put me on Sinner's Squad Friday. I had to paint walls the whole fucking morning for taking four days off. Their values are so screwed up."

"It was your choice. You knew the consequences—whether they're fair or not."

Of all the subjects we discussed, her threat of suicide provided the best example of what I was attempting to point out to her— that we all have choices and those choices carry with them certain consequences. There had been an established pattern that I would not accept. In interaction with her parents and previous therapy, Jennifer would pull the suicide routine when she thought she was losing control of any given situation. She had often found it an extremely effective way to gain control of her audience. At this point, banking on our involvement and knowing her patterns, I was reasonably sure that the threat of suicide was manipulative. We handled the discussion of suicide the same way as all other topics.

"Suicide? Sure, that's one alternative."

"It's the only way to escape all this bullshit."

"Let's see if there are any other choices first, and then if they don't work, we can always return to suicide."

Eventually all this verbosity on both of our parts began to make itself felt; Jenny was internalizing some of the ideas. Whenever she wanted to go to a concert, for example, I'd hit her with some of the ideas we'd discussed earlier.

"Tell my parents I can go to the concert. They'll accept your word."

"Call them yourself."

"But they'll say no. You know that."

"Then that's your answer."

"That's not fair."

"I don't see why not. They let you go to a concert last weekend. It's not unreasonable to say no occasionally."

"No one trusts me. No matter what I do, no one trusts me."

"What have you done in the last six months to deserve their trust?"

Here she would mention very remote things—positive thoughts or feelings she'd had. She might have wanted to call home once or twice (though never following through on the urge). Never could she think of something concrete, however.

I would tell her that the only standard by which we're judged is what we *do*—our actions, not our thoughts. "What have you *done* in the last six months to deserve their trust?"

Naturally, she would draw a blank, and the concert furor would die a peaceful death by the end of the session.

As a result of these sessions, there were noticeable changes in Jenny by Thanksgiving—all of them positive. She had made many friends at Mendon, and therefore enjoyed the new school in spite of herself. She continued to excel in her courses, and the teachers fed her genuine encouragement. Jenny had also been elected to serve on the Committee for Disciplinary Action, a responsibility she took seriously.

She worked with the students who broke the rules on drinking, drugs, cohab, among others, offering any constructive support she could. With drugs occupying less of her free time, Jenny seemed to follow through more on her various commitments, too. In short, her self-worth grew steadily because of these successes.

One suggestion that helped her immensely was discontinuing the journal she had been keeping. I suggested she stop keeping it because Jenny seemed to exacerbate her own states of depression by writing in it. She wrote in the journal only when she was depressed or upset, thereby dwelling on the very feelings she should have been trying to forget.

All these changes pointed out to Jenny, if not to the rest of us, that she had made it to Thanksgiving—and quite successfully. Whether or not to remain at Mendon was no longer a question. By now she wanted to stay. In preparation for the holiday break, therefore, we sat down to plan out how she would spend her time: how much of the break she should spend with her father at home and how much she could spend with her friends in the city. Vacations are long at Mendon—school closes for ten days at Thanksgiving.

At first she offered to spend one day with her father and the remaining nine days in the city with friends. No way was he going to accept such a proposal, I argued. Eventually she modified her plan to allow equal stays in both places—five with her father and five with her friends. Her mother remained out of the picture. And during those five days in the city, her father would have the name of the friend with whom she was staying, although both he and I had doubts as to whether or not she would actually be staying there.

Prior to my session with Jenny, her father and I had discussed this point, and we both saw the importance of not pressing Jenny on her whereabouts in the city. If, after all, she did stay with David under the guise of being with another friend, it was not important. Maintaining trust at this point was the crucial factor in Jenny's development, whereas to interfere with her seeing Dave and the other "Manson crowd" would only damage the progress we had already made. She had to let go of those friends of her own free will—or not at all.

Upon returning from the holiday, Jenny admitted to seeing Dave and the others. I asked her if that was playing fair, to complain of the lack of trust on her parents' part and then to lie outright to them. No answer. She was never able to answer such questions any more. And that meant we were making progress.

During the short period between Thanksgiving and Christmas, Jenny continued to improve. She laughed more in the sessions, seemed more alert, and involved herself in various extracurricular activities—all contributing to a gradual amnesia of past friends and parties left somewhere back in New York. She even adopted one or two of the students at Mendon who were struggling with serious drinking problems. She took it upon herself to be available whenever one or the other of them needed somebody to talk with. She helped them toward better ways of using their time, and generally provided support whenever they needed it. At last she was beginning to focus on others, not just herself.

It was around this period that Jenny said to me, "You know, Ann, you've restored my faith in adults." When she was ready to leave for the Christmas break, that same positive attitude permeated most of her thoughts. She had resolved to see Dave in the open and to have her parents accept that fact. She agreed with me that they probably wouldn't accept him, and though she didn't agree with their opinion, Jenny had begun to take this difference of opinion with more maturity. She still hadn't come to grips with her feelings toward her mother, but she had resolved many of her emotions concerning her father. She now knew she could learn to deal with him, to understand him, and over the holiday she would concentrate on exactly that. Finally, when the session ended, Jenny threw her arms around me, wishing me a Merry Christmas and telling me that now she realized she *did* have a choice between things which could either help or harm her. I was ecstatic.

January, a brand-new year, and disaster. Complete and utter disaster. The very first session, Jenny came in glassy-eyed and clearly high on more than life. As if reliving the first session all over again, I listened to her rave against the fucked-up people in the world. Mendon was once again a screwed-up school she detested; she counted the hours and minutes to her return to New York. All her comments were negative, and so was her subject matter. So . . . we started all over again—or seemed to.

One subject that enraged her was her parents' reaction to an incident that had occurred over the break. While staying at her father's estate in New Jersey, Jenny had entertained a city friend of hers at the house for two to three days. Mr. Wykes was on a business trip but Jenny's stepmother was at home. Apparently, Jenny and her friend had spent much of the time alone in her room. Though they hadn't been engaged in anything that might have merited suspicion, Jenny's stepmother had jumped to conclusions about what they were doing.

"I can't fucking believe it! Who do they think they are? What do they expect me to do?"

Again I broached the subject of accepting someone's values versus respecting those values. No dent. I learned later that she had called her father up the night of the bedroom incident and discussed the situation with him, finally hanging up on him.

However, the thing that eventually led to the big blowup between us was a rock concert. Jenny called her father, asking permission to go to a Grateful Dead concert in New York. To her, the request seemed reasonable. In the space of two weeks, however, she had already attended concerts by the same group in Boston, Hanover, and Burlington, so his saying no to the concert in New York did not seem too outrageous to me. When it became clear that I would offer no support in changing her father's mind, Jenny switched tactics and began manipulating her mother. Thrilled at even hearing from her daughter, Jenny's mother consented quite easily to the request, especially since Jenny had promised she would stay with her sister that night. In short, Jenny had even involved her sister in the affair by asking her to vouch for where she would be staying the night of the concert.

To complicate the story even more, her father caught wind of Jenny's new tactics, and explaining the full situation to his ex-wife, he then called Jenny to tell her that the word was still no. From there, Jenny asked me to intercede one last time, and that's when I literally blew it.

It was the session after her father had told her no for the second and final time. She strode into my office, furious at the whole world.

"Look, couldn't you do this one favor for me? Just this once? It's necessary for my peace of mind."

"No, I'm not going to step in for you. I don't think you need it, and I don't think you particularly deserve it. What have you done for them lately?"

"I thought you were supposed to be my friend!"

"I am your friend, not your puppet—somebody whose strings you pull."

"Jesus, is that fucked up or what?"

That's when I exploded.

"Jenny, you're spoiled! What you really need is a good licking, not the Grateful Dead, and a good crash course in taking no for an answer!"

"Oh Jesus, the whole world is fucked up! I don't have to sit here and take this shit!" And she walked out.

Semesters are much shorter at Mendon than at most other schools. Before long it would be spring vacation, and three long weeks before Jenny would be returning to Mendon—three weeks that she would spend in New York with David and all her old friends. Undoubtedly, that had been the last I would see of Jenny.

Her father handled the news in his usual sensible manner: "Well, that's all right. You did what you could. The rest has to come from her."

When Jenny telephoned me after the spring holiday, I was more than surprised. In our first session, however, she explained what dynamics over the break had eventually led her back to me.

After returning home, Jenny had been allowed to stay with certain friends in the city from time to time. Through an old girlfriend, she met several new friends, and together they had attended poetry readings and plays. The blowup between Jenny and me had already shaken her a good deal—she said that after she left my office she had cried all the way back to Mendon—but meeting these others over the holiday had helped influence her even more. They would sit around a fire at night and exchange personal stories with one another, sometimes stories they hadn't even admitted to themselves. At one point, they told each other incidents they weren't proud of. No one criticized or passed judgment on the other, but rather listened and then accepted that person in spite of what had been told. Such solid support helped Jenny immensely: "Truth was the best high I'd ever experienced."

On the way back to school, yet another incident occurred to reinforce Jenny's change. She got food poisoning, and instead of taking the bus up to school that night, she stayed with a friend in New York to recuperate and did not take the bus to school until the following day—a day later than she had planned. Her mother tried calling her at school when Jenny was still in New York. The school had no idea of Jenny's whereabouts and her mother panicked. In no time, the police were notified, and by three in the morning, police in Florida, where Mr. Wykes and his wife were vacationing, were knocking on their shutters, to ask if they knew the whereabouts of their daughter. In spite of this alarm on the part of Jenny's mother, her father and stepmother now trusted Jenny; they were sure something had occurred to justify her late arrival, and they were willing to wait and find out.

This trust they both placed in her added to Jenny's personal strength just that much more.

Back at school, Jenny explained why she had come back to me. My friendship meant a lot to her. By exploding and calling her spoiled, I had forced her to think about herself in a new light—though initially it had only angered her. What I considered a gross mistake on my part, therefore, turned out to be a crucial catalyst in the whole process. But it was only because of the great degree of involvement each of us had with the other that a potential disaster had been avoided. Only because Jenny felt she had found a friend in me was I able to get away with such a tactic. Even then, I don't think I'd react in the same way if I had to do it over again.

Some months later Jenny decided to share with me a note she had written to herself about the incident.

When I first started seeing Ann, I was very unrealistic about life and was quite self centered but with reason because I had been very hurt. For the first 4 or 5 months I talked a lot about rebelling but never actually did that much. Later on all I thought about was getting my way. I was right in thinking of ways to make myself happy but I was not thinking of the situation I was in or thinking of others. Then one day Ann and I got in a fight and she told me I was spoiled. I got really pissed off and walked out on her. This was the beginning of me getting it together. I had formerly trusted Ann very much so I began to take into account what she had said. I began to compromise with people and find a happy medium which would make everyone happy. By doing this I ended up getting more rewarded then by just getting my way because it made me happy that other people were happy with my decision.

As it turns out, Jenny finally left Dave—of her own free will. The last time she went out with him was to a concert. On the way to the concert hall, he periodically left her side in pursuit of scraps of paper and litter blowing along the pavement, hoping there'd be some cocaine on them. Jenny decided then she didn't need such a life.

"You know," she once said to me, "when you're wasted that's supposed to be good, and when you're sick that's supposed to be bad. But in both cases you look the same."

To show that both my involvement and my caring were sincere, I would invite Jenny out to our house for weekends. For one thing, she had no home of her own: she no longer lived with her mother. She didn't enjoy visiting her father's home, and the atmosphere at Mendon grew stifling at times. I felt that if she was to experience some kind of family life, she might as well start with our house. Inviting Jenny over for a weekend was another way to share parts of my life with her. A relationship where only one does all the sharing and opening up quickly grows false and cold.

Jenny refused these invitations, but other than that we were getting along even better than before. Jenny was starting to make plans with her life at this point, and I would offer suggestions from time to time, but as a friend more than as a therapist. She decided to buckle down with the academics and graduate early from Mendon—which she is doing with straight As. She still hasn't taken up the violin or riding again, but she now spends a great deal of time with the guitar—and in a serious way. She still admits to smoking pot, but only occasionally; now she doesn't need it. And if she sleeps with someone now, one can be sure that the relationship is no one-night affair, for Jenny no longer seeks acceptance through sex. Finally, Jenny has become a much-respected figure around the campus. Students come to "rap" with her or to discuss their problems, and she is always willing to listen.

As for handling adverse situations in a mature way, listen to this incident:

A student she knew asked to borrow her tape recorder, and though she did not normally lend such valuable items, Jenny told him that if he was especially careful with it, she would be willing to lend it. When he returned it, the recorder malfunctioned to the point that it thoroughly digested one of her own tapes the first time she played it. Jenny approached the borrower with the problem, but he didn't seem disturbed at all.

"What are you going to do about it, Nicky? It doesn't work any more."

"Nothing."

And that ended that.

"It may have cost me a few dollars," she told me later, "but I learned my lesson. I just don't lend my things out now."

Acquiring the ability to cope with just such attitudes of thoughlessness or moral indifference best exemplifies the beneficial effect Mendon has on its students. At first glance, an atmosphere in which one hundred twenty students care about no one but themselves would seem to encourage more of the same behavior. Ultimately, however, this atmosphere somehow seems to open their eyes; by graduation, many of the students have pulled out of their own egocentricity. Perhaps the students all provide a mirror image of one another, creating a positive effect out of the initial negative one. Whatever the answer, many of the students leave Mendon having learned some very important lessons about themselves as well as about others.

Jenny, for example, no longer asks "why." If she can't deal with someone, she accepts that fact and goes from there. Now she accepts her mother for what she is, and she accepts where they both are in relation to one another. They get along quite well now; in fact, they'll be visiting one another this summer.

As for her father, she loves and respects him very deeply—and with reason. His intelligent, common-sense approach to the whole affair certainly stands as a most important factor. Without his calm and trusting cooperation, my job would have proven ten times as difficult.

And though her family is wealthy, Jenny cannot be called spoiled any longer. She would like a guitar this year, but realizes the cost involved; consequently, she is asking for a combined Christmas/birthday gift. For certain others at Mendon, a Maserati wouldn't suffice.

I showed this chapter to Jenny for her opinion on my perceptions, and she agreed with all of them. What's more, she singled out my refusal to pass judgment on her actions as the most important factor. Now she does most of what her parents want her to do, but for that to happen, they had to stop pushing. Jenny's rebellious nature immediately surfaced whenever someone shoved values at her. By not labeling her actions right or wrong, I enabled her comfortably to make the most sensible decisions on her own. As Jenny stated herself, "I was right in thinking of ways to make myself happy, but I was not thinking of the situation I was in or thinking of others."

In our last session together, we talked over Jenny's plans for the future, and she wrote the following evaluation of the past few years:

I certainly have come a long way this year. I started as someone who only got happiness through sex, I was totally dependent upon Dave and totally miserable with my mother. I learned to find happiness in other ways. I'm no longer dependent upon Dave and I am able to understand my mother more. I don't drink or take drugs anymore but I do occasionally get stoned. When someone used to offer me a drink, I would have to fight myself to refuse. Now I don't even have to think about it because it's just not there anymore. I don't have the craving to drink or take drugs. I used to have sex with people if they were nice and also to get accepted. Now I can't have sex with someone unless I know them very well and really care for them. It's the same as the drinking. I used to fight myself off, now it's just not needed because I've changed. I have a much better relationship with my father now. I am able to see his view. Therefore, we are able to make compromises. I go to boarding school, I've worked hard this year so I am able to graduate a year early. I learned a lot about people but most of all about myself.

After graduating early this year from Mendon, Jenny plans to travel through the United States for a while, collecting her thoughts as she goes. However, I am sure we'll keep in touch. Why am I sure? Listen:

"Jenny, that invitation to come and visit for a weekend still stands. I hope you'll take us up on that sometime."

"I really want to, Ann, but I'm going to be leaving soon. I don't know when I could . . . well . . . you know, I could stop by next weekend on the way home. Would both Friday and Saturday be an imposition?"

"Not at all, Jenny. I'd really like that."

2

"Be My Friend"

A Young Adult Finds Direction

E. Perry Good

"I've been seeing this psychiatrist, and nobody really thinks it's doing me much good. My mother wants me to come see you for therapy, but I'm really sort of hesitant about the whole thing because I think reality therapy is just some other therapy that someone thought up so they could put their name on it and become famous and rich."

Rebecca was clearly not enthusiastic about becoming my client. She had been seeing a psychiatrist three times a week for about three years, and her parents didn't think he was helping her. Her mother, an acquaintance of mine, had asked me to phone her. As our conversation continued, Rebecca said, "Perry, I just want you to be my friend. I'm sick of the whole idea of seeing a therapist. Anyway, since you know my parents, even though it's just slightly, it won't work for you to be my therapist because you won't be objective."

"I want to be your friend, Rebecca, but I don't have enough free time to see you as often as you would like, and since I have to pay my bills, I would like to be a paid therapist who is also your friend."

We finally agreed that I would start seeing Rebecca for therapy the next week. I had practiced reality therapy for several years, but in institutional settings, and I was in the process of finding an office in order to do more private therapy. I met Rebecca the first week at her house; subsequently we met at the dance studio of a friend of mine or in Jason's Hamburger Shop or even, once, in a department store. At first I was apprehensive about seeing Rebecca without a proper office, but I quickly ascertained what I had suspected. Reality therapy doesn't always have to take place in an office, and it can sometimes be more effective if practiced "on location." I believe I was able to be more creative and flexible in my therapeutic relationship with Rebecca because of I didn't yet have an office. I now try to see clients as much out of my office as I do in it.

When Rebecca greeted me at the door of her parents' house, she was extremely excited because André Watts was making one of his rare television appearances. Rebecca majored in music in college— classical music is one of her great loves. I told her that I could wait if she wanted to see the performance, but she said it would be rebroadcast, so we decided to go for a walk. I thought that would be better than staying in her parents' house, although there was lots of room and we could have talked in private. I felt Rebecca would be more open if we weren't in that environment.

When we first started therapy, Rebecca, who was about five feet eight inches tall, weighed about one hundred and fifty pounds, and she had thick, dark, wavy, unkempt hair. Her face was lifeless, her eyes vacant, and she seemed very childlike. She didn't appear to be very alert or very intelligent, although a person who had known her since she had been born twenty-two years ago (a friend of her mother's, the woman who had convinced me to take her for a client) had told me that Rebecca had been vivacious, curious, and quite intelligent before she began to receive psychiatric care and had been placed on a drug.[1] That vision of Rebecca was the thin hope I carried through the first few months of therapy when I wasn't sure that reality therapy—or any other kind of therapy—was going to help her.

When we left Rebecca's house, we went to the park for a walk. Although it was late November and chilly, we strolled along the river to a bench, where we sat and talked. Rebecca immediately started to talk about her past. I said, "I don't want to talk about that with you."

"That's what all my other psychiatrists talked about. If you don't talk about my past, we'll never get anywhere."

I replied, "I don't believe that's true, Rebecca. In fact, it might be true that you never get anywhere *if* you talk about the past. In

---

[1] Rebecca was taking chlorpromazine, a strong, often paralyzing drug psychiatrically prescribed under a variety of trade names.

any case, as you know, I'm a reality therapist. We don't think it helps to talk about the past, so we don't do it. With me, we'll talk about what you're doing, and what you plan to do. What *are* you doing right now?" I said.

Rebecca said that the only thing she was doing was taking a class in math at a nearby college so she could go back to school and take premed, since she wanted to become a doctor. She then began to cry and said. "I've lost any semblance of independence. I can't take care of myself, and it really bothers me. I think it might have something to do with the drug I'm taking. I've really felt strange since I started taking it two years ago. It was prescribed to me by a psychiatrist I started seeing when I was in college. I had just found out that my mother had cancer of the lymph glands. Although there was a treatment for it, and I knew she was in no immediate danger, I also knew that it meant she had a limited time left to live, and that really frightened me. I was also confused about whether to major in music or science. After the psychiatrist prescribed the drug, I kept going to the health center because I thought something was really wrong with me. When my mother's cancer flared up a year or so later, I became very upset. A teacher sent me to a health center, and one of the psychiatrists called an ambulance and put me in the hospital. I mean a mental institution. It was horrible, I was there for a month."

"How much are you taking now?" I asked.

"Two hundred milligrams," she said, "but I want to stop taking it."

Rebecca told me that soon after the drug had been prescribed, she had gone to the health clinic in her college saying that she felt "funny." I know that some people have extremely bad reactions to that drug. The only way to find out if she was one of these people was to take her off the medication. Rebecca wanted to get off it, but she was also afraid. I consulted a medical doctor about how to reduce her dosage in a safe way and convinced her that if she had trouble, we would handle it.

It was two months before she was completely off. During that time, Rebecca saw me twice a week. She had been seeing her psychiatrist three times a week, and I thought she needed the support of seeing me at least twice a week. Our sessions were not regulated by the clock. Sometimes Rebecca stayed as long as an hour and a half. She said, "I really like not having the pressure of time during our sessions.

I don't feel as if I have to constantly filter out what's super important and what isn't. It gives me a chance to talk about issues and discuss relatively minor things that are bothering me."

I knew at the beginning of our therapeutic relationship that one of the things Rebecca needed most was a friend, someone to talk to—not only about major problems in her life, but about everything. When we began therapy, she was living at home. Her most immediate problems were that she lacked friends and a way to support herself. Her parents had told me that she had been acting so "out of it" that none of her old friends ever saw her. In fact, she saw no one socially. And it would be hard for her to find a job, since as far as the job market was concerned, she was just another liberal arts graduate with no salable skills.

Our next meetings were held in my friend's dance studio. It was a bit overspacious, but I managed to create a small, cozy space for us by using a small area rug and two comfortable chairs. We also had a small hot-water heater so we could make coffee and tea. Of course, at the end of each session I had to dismantle my temporary "office," and sometimes I felt like Lucy in Peanuts with her "Psychiatry, 5¢." I told Rebecca that I traveled often and our meetings would have to be flexible. She was pleased to hear that I taught reality therapy, and she didn't seem bothered by the fact that I wouldn't be there at exactly the same time each week. I assured her that she would always know where I was staying when I traveled, and we would talk on the telephone. She said she didn't care if we didn't have a regular meeting time as long as we could make up the time later if we missed a session. I told her that we would, and we always did. During the first three months, we talked on the telephone every time I was away. Rebecca was amazed that I would call her to ask how or what she was doing. She seemed amazed at my availability and her easy access to me. I told her that she could feel free to call me up if she needed to talk to me, but to remember that I had a family and other things to do and to try to make those calls only when they were truly important. She didn't abuse the privilege.

During our first two or three sessions, while we were still in the process of becoming friends, she came in one day and said, "My mother says I need a new coat. She's been bugging me to get one for two months. This navy jacket is old and has these little white balls on it."

"Do you think you need a new coat?" I asked her.

"Yes, but I don't know where to go to get it, and I don't really know what kind of coat to get," Rebecca said.

"Do you have the money to buy a coat?" I asked.

"Yes, I have it in the bank, and I also have a Master Charge card."

"Do you want to go see if we can find one now at Montaldo's? It's right around the corner from here," I said.

"You mean right now, during our session?"

"Yes, we can finish up what we're talking about and go over there in a few minutes. It would be a great surprise for your mother and a relief to you."

"It sure would," Rebecca said.

When Rebecca mentioned the coat, the idea of trying to get it immediately had two primary purposes from a therapeutic point of view. One was that it would give Rebecca an instant success, which she badly needed at this point in therapy; she had nothing going for her. I knew, after looking at the coat that she was wearing, that her mother would give her lots of positive feedback on a new one—especially since Rebecca told me that her mother had been urging this for months. I also thought that Rebecca's need for a friend to do such things with her was so acute that it would be good for her to have that experience. Rebecca didn't have enough strength then to buy the coat herself, and she didn't want her mother to have to go with her to pick it out. I know I don't like to buy a major item like a coat without another opinion that I trust, and Rebecca didn't have another person like that in her life. So I became that person.

We bought the coat, and it looked terrific on her. As she looked in the mirror, I could almost see her self-worth take a leap forward. When she came in for her appointment the following week, she told me that her mother liked the new coat and had been overjoyed that she had gotten it—and it made Rebecca feel better to wear it. I think this was the first time she realized that fulfilling her current needs, and not talking about the past, was what mattered—what made her feel better. She had been spending so much time thinking about what had happened to her in the past that she had lost touch with the present. Buying the coat had given her the idea that she could do something positive about what was happening now. After the coat, she simply became more hopeful. I think that was the first time she thought she might be able to solve her problems.

The most acute problem now was finding friends. She didn't seem to have any concept of where to go to look. After spending a couple of sessions exploring ideas about where she might find some people who would interest her, she told me that there was a choral society she wanted to join. That week she made a plan to call the director of the society. When she arrived for her next session, I asked, "What did the director say? Can you join?"

"I haven't called him. I didn't have the nerve," she replied.

We were in my friend's dance studio and there was no telephone, but I knew the fellow across the hall had one, so I said, "Would you call him now?"

Rebecca said, "There's no phone."

"There's one across the hall—we can ask to use it."

When she returned, she looked jubilant. "The director was really impressed that I had been a music major at my college, and I have an interview with him on Tuesday." She was surprised that this respected man thought something she had done was good. For Rebecca at this point, there was nothing she had done that she felt that good about—or, in reality therapy terms, nothing she felt she was truly successful in doing.

Since our first session, I had been encouraging Rebecca to find a job. She had gone to some employment agencies, and finally, while I was away on a trip, she had gotten a job as a filing clerk with a wholesale distributor. She wasn't crazy about the job, but we talked about its being temporary.

She was still on the drug, although her dosage was being reduced, and she was very emotional. She was tense and anxious about not doing well in her math course. We talked about how she could handle this, but she carried her math book everywhere she went and was obsessed with the course. I asked her if she took her book to work, and she told me she did. She said she didn't study during work hours, just at lunchtime when she ate a sandwich in the office. I had an idea that her obsession with this course would be noted by her employer, and that it would not make a good impression.

It didn't. When Rebecca arrived at our next session, she was in tears, saying, "I've been laid off."

I said, "I think what you mean is that you've been fired." I wanted Rebecca to face the fact that she had not been doing an adequate job. She was offended that I had told her she had been fired, but after she calmed down, we talked about her situation. I told her that although it wasn't great that she was fired, it could be worse. She had a place to live, parents who loved her, and an education. I lived in an economically extremely deprived area, which Rebecca knew, and I talked about what it meant for someone in my neighborhood to lose a job. Sometimes it meant a whole family would go hungry. I told her that although she was having a hard time at the moment, she was really a comparatively lucky person.

As a therapist, I don't usually "preach," but in Rebecca's case I took a chance, and it worked.

She said, "You're right. I never realized how many things I do have. I shouldn't go around thinking I'm at the bottom of the barrel all the time, because I'm not."

Rebecca spent the rest of the session deciding what she would do now that she had been "laid off." It was only two weeks before Christmas, and her math final was coming up in early January. She decided to try to help out at home during Christmas and to be cheerful, which was something new for her.

Even though Rebecca left the session in a better frame of mind than when she had arrived, I phoned her that night. I apologized for being so harsh that afternoon. I said that because I cared about her, I wanted her to accept some responsibility for what had happened to her. I had phoned because I did not want to break our involvement, which I realized was more important to me at that time than having her face up to the responsibility that she had something to do with getting laid off. Later in therapy that might not have been true, but at this point it was crucial that our friendship continue. It was our involvement that was giving her some of the support she needed to make changes in her life. Without it, she would never have the strength to take any responsibility for herself.

My sense that this session had been a turning point was confirmed later, when Rebecca told me that no one had ever before pointed out to her the reality of her situation in a positive way that she could understand.

"My mother is in the hospital," Rebecca said at the beginning of our next session, "and it's only three days until Christmas, but they think she'll come home Christmas Eve, when we're having a family dinner at our house." Rebecca and I spent the rest of the session planning Christmas dinner and how she could manage to buy the food, cook it, and serve it. She carried out the plan very successfully, and her parents were so delighted with how she had coped with the responsibility that they called to let me know how pleased they were with the therapy.

She decided not to try to find another job until after Christmas and after her math exam. She so desperately wanted to become a doctor that she had taken the first course she could find in an Ivy League college—her math course. Her sense of reality was so distorted that she had convinced herself that a music major who hadn't even done that well in college could take some premed courses and be accepted into medical school.

I realized that this was a major hurdle to cross in the therapeutic process with Rebecca. She was clinging to the idea that she could get into medical school if she made good grades in the premed courses. My experience had taught me that even people who had top averages in college were having a hard time getting into medical school, and it didn't make sense to me that Rebecca thought she had a chance of getting into one. I felt my job as her therapist was to help her to evaluate her chances realistically and make a decision based on facts, not emotion.

Rebecca knew the facts, but it was difficult for her to face them:

1. She had no money to go to school for two years for the prerequisite courses.
2. She was in no state of mind to pass the courses.
3. Even if she did pass them, her chances of getting into medical school were still slim.

I had now been seeing Rebecca for a month and a half. She still chose to live in a dream world because it was too painful for her to look honestly at her life. She had graduated with a degree in music. Her great love in music had been in performing, and she had not been able to excel in performance. That is not to say that she is a poor musician. It's just that to be a performer one must be exceptional, and she was not. Coming from a family of achievers, Rebecca was not willing to settle for second best.

Since she had "failed" at what she wanted to do in music, she chose to go in an entirely different direction—medicine (her grandfather, whom she very much admires, is a well-known researcher in medicine). In this case, too, however, she would not consider being anything in the medical field except a doctor, because in her family you were the best, or it was a disgrace. Or so Rebecca thought.

She was also very idealistic and kept saying she wanted to help other people, she didn't want to be just a music historian or spend all of her life in books. She wanted to be helping others directly.

My speculation was that this had something to do with her mother's having cancer, and Rebecca's feeling helpless to do anything about it—but we didn't discuss this. We kept talking about the facts.

The first test came after Christmas, when Rebecca had to decide whether to enroll for another course or look for a job seriously. I felt that her chance for success was much greater in the work world, even though she had been fired from one job. It worried me that she would be carrying on with a totally unrealistic plan for her life (i.e., trying to enter medical school), and one that I felt was surely doomed to fail. As a responsible reality therapist I could not allow a failing person to set herself up for continued failure.

"You're really insistent that I shouldn't go back to school this semester, aren't you?" Rebecca said.

"Well, Rebecca, it's your decision, but it's my opinion that you've never thought of school as a means to an end, which is getting a job. It seems to me that you want to go to school forever. Why don't you quit for a while and see what it's really like out there? College will still be there if you want to go back in a year. I'm really glad that I went to work when I graduated from college. I think I did much better when I went back to graduate school five years later than I would have if I had gone directly from my undergraduate studies." I believe that part of being involved with a client is sharing your life's experiences when they can help.

"Maybe it would be a good idea to get a job, earn some money, and try to get another place to live. I'm sick of living with my parents," Rebecca said. "But I don't want to work in the same kind of place that I did before. That was horrible."

"Let's see what your options are. Do you know anybody who might be able to help you with a job?"

"My uncle is one of those people who knows everybody, but I couldn't ask him. I wouldn't want to get any special treatment. I want to be independent," Rebecca replied.

"But Rebecca, the whole world works on relationships. Most of us are far from independent. Furthermore, would it hurt to have lunch with your uncle? I doubt that he'll have a job for you on the spot, but he might be able to give you some advice," I said. Rebecca decided to call her uncle and have lunch with him.

At our next session, she said, "Guess what! My uncle is on the board of a museum, and he called them. They had a job opening. I went down there and had an interview, and I think I got the job!

Do you think I got it only because my uncle is on the board?"

"If you get the job, I think it will be because they thought you could do it," I said. "Even if your uncle is on the board, they wouldn't hire you if they thought you weren't qualified. It's not exactly a family business, it's a big public museum."

Rebecca got the job, and although initially she felt it was because of her uncle, which was true, she began to see that she could do the work. In fact, she was extremely good at it, received an increase in salary, and began to write a monthly newsletter.

At about this time, Rebecca was finally off drugs. There was a big change in her appearance and in her personality. She began to look like a different person. She was no longer sluggish, and her eyes looked lively. She lost about fifteen pounds and had her hair cut in a short, becoming style. She bought herself a gold skirt and sweater. I'll never forget the day she arrived in my office, her stylish hair, her new figure, and with that outfit on. She walked differently. She greeted my partner, which she had never done before, and even exchanged words spontaneously with some other people in the office. She had gotten rid of her tendency to hunch over, and no longer responded in monosyllables while looking the other way and attempting to "hide." It was a transformation. I think this was when she started to see herself as a successful person instead of a failure. Her identity had actually changed.

She still had major decisions to make in her life, but at this point she was in a much better position to make them than she had been three months previously; she had some strength with which to make them.

We still had to talk about what she would do with her life, but two other decisions had to be made first. These decisions were especially difficult, as one depended upon the other. She needed to move out of her parents' home, and she needed new friends. It was frightening for her to think of moving and making the effort to find a place, since she didn't have any friends who wanted to live with her and could not afford to live alone even if she had wanted to do so.

Our first new plan was for her to go look on the bulletin boards in the two colleges in our town to see if anyone was looking for a roommate. "I'm really frightened. How can I know who I'm going to run into just from names on a bulletin board?" But she did check into it, and this did, though only coincidentally, help her to move out of her parents' home.

While at the college checking for housing, Rebecca decided to look up an old friend. He invited her to a party, where she met a girl who was sharing an apartment with another girl. They were looking for a third girl to share expenses. When Rebecca came in for her next appointment, she said that she wasn't crazy about the girl, but that she thought it was better to take the aprtment with her than with a total stranger. She moved in with this girl and one other girl, and although they didn't become close friends, Rebecca felt independent being out of her parents' house. She bought a bed, fixed up her room, and generally felt things were going well.

In the summer she moved because of a terrible experience in the apartment. A window had been left open, and one of the girls had been raped in the middle of the night. All three girls were naturally upset. I was amazed, however, that Rebecca was not more upset. She handled the situation very rationally. She didn't move immediately, but decided that she wasn't comfortable living there any more and had no real investment in staying.

"Guess what! A friend I knew in California called yesterday, and she's looking for a roommate!" Rebecca excitedly told me. "She's a concert pianist and has won all kinds of awards. Plus I really like her so much!" Rebecca moved in with this girl, whom she respected enormously. Julie got Rebecca some dates and was a real link to Rebecca's peer group. It seemed a miracle to me that this friend arrived just when she did.

Rebecca started dating a medical student, and although she wasn't "in love" with him, he added to the general sense of well-being that was developing in her at this time.

Rebecca's mother was again receiving treatment for cancer, and Rebecca's general improvement was a great relief to her. She knew she was not getting better, and she also knew that in another year she would have to go off the "miracle" drug that had kept her functioning for the past four years. Rebecca during this period was beginning to accept her mother as a person and to come to terms with her mother's approaching death. "I am trying to spend at least one night every weekend at home so I can be with Mom," she told me. "I know that when she gets sicker, I'll really regret it if I don't. I think I'm beginning to get to know her better than I ever have."

A recurring theme in her therapy was the question of what Rebecca was going to do with her life. Although she was working at the museum and doing a good job, she knew she didn't want to do that "forever." The choral society was a fulfilling outside interest, but she was extremely concerned over her future. The decision for her to work for a while had given us time to talk about possibilities for her career.

Rebecca was still determined to go to medical school. I was still sure it would be a devastating failure and felt she had to realize this. She had had about six months of successful experiences, and she was feeling and doing so much better that I was afraid for her to make a try for medical school and fail. As her therapist, my first attempt to help her find an alternative was to explore her interest in music—to see if she wanted to go to graduate school in music. After a lot of thinking, Rebecca still said that she wanted a profession in which she could help other people, and she didn't think music was it.

At that time, I had been doing a reality workshop in Maine for a community health program, and I started talking to the nurses there. I became quite fascinated with the diversity of their jobs. Some were midwives, some were nurse practitioners—their jobs seemed demanding and responsible to me. When I returned home, I breezed into my office for Rebecca's appointment and said, "Why don't you become a nurse? I met some nurses doing interesting things in Maine."

"Are you kidding? Nurses just take orders from doctors. I don't want to be a second-class citizen. No, if I can't be a doctor, I don't want to settle for second best."

"But Rebecca, these nurses I met are really doing three-quarters of what doctors do," I said.

"Well, I don't think it's a good idea," Rebecca said.

I was quite miffed. I thought I had come up with a reasonable alternative. But Rebecca wasn't interested in any plan that deviated from what she wanted—to be a physician. She had from time to time said that she knew she *might* not make it, but she had never said, "It is foolish for me to try to get into medical school at this point in my life." After months of discussing the pros and cons between music and medicine with her, I had made a common mistake. I thought Rebecca had made a value judgment and was ready to move on, but when I suggested an alternative to her, she wouldn't even consider it. She had not made a value judgment, and until she did, she could not move ahead with a realistic plan for a career.

So, relying on my involvement with her, I said somewhat harshly, "Do you believe that you will get into graduate school in premed?"

She replied, "Well, I think my chances are close to nil. I think I could pass organic chemistry and physics, but deep down inside I'm not sure."

"Okay, Rebecca, tell me this—is it worth two years of your life and seven thousand dollars to take premed and find out you can't get into medical school?"

"No, I don't guess it is, and anyway I don't have seven thousand dollars."

"Can you think of another way that you might be able to get what you want in the end?" I said.

"Well, if I went to nursing school and was very successful, I might be able to go on to medical school."

The next week Rebecca said, "I was riding on the bus the other day and thinking I'm sick of not doing anything interesting. I'm tired of the museum. I just decided to make a decision and go ahead and do something. And it's going to be nursing school."

She had finally made a realistic value judgment for herself.

We made a plan for her to send for nursing school applications, because even after getting over the hurdle of giving up medical school for the moment, we weren't sure that she could get into nursing school.

When the applications to nursing school came, two new problems arose. The first was that Rebecca had to take some courses to fulfill the requirements. At first she wanted to attend only an Ivy League college. I was concerned that she wouldn't pass her course, or wouldn't do well, and I told her this. She said, "But prestige is really important in my family. Nobody goes to City College." We kept discussing the issue, discussing the tuition both places (City College being considerably cheaper), and Rebecca decided to give City College a try.

She took a course at City College—and made an A on it. She then took others, and eventually she became a tutor there. This work was a big help in terms of revising her opinion of her scholastic capabilities. She began to think of herself as a serious student who could do good work.

The other problem that came with the applications presented an even bigger dilemma. Each application included a health form. On the form was the inevitable question, "Has your patient ever seen a specialist, for example, ophthalmologist, gynecologist, or psychiatrist or been in a mental hospital and if so please write down the prognosis of the diagnosis."

Rebecca was in agony when she saw this question. Her family doctor, who was the logical person to fill out the health form, had recommended her to a psychiatrist, so we knew that he would answer yes. Rebecca had not only seen a psychiatrist when she was in college but she actually had been put in a mental institution for four weeks after a breakdown. We were both sure the psychiatrist would put that information on her medical form if he filled it out.

I was convinced that if she put "yes" on the questionnaire, she would have no chance at all of getting into nursing school. She is basically such an honest person that she felt that she couldn't lie about it. She also believed me when I told her that I didn't think she would have a chance of getting into nursing school if she said yes.

She asked me to ask Dr. Glasser what he thought, and I did. He said, "I think it should be illegal to ask on an application if a person has been mentally ill. Who can define mental illness? The definition that you are mentally ill because you see a psychiatrist is circular and damning. Because psychiatrists put people in mental hospitals, the fact that a person has spent time in one is equally circular and damning. I don't think she'll get in if she answers the question factually." I knew that he would say this, but Rebecca appreciated the fact that I would ask specifically on her behalf.

As we discussed this issue more and more, Rebecca began to realize that she hadn't chosen to go on a drug—it had been given to her. I believed that she had been adversely affected by the drug and that it could very possibly have been what landed her in the mental hospital. As her view of her past treatment became more clear to her, Rebecca became more willing to take a stand on the issue. Or should I say, became more willing to ignore the question. I also told her that I would be willing to go to court with her if it should ever come up in the future.

I believe strongly that if our society keeps asking questions like this of people we may destroy the future for those people who have had therapy. If people overcome their past only to have to answer for it over and over, there is no point in change and growth. When Rebecca took the health form to her doctor, she simply told him that she didn't want that part filled out because she thought it would hurt her chances of getting into nursing school.

The doctor took a strange way out. He sent her the form back a week later with the question left blank. Then, a week after that, after Rebecca had sent the form off, he sent her a note saying that she should take it to her psychiatrist. I decided that he simply wanted to be covered in case the question ever arose.

At this point, I told Rebecca that I was going to have lunch with her mother to tell her about the decision to go to nursing school and how I saw it. I knew her mother was not enthusiastic about nursing school, but I felt that the main worry was that Rebecca couldn't do the work, or wasn't emotionally able to handle the experience. I explained to Rebecca that since her mother was paying for the therapy, I felt that was my obligation.

I explained to Rebecca's mother how I viewed the situation, and she felt better. She was so pleased by her daughter's progress that she didn't have much else to say. We also talked about her cancer, and she told me that she realized she didn't have long to live. Part of the urgency that I felt about Rebecca had to do with this—I knew how important it was for her mother to see Rebecca well and functioning.

When Rebecca started to send applications to nursing school, I noticed a big change in her ability to do things for herself. I had always kept a yellow pad on the table in my office, and from time to time I would ask her to write down a list of things she wanted to do or a plan we had come up with together. That day she said, "Where is that pad you always have here? I need to write this down." I realized that she had taken a big step. No longer did I have to remind her—she was taking the responsibility herself.

It was also at that point that she bought a wallet and a calendar for appointments. Her success identity was growing. She was acting like a successful person. She talked about goals and how she was going to reach them. She planned her time well—she bought clothes, exercised, took courses, and she dated. She was seeing me less and less because she was too busy for therapy.

That is the ultimate goal of therapy for me as a therapist. When Rebecca told me that she was too busy to come one week, I knew we were almost finished.

We had our last regular appointment one year to the day that I started seeing her. I had seen her for six months twice a week and for six months once a week. After that, I saw her occasionally if she had a problem with which she needed help, or we met for lunch occasionally. She would buy lunch for me instead of paying me for a session, since she didn't have much money.

In the spring, Rebecca was accepted at an Ivy League nursing school, one of the best in the country. She brought her acceptance letter to the hospital, where she and her father drank champagne with her mother, who was much worse.

That summer, Rebecca realized that her mother hadn't long to live, so she took time off and went to stay with her father and visit her mother, who had been hospitalized near their country house. She and her father commuted to the hospital four hours each day to see her mother.

Two weeks before Rebecca started nursing school, her mother died. Rebecca was the family member who held things together. She planned a memorial service for her mother and participated in it. Then she came back to the city and, by herself, got ready and entered school.

A year later, she was on the dean's list and was an outstanding student in activities and all around.

3

"If Only My Spouse Would Change"

Marriage Counseling with a Young Couple

Gary Applegate

They came to see me together with stories of their boredom with each other, accusations of affairs—unfortunately not with each other—and a deteriorating sexual relationship, the frequency being zero for the last three months.

Tim, thirty-two, and Elizabeth (who liked to be called Liz), twenty-eight, had been married for eight years, six of which had been traumatic. They had dated each other for a little over a year before marrying, and neither had been married before. They had no children and lived in a West Los Angeles apartment with a cat named Easy. Both had professional careers, Tim in corporate middle management and Liz teaching in a secondary school. Neither had any major physical problems, except for Liz's situational headaches and Tim's terminal case of nail-biting.

My first session was spent getting to know them by making friends. I look for things we have in common and share them, compliment specific things that I see or hear, and eventually do an activity with my clients—take walks or go out to lunch.

With Tim and Liz, I started by asking Liz what was happening in her life that had caused her to call me for their appointment. She was attractive and casually dressed, though with just a bit too much eye makeup and dark red lipstick (we used to call them "bee-stung" lips). Her first statement was that their marriage was going nowhere and, in fact, hadn't been anyplace in the last four years. She complained that Tim came home very late, wasn't interested in having sex, had stopped complimenting her, and that they rarely went out and had very little fun with each other when they were alone. I thought, How challenging to deal with positive people.

After hearing Liz's complaints for about ten minutes, I stopped her and asked a question I sooner or later ask all people with relationship problems: "What are you doing, Liz, to hurt this marital relationship?" Her monologue stopped. What I heard then was much more appropriate. She said she probably was complaining too much and drinking too much, but quickly added that if Tim would come home on time, she wouldn't need to complain or drink so much. I simply repeated, "Just tell me what *you* do to hurt the marriage."

Repeating a question when people go off on tangents is an important technique in keeping control of the session. The therapist may have to repeat it several times, firmly and with no concern that it will drive people crazy or out of the office.

Liz responded by saying that she didn't always fix herself up when Tim came home, that she didn't watch her diet or exercise as much as she should, but that was all she was doing to hurt the relationship. I then asked her specific questions I consider necessary so the client can later make specific plans to change behavior.

I asked her how her day started and specifically what she did with or for her husband in the morning before they went to work. She squirmed a little in her seat and shyly said that she was not a morning person. (Drinking will do that, I thought.) I asked other questions in a more or less chronological order that gave me information about her day. When I asked her how she greeted Tim when he came home from work, she said she usually complained either directly or with sarcasm about his being late or, if he were on time, she usually just acknowledged he was home. No hugs, compliments, or enthusiasm.

I asked other questions, such as when was the last time she had told Tim that she loved him or complimented him? What (if any) were the compliments? What was she doing each day for achievement in her own life? How did she react to Tim when he caused her to feel stress, and what were her goals for her life? I then asked her if she wanted to stay married and do nothing to change the marriage, get a divorce, or work on the marriage by changing herself. (I ask these questions so I am clear in what direction the client wants to work.) She said she wanted to work on the marriage.

I then turned to Tim, who had been sitting and listening. I suspected that he would be amazed at Liz's specific answers and confessions of irresponsibility. He was an interesting-looking man with red hair, a mustache, green eyes, and a face that looked years younger than his age. At first he seemed bashful—almost shy.

I asked him similar questions, like, "Tell me what brought you here?" He started with his feeling of being unloved and not needed, but quickly changed to state that Liz drank too much, complained too much, and seemed to have no interest in having any kind of sexual relationship with him. He said these were the main reasons why he was here. It's interesting how he still started with how Liz had to change after hearing what questions I had just asked her. I am never surprised at how much people expect others to make changes. Other people will change and my life will be better, they think.

I asked Tim if he would tell me what he was doing to hurt the marriage. His response was, "Well, I guess at times I come home too late from work and I don't always give my wife good-quality time when I am at home." He also said that he hadn't approached his wife for sex in the last three months and added, "It's tough to approach an alcoholic who doesn't even care about herself."

This attack started an argument, which I stopped by asking Tim my same question over again. What was he doing to hurt the relationship? I feel there is no need to listen to people argue in my office. I gain no useful information except that they know how to hurt each other, a fact I usually assume before they come in.

Tim mentioned a few more things he was doing to hurt the relationship, and then I began my specific questions. They were similar to the ones that I had asked Liz. What was he doing each day to approach her from the early morning to late evening? What was he doing to have fun with her? Was he complimenting her and being consistent in what he said and did? What was he doing to achieve strength in his own life? Tim felt very good about his life away from his marriage. His job was going well, he had recently received a promotion, and he felt his future with his company looked very bright. I also asked him if he wanted to get a divorce, stay married and not work on improving his marriage, or work at making his marriage a better one by changing himself. He said he wanted to work at it. I listened to Tim answer my questions for about twenty minutes, and the first session was about over. I summarized to both very specifically what I had heard each tell me. I had done periodic summaries at about ten-minute intervals during the session, as I do with all sessions.

The reason for summarizing is threefold. First, it lets the clients know I am listening and demonstrates to them that I feel they have worth and that I am attempting to care. Second, it gives the clients a chance to hear their own script, something they may never have listened to before. Third, it gives the clients an opportunity to correct my misinterpretation of any of what they have said. The final summary also serves as a way to indicate that time is up and the session is over.

I did not get into a specific plan to change their behavior except to make appointments with each separately for the following week and to get a commitment that they would come to see me. I might add that rushing into a plan without extremely specific information on a client's present behavior can be a grave error. Remember that without specific details you probably won't be able to make specific plans. There will be plenty of time for good plan making after you have made friends and found out specifically what people are really doing.

After this first session I saw them separately, and only on rare occasions would I see them together. I do this now with all of my clients who are having trouble maintaining a relationship. The rationale for this is that they will have no one to argue with during the session. I primarily try to get them to realize that they must change themselves and not work on expecting the other person to change. Just about 95 percent of the people who come in for a relationship problem—whether it be marital, parent-child, employer-employee, or friend-friend—are initially saying the same thing. "If the other person would change, my life would be better."

I believe that change is very difficult. If you don't believe me, try to eliminate a food you have used all your life from your diet—salt, for example. You will find you have to concentrate very hard. It will be very difficult not to reach for the salt shaker. The point is that if a simple personal habit change is difficult to achieve, then how successful might you possibly be at changing someone else's habits? It's a waste of time and energy for both me and the client to work to control others.

In the second session I saw Liz, and I started the hour by asking her what she had done in the past week to make it a positive one for her. I like to ask this question because it helps people to see immediately the relationship between what they do and their positive feelings. But many times the answer is, "Nothing." Some patients say that the week has been terrible or no different from any other boring week. If you focus on their negative script and allow them to elaborate, then they have control because they have not answered your question. Just repeat the question, and to help them, ask specific questions such as any of the following: Did you give to anyone, including yourself, this week? Did you achieve something? Did you tell a joke? Did you go any place that was fun or different? You can be creative and get more specific in your questions. In fact, the more different or unusual, the better.

Liz answered my questions with the answer that nothing had really changed except that for two nights Tim had come home from work earlier than normal. I quickly switched back to what she was doing to make the marriage better. She told me a few things, like she had given Tim a compliment about his appearance and she hadn't had a drink for four out of the seven nights.

After summarizing and getting some more specifics about how her week had gone, and sharing with her a few things that had happened to me, I asked Liz to list what she and Tim had in common. This is usually a good starting point for making plans to do things together. I make sure the following areas are covered in terms of comparing how it was when things were good with how it is now. How do they have fun together? How are their energy levels similar? What time do they go to bed and get up? What is their sexual drive? Do they participate in active sports? How do they feel about money? How much do they spend? Save? Want to make? What do they do for intellectual stimulation? How important is thinking? Their emotional life? Can and how do they reveal their feelings? How do they solve problems—from a logical point of view or from an emotional one? (This area of problem solving can lead to many more problems if there are great differences in their problem-solving approach.) Where does religion enter into their relationship and how important is it to each partner? What is their philosophy of man? Do they see man basically as good or evil? While I am asking these questions, I share information about myself so that the relationship is friendly and not one-sided. People find it easier to talk about themselves if I've said a few things about myself first.

Liz told me she had very little in common with Tim. They used to go out and have fun, sex used to be terrific, they used to go to plays and lots of movies together, but now all they seem to have in common was a mutual dislike, each for the other, and a love for the set of china dishes that her mother gave them for their wedding gift. However, only three pieces were left, the rest having become casualties of the relationship. I asked if she were a thrower or a dropper. She said a very definite thrower, with a pretty good curve. I asked if she were a baseball fan, and she told me she used to play softball. She added that Tim liked to watch the Dodgers play and had been an athlete in college. She said kiddingly, "I think he was a javelin catcher."

At this point, I felt I had enough information to make a plan. When making the initial plan with about 95 percent of the people I see, I do it myself. I have found that most people don't know how to make good plans, as they don't always see all of their alternatives. As therapy progresses and people learn about good plan making, we make the plan together. You know that therapy is just about over when your client comes in, states the problem, and then tells you his or her plan to make things better. That's in essence what strong people do to remain strong. I don't worry about being too directive in making the plan. I am always asking for a value judgment about present behavior, and this lets me know if my idea or plan has the potential to help the client feel better.

Since both Tim and Liz like baseball, I thought immediately about making a plan for them to go to a baseball game together but realized that just going to a ball game once a week wasn't going to change any habits. So I kept the baseball plan in my head and saved it for later.

Instead, I asked Liz if she could hug Tim when he came home from the office every night for the next six nights, no matter what time he came home and no matter what she was feeling. We talked about how difficult it would be for her to hug him if he were late or if they had had a fight that morning. I asked Liz if he would like her hugs, and she thought he would. I asked if hugging would help the relationship, and she said yes. I then asked for a commitment. She made the commitment to make this change, and with that I summarized the session, made an appointment in six days, and ended the session. With her, she took a copy of the plan sheet she had filled out (a duplicate of which follows).

A GOOD PLAN IS:

1. *Simple,* that is, not complicated.
2. *Small,* both in terms of what is done and the time frame it is done in.
3. *Something to do,* not stop doing.
4. *Dependent on what you do,* not on what others do.
5. *Specific,* as to what, when, where, how, how many, with whom.
6. *Repetitive,* something you can do each day or often.
7. *Immediate,* that is, something that can be done soon.
8. *Making a commitment,* which is important in developing responsibility.

MY PLAN IS: DATES AND/OR DAYS

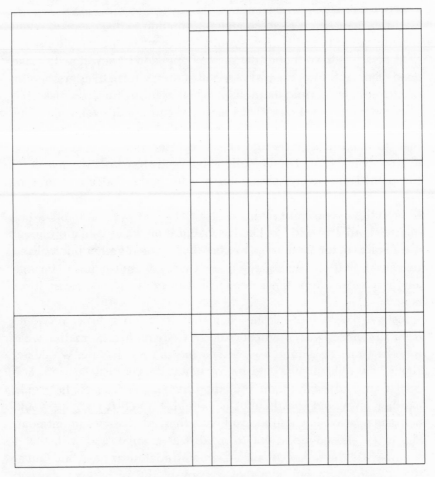

Each patient and I have a copy of this plan sheet, so there is no problem determining what specifically the plan is or later how it went. We go over it together and discuss how a good plan meets all the criteria on the list.

The next day I saw Tim for our first session alone. I felt it was going to take more time to get to know and make friends with him, so I spent the first twenty minutes just sharing what we both did for fun. We found out that we both liked to play practical jokes. While in high school we had both put clear plastic wrap on toilet seats in the girls' rest room.

When we got into the problems with his relationship with his wife, Tim confided that coming home to Liz after work was a terrific turnoff. To avoid her, he stayed as late as he could at the office or went somewhere after work.

As I had done with Liz, we covered areas of compatibility. In most areas, he agreed with her. I asked specific questions about what he dreaded about coming home. He told me it was boring being with a lady who was drunk half the time and complained for the other half. At this point, I went through his evening—what he did from the time he got home until he went to bed. He was doing nothing to have fun at home or to approach his wife positively.

I asked for a value judgment as to whether his behavior when he came home from work was making his life happier or his marriage stronger. He said, "No," and I suggested that for the next five workdays he make a plan to be home by seven o'clock and that he ask his wife to do something they would both enjoy doing together for about half an hour each night. I made some suggestions, like taking a walk together after dinner, making dinner together, playing a game like backgammon, or even taking a bath together. It could be something different each night, but he had to ask his wife to do something each evening. We talked about how difficult that might be if she had been drinking when he got home or if she started complaining. I pointed out that his feelings about their marriage and Liz would stay the same if he didn't change. I also pointed out that with his change, he would feel better about the marriage and himself. He was in control about asking, and that was to be his change. Whether or not she accepted was her choice.

I then got his commitment that he *would* be, and not just try to be, home every workday by seven and ask her to do an activity for each evening for the next five days. I summarized the session and made an appointment for the next week.

The third session, with Liz, started with my review of how she had done with her hugging of Tim. She said first that Tim had been getting home by seven each work night and she had, in fact, hugged him each night. She showed me her plan sheet with her nights checked off, and I asked her if she felt good when she approached her husband and hugged him. I want people to see the relationship between feeling good and their behavior. I then asked if she would do the same plan next week. She certainly didn't have a hugging habit yet, but with practice, no matter what Tim did, she would get it. She made the commitment.

We then started talking about other things that she would like to change in her life. I asked her how often she drank and if she or Tim considered it to be a problem. She admitted that occasionally she drank too much and that Tim did feel it was a problem. I asked her if her drinking was helping her marriage and she said that it wasn't, but that at times it did make her feel good, especially when she felt that Tim didn't love her. I summarized her statements that when she drank Tim complained, that drinking wasn't helping her marriage, and that she felt drinking was reducing a stress.

I asked her if she wanted to stop drinking and if she wanted to start doing things that would help her gain self-worth and reduce her need for alcohol. She said yes, if she only knew how. I told her it was my job to know how, hers to act.

I told her to begin by making a positive list of her good qualities. She could divide herself into four areas, physical, intellectual, emotional, and behavioral. She was to write down at least five things in each category every day for the next seven days. We went over some examples, like having pretty blue eyes and an excellent memory for names, being sympathetic to people, and being a good cook (especially of spaghetti). She had to know exactly what I meant. She made a commitment to do this and continue the hugging. She filled out the plan sheet, I summarized the session, and we made an appointment for the following week.

When Tim came in, he was ready to complain about Liz's uncooperative attitude—not doing what he had asked for half an hour each night. I quickly referred to the plan sheet and asked him only what he had done. Had he come home each workday by seven, and had he asked Liz to do an activity for half an hour? He said he had come home for the first three nights, but not the fourth or fifth. He also said that he only asked for two nights and then started to tell me why he hadn't followed through. His excuse was about to begin when I cut him off.

When people come in with excuses, I never ask why they didn't complete the plan. Instead, I go through the following steps. First, I ask myself, am I involved with the client? Did I spend enough time to get to know this person? In Tim's case, I felt I had. Next, I ask myself if this was a plan that had met the criteria of a good plan. Tim's checked out. Next, I ask the client if this was a plan that he or she wanted to do. Tim said, "Yes." If the answer to any of my questions had been no, I would have stopped at that step, spent time becoming more involved and then changed the plan to meet the correct criteria. Then I would have asked Tim to commit himself to a plan that he wanted to do. Since Tim's answers were all yes answers, I went on to ask for the excuse. I believe there are two kinds of excuses. There are reasonable ones like "I had the flu all week" or "I was called out of town unexpectedly." These are only going to happen once. If I hear a reasonable excuse, I just repeat the plan. The other is a weak excuse like "I just forgot" or "I got drunk" or "She wasn't nice to me." With these I get very confrontive, by pointing out what is now happening, the consequences of such actions, and the fact that it's the patient's choice.

With Tim, the excuse was that Liz didn't want to do anything with him, so he had stopped asking and had stopped coming home before seven as well. After I confronted him with the positive and negative consequences of his behavior and his previously stated choice to improve his marriage, he said he would try to do better. I was still far from confident that the plan would be successful.

We talked about the specifics of what he was going to do, then discussed how he could sabotage the plan. After that we went over all the potential excuses we could think of and discussed how they were all just excuses. I then asked for a firm commitment. He recommitted himself to the plan and wrote the agreement on his plan sheet. I summarized, talked awhile about things in general, and then made an appointment for the next week.

My third session with Liz started with a discussion of her "positive" list and how she was doing with her hugs. The list was quite honestly better than I had expected it would be, and she had indeed kept up the hugging. She told me that she liked Tim more and looked forward to seeing him when he came home. He had been coming home and asking her to do things with him.

We talked next about what she did for fun on her own. She said, "Really, nothing." We talked about the possibility of doing things with other people when Tim was not around. Maybe one night a week she could plan an activity with a friend. She told me that there really wasn't anyone she considered a friend and hadn't been for a long time. I asked her if she had ever had a best friend, and if so, what had they done? She said that when she was in college she had had a best friend, and they had played tennis, ridden bikes, and double-dated a lot. It was a great time of life for her, and she had had no drinking problems.

To get back the good feelings and to stop drinking, she would have to start to make some friends and do things with them. But how? I went through her typical day again, looking for women with whom she had contact, to whom she could say hello and maybe start a conversation with the intention of eventually making a plan to do something together. There was Gracie the gossip, Cathie the complainer, and Doris the dull one at her school, none of which she now chose to approach. There was, however, a neat neighbor whom she saw in the community garage almost every day when she was coming home from work. They had had a few brief positive exchanges, and Liz had often thought that she would like to pursue the relationship.

I suggested a plan for Liz to approach her neighbor in the garage or at her apartment the next day. I asked Liz to start the conversation to see what they had in common and to get her neighbor's phone number and make a plan to do something together.

The hugs were to continue. She was also to read her "positive" list each day, and the new plan was added to the plan sheet.

During the next ten weeks of her therapy, Liz and I worked primarily to develop behaviors that would increase her confidence to make and maintain friendships. In these sessions I was still providing most of the ideas for good planning.

First she started taking and then reading the newspaper for at least half an hour every morning before she left the house. We, in fact, spent time during our therapy session discussing current events, sports, and other new information that made Liz more interesting. We made specific plans concerning which people she could talk to and when she could talk to them. We talked specifically about what she was reading.

She liked to laugh and have fun but felt she was not a lot of fun herself. We talked about jokes and how and where to learn them, how to practice her timing alone, when to tell the jokes, and then made a specific plan for her to tell the same joke as many times as she could in a seven day period. By the end of the seven-days she knew that joke!

To help her friendship with her husband, she persuaded Tim to take a tennis class each Saturday morning with her, and they played on Sunday for at least an hour. On some Sundays they would ask Judy, Liz's new best friend who lived in the building, to get a date and play doubles.

Remember that baseball idea? When we started therapy it would probably have been a bad plan. During our tenth visit, though, Liz brought it up, and I encouraged her, since things were now going so well, to find out about leagues they could play in and ask Tim. She did both, and within a few weeks they were playing on a coed softball team two nights a week. From this point on, we were making more and more plans together, rather than my taking the major responsibility.

With all these new alternative behaviors, two very significant things started to change. First, sex improved to the point where Liz was approaching Tim and feeling comfortable about doing so, and second, she seemed to have chosen to stop drinking entirely. Both problem areas started to change when Liz started doing things for herself and with her husband that made her and her marriage stronger and more fun.

With Tim we continued along much the same way, with some additions for his needs. By the eighth week we were making plans *together* to help him become more assertive in order to overcome his shyness and build his psychological strength up to the point where he could tell Liz what she did that was painful and what she did that was good. In the fourth session I gave Tim a plan to do one positive thing for or say one positive thing to Liz each day. We made out a list of what he could do or say in my office first, and then he recorded it or he did it on his plan sheet—the way the hugging, coming home on time, and spending half an hour together had been recorded. These plans became habits because they were assigned over and over again and therefore practiced each day.

As time goes on and people get stronger, I give plans that may not necessarily be repeated each day. For example, after the ninth week Liz and Tim were to give a party together, and Tim was to call all the people on the party list, some of whom were Liz's new friends. At the party both were to practice changes they were trying to make, like approaching others first, having things to talk about, telling a funny story or joke, drinking beverages other than alcohol, and having specific positive things to say about themselves and others at the party. I discussed these things in detail with both of them.

I was quite pleased with how things were going. There had been only occasional minor slip-ups but then, in the eighteenth week of therapy Liz came in with a major negative change. She had started drinking again and had been doing so for the last four days. I asked her to go over, specifically, what she had been doing for the last seven days. She started to tell me that Tim had been late the last six nights, but she caught herself (possibly because of my nonverbal behavior showing annoyance and disapproval) and said, "I know it's what I have been doing and not Tim." She then admitted that she had stopped doing things that had made her feel good—hugging Tim, complimenting him, doing things with other people, and so on, and had gone back to old habits where others controlled her feelings. During this session I pointed out, through summaries, what she was now doing and what the consequences were. I also brought in the positive things she had done since therapy started and the consequences she had felt. It was her choice, since she had control, to feel good or feel bad. I also quickly added two specific things she could do for the next week—go to the softball game alone and be with friends there if Tim were late and couldn't go, and hug and compliment him each morning before they left for work. I didn't spend a lot of time finding out details about the drinking or her feelings toward Tim for not coming home on time. I just pointed out, through summarizing, what she was doing, what positive things she had done, and what she could specifically do now.

The following week she reported no improvement. She was still choosing to drink and not take positive control of her life. At this point, I felt it was very important not to panic and not to do anything significantly different from what I had done the previous week. I continued to point out her behavior, her choices and their consequences, and what, specifically, she could do differently.

After nine days of drinking and feeling sorry for herself, she stopped. There was no magic or easy way—just hard work on her own. In our twentieth session things had gotten much better. She not only had started to do the things I had suggested, but had come up with two other plans on her own. She wrote Tim love notes and hid them in his pockets each morning, and she invited him out to his favorite restaurant for dinner.

It was at about this point in my sessions with both Liz and Tim that the plan making was starting to move into the third phase. I would still start the sessions with questions about their commitments from the previous week, and what new things had happened since I last saw them, but now I would also ask what plan of action they had to make their lives better for the next week.

They were now making plans to solve their own stresses. They had learned how to look at what they were doing and not so much at what others were doing to them, how to set up plans that met the criteria of what a good plan is, and how to build upon strengths in their lives, not weaknesses.

I saw Liz and Tim for about twenty-three weeks on a once-a-week basis, with a few missed appointments. As I do with most people who work to get stronger, I scaled down gradually to seeing them every other week, then once a month, and finally occasionally when they would call. I haven't seen or heard from either one of them for the last two years. I assume they both are still choosing, successfully, to work on their problems each day to make their lives better.

4

Reality Therapy

An Explanation of the Steps of Reality Therapy

William Glasser, M.D.

As the steps of reality therapy were worked out in practice, it became apparent that, with skill, this approach could be used successfully with anyone who needed help. Some people are more difficult to treat than others, but regardless of the client's problem or level of maturation, a creative and tenacious therapist can in almost all cases help people significantly to improve the way they lead their lives.

Reality therapy is based upon the theory that all of us are born with at least two built-in psychological needs: (1) the need to belong and be loved and (2) the need for gaining self-worth and recognition. We spend our lives trying to satisfy these needs, and whenever we can't satisfy them, we suffer. But even our suffering is, in a way, an attempt to fulfill the same needs. Children acting up in school to gain attention are briefly satisfying their need to be recognized and to feel worthwhile. A depressed person uses depression to ask for help, reduce anger against others, and rationalize that "I can't do anything to help myself because I am so depressed." Alcoholics drug themselves with alcohol so they feel good and thus gain the false impression that their needs are satisfied, even though their lives are falling apart. All these actions are destructive to the relationships with people such persons need. To help people, therefore, we must help them gain the strength to do worthwhile things with their lives and at the same time become warmly involved with the people they need.

Reality therapy is a process in which we teach people better ways to fulfill their needs than they have learned so far. The therapist must become an important part of the helping process. Even though, in many cases, clients may have a devoted family and close friends, they still need to experience care and concern from the therapist. Therefore, step one of reality therapy, *make friends,* is to establish, as soon as possible, a warm, supportive relationship, and throughout therapy to insist that clients take a hard look at the life they are choosing to lead. Unless this kind of friendship is woven deeply into the fabric of therapy from beginning to end, the helping process will rarely be effective. The ways this is done will be illustrated in depth in the cases discussed in this book.

Because it is so necessary that clients examine their lives, the title of this book, *What Are You Doing?* is heard over and over again, almost as a refrain in the treatment process. Always the emphasis is on the present—what are you doing now and what do you plan to do in the future? This does not mean we deny that problems may be rooted in the past. Everything we do today is in some way related to everything that has happened to us since birth. But since we can only correct for today and plan for a better tomorrow, we talk little about the past—we can't undo anything that has already occurred. Therefore, the reality therapist takes account of the past, believes in it, but deals with the present because dealing with the present respects the whole past.

Reality therapists, however, on some occasions do ask about the past. We are not trained to be rigid in any way, and if we believe that knowing about the past will help us to plan for better behavior now or in the future, we encourage therapists to move in this direction, but with the strong caution *that what they should look for are past successes.* From these, rather than past failures, or misery, we can help the client to do better now. Take, for example, a client who is having difficulty in his marriage—it would be very important to look back into the past to find out when the marriage was going well and rebuild from that past success. What should be avoided is looking back for past failures. We have our hands full with dealing with present failure; we need not look in the past for more.

Also important, as we focus on present behavior, is not to ask clients how they feel unless that feeling is firmly tied to what they are doing now or plan to do in the future. We believe that our behaviors are a combination of what we do, what we think, and what we feel, but to the people who are upset it may seem that how they feel is most important. We must not be misled by the importance of the feeling to them, but must keep in mind that even when people are extremely depressed their depression comes partly from what they do (perhaps sitting around the house a great deal), partly from what they think (that maybe they are worthless), and partly from what they feel (which is the emotion of being depressed). But of these three components we have discovered that to help clients we should focus upon the doing part—in this case, the sitting around the house.

Therefore, step two of reality therapy is to focus upon the clients' daily activity and *ask people what they are doing now.* All the clients in this book are continually being moved toward facing what they are doing and accepting that they choose at least this one component of their behavior. If we were to try to get clients to accept that they choose *all* their behavior, they would almost all argue that "I don't choose to feel this way," and perhaps also that "I don't choose to think upsetting thoughts." Rather than get involved in this argument, which is pointless because there is no way to win it, we try to select the component of their behavior that they are most likely to admit they choose, which is their activity. We are, of course, concerned with what they are thinking about and how they feel, but we don't ask about either of these, especially not about feelings, unless these two activities are closely related to their daily behavior. This doesn't mean we don't listen if people complain. Not to listen would be heartless, but as they complain, usually about how they feel, we try to relate this to what they are doing. For example, if a depressed person complains that he or she sits at home alone all day feeling miserable and thinking unhappy thoughts, we will listen to the misery, but we will stress the sitting home. We will ask, "Is that what you choose to do?" and although the client is telling about the misery and the upset, we will focus more and more upon his or her activity, or the lack of it. We have found that depressed people can change the sitting much more easily than they can change the depressed feeling or the miserable thoughts. We've also discovered that when they start to move around and become more productive, they will be less depressed. Therefore, talking about how a person feels or thinks, without strongly relating it to what he or she is doing, is always counterproductive.

Another frequent example of this same process is seen when we deal with extremely upset young people who are angry, hostile, and acting out. If we ask them how they feel, it seems that our listening recognizes, and to them justifies, how they feel and usually causes them to become more angry and more rebellious. Asking less about how they feel and more about what they are doing, and then working out a way that they can do better, causes them to feel less frustrated and more worthwhile, and then the anger is reduced. The anger is not a cause of their ineffectiveness, it is the result of their inability to do the things they need to do to satisfy their needs. Ann Lutter demonstrates this in working with Jennifer, as shown in Chapter 1.

Step three of reality therapy is the question, *Is what you are doing helping you?* Once the person accepts that he or she has chosen any part of his or her behavior, that person is ready for this question. It can be asked in a wide variety of ways. The therapist may inquire, "Is it working out?" or "Is it what you want to do?" or "Is it the kind of thing that's going to make life better for you in the future?" There are many variations, but basically the importance of this step is to get the person to judge whether or not what he or she is doing is effective right now.

If there is a specific time in reality therapy when people begin to change, it is when the client evaluates what he or she is doing and then begins to answer the question, "Is it helping?" People do not change until they decide that what they are doing does not help them to accomplish what they want to. This question gets right to the core of the theory of reality therapy: Are you doing what will help you to fulfill your needs? It is important here at step three for the therapist to remain nonjudgmental—the client must answer this key question. In most cases, once clients become aware of their behavior, they quickly see that what they are doing isn't helping. But in some cases, when they don't know how to do better, they don't want to face this; it is too painful. Here the therapist may have to offer an opinion, but when it is offered, the emphasis must be that it is only an opinion. What is important is what the client believes. In rare instances, as in the chapter "Coming Out of the Corner," when the patient is a seriously disturbed psychotic client like Henry, the therapist in the beginning will have to make the decision for him, to actually tell him what he is doing is not helping. But, as therapy proceeds, even the most recalcitrant client will begin to make this decision if the therapist keeps asking, What are you doing? As they focus more and more upon their behavior and as they gain strength, a little understanding, and a few better behaviors, even clients as upset as Henry can begin to evaluate that "What I am doing is not helping me."

There is an obvious modification to this important question in the case of out-of-order school children, whom we ask, "Are you breaking a rule?" or "Is it helping you break the rule?" The emphasis is on the broken rule. We inquire about this to help make young people aware both that there are rules and that they must take responsibility for their behavior.

The fourth step of reality therapy is *to help the client to make a plan* to do better. A large portion of the time spent in reality therapy is spent in planning and in checking with the client on how the plans are being carried out. As you have seen in "Be My Friend," the planning was long term and complicated. In "Big Returns on Little Plans," the plans are simpler. But there must always be a plan. People who go through life without some sort of long-term plan, usually divided into a series of small plans to reach larger goals, are like ships floundering without rudders. Over and over throughout this book is a refrain—let's make a plan, let's work something out, let's figure out a better way, let's see if we can plan to do something that is better than what you are doing now. While it is preferable for the client to make the plan, this is not a fixed rule. In many cases, especially with upset people, the therapist may have to offer a plan to get things started. What I've discovered over the years is that it is rarely important who makes the plan. Ultimately if it is accepted, it will become the client's plan. No one does something very long for someone else. We do things for ourselves, but very often, especially when working with skilled therapists, people find themselves in agreement with what someone else has suggested. The idea that the therapist doesn't invade the planning aspects of a person's life is to me like an oven salesman watching the Ancient Chinese burning down their houses to roast pigs and not stepping in to say, "Wouldn't an oven be better?"

Making plans is, in many instances, teaching, and we teach all the time. People don't learn what they don't want to learn, but teaching becomes effective as soon as people who hurt discover that they can learn a better way. Wouldn't it be silly for an algebra teacher to say, "When you get the urge and inclination to figure out algebra, I will check and see if you are right." In therapy we are constantly teaching, training, and showing people, most of whom accept our teaching because they believe it makes sense for them. For example, recently I worked successfully with a young woman who felt incapable in every area of her life. She was almost immobilized by her image of herself as a failure. Rather than see her in my office, where I was sure she would do nothing but complain a great deal about her inadequacy and blame it on her parents and employers, I suggested that if she would run daily I would run with her twice a week. We talked during and after. As our runs approached five miles, she began to believe she was a good runner. Then we were working from a little success instead of all failures, and I believe her acceptance of this suggestion was crucial to the progress that she later made in every area of her life.

Perhaps most often the plans are made jointly between the therapist and the client, or the therapist encourages the client to plan with someone else who is important in his or her life. How the plan was initiated or who it came from doesn't matter. What does matter is that the client begins to follow the plan he or she believes will help.

When clients do this, they are becoming more responsible, and the concept of responsibility cannot be stressed too much. Steps two, three, and four are what I call the "responsibility steps." When clients accept that they choose what they do, when they evaluate their behavior and conclude that it is not working for them, they begin to see that they must become more responsible. Step four then naturally follows, because the responsible person makes a plan and follows it through. Over and over the therapist urges clients to take this responsibility, to accept that no one in the world is going to do things for them or live their lives for them. The therapist can help for a while, but all therapy can do is get this process started. In the end everyone has to be responsible for his or her own life and for living in a world much larger than the limited world of therapy.

Because there is so much human involvement and detailed planning, some people are concerned that reality therapy makes the client too dependent upon the therapist. In practice, this has not turned out to be a problem. I have had clients who have become extremely dependent upon me for long periods of time, but when they finally gained strength, they got along well without me. We have to face the fact that none of us is independent, that those who cry most for independence have not faced the fact that if they are strong and successful they are almost always surrounded by a group of supportive people.

We are more likely to become dependent upon another person

when we are not helped to plan and to move toward better behaviors. To keep someone dependent upon you, ask the person often how he or she feels. When people discover that you are a sponge for their complaints of mistreatment and unhappiness, they may feel better for the short while you are there. If this happens over and over again, it is like taking a drug. The complainer feels better for a while, but since he or she is not doing anything to improve life except talk, the brief good feeling that ventilating provides quickly wears off, and the client looks to the therapist for another feeling "fix." In reality therapy, there may be a deep dependence for a while, but as soon as the client develops behaviors to cope with the world, he or she begins to move away from the therapist and the limited arena of treatment. Even the loneliest of clients eventually learns that there is more to life than a relationship with a therapist for an hour or two twice a week.

5 The fifth step of reality therapy is *commitment to the plan* worked out in step four. This is an important step because it helps a person again to see "I'm responsible, not only to myself but to my therapist and others who care for me." Commitment means "I'm no longer alone. What I do now is not only for myself but also for someone else." When the client says, "I will really do it," to the therapist, it provides a sense of strength, a sense of purpose, and as such it becomes important to reality therapy. Not much time is spent on commitment, yet this small amount of time, the idea that you are not doing this just by yourself, but that you are doing it as a committed plan of action to someone else, makes it more likely to occur.

6-7 The next two steps, six, *no excuses,* and seven, *no punishment,* go together. Obviously in a world where excuses are readily accepted, many people hesitate to do their best. In reality therapy, when there is commitment to a plan, there is no excuse for not following through. When the client does not follow through, the therapist asks, "When will it happen, when will you get it done?" or asks "Do we have to renegotiate? Maybe we have to drop this plan and figure a new one," but under no circumstances will the therapist accept an excuse. The accepting of an excuse is saying to the person, "I accept your inadequacy, I accept your misery, I accept your inability."

The reason most of us accept so many excuses is that, although we live in a punitive world, people don't ordinarily like either to punish or to be punished. So it seems that we are always looking for reasons to excuse behavior so we don't have to hurt or get hurt.

In nonpunitive reality therapy the clients are never put down for not having done what they said they would do. If we don't put people down or punish in any way, we are justified in being firm about not accepting excuses, because without punishment or rejection there are no good reasons for excuses. A teacher might say, "If you disrupt my class, I am not going to punish you, but I do insist we work out a better way. It is not important to me why you did it, I'll accept that you have a good reason, but as I said, regardless of the reason, we have to solve the problem. We have to figure out a better way for you to follow the rules."

Ordinarily, however, except in raising children or teaching school, the subject of punishment never comes up directly. Some clients, however, when they fail, expect punishment. They expect the therapist to take a hard and critical attitude toward them, and they tell us so in a variety of ways. But a good therapist does not fall into this trap. We don't criticize, because if we did, they would use our behavior to continue excusing their inadequacy, a game they played for years with those around them. By not being punitive we do not get involved with this inadequate way they live.

If, however, you are teaching school or raising children and they refuse to follow the rules, you must do something that could be construed as punishment, or at minimum a sanction. That is, you can't let children break the rules and disrupt the situation, whether at home or school, without having some reasonable consequence for their behavior. What we have worked out, we believe, is the most reasonable of all consequences, that is, temporarily to deprive the young person of freedom until he or she is willing to work out a better way. We ask that the child sit in a chair or go to a comfortable room, either at home or school, until he or she can make a plan to follow the rules. Of course, we first try to help, but if the child continues to refuse to follow the rules, we say calmly but firmly, "Sit here until you can work out a better way." A calm, quiet place to sit, to read or do school work, or even sleep, provides the child with an opportunity to get over the upset and to think of a plan to follow the rules.

This simple, consistent sanction is much more acceptable to any child than striking a blow or using a put-down phrase and gives them a chance to change. Children like the refuge of a place to sit as long as they are not sentenced there. Our chair or room is not jail. It's a calm, comfortable place to sit until the child can figure out a way to begin to follow the rules. As soon as they have calmed down, usually after a short while, the helping parent or teacher comes and says, "Come on, it's foolish to be sitting here, let's get going and figure out how to solve the problem." This is a reasonable consequence that we advocate. It doesn't hurt, it doesn't put people down, it allows them a rest and a chance to gather themselves together and lasts just long enough so that they can begin to work out a better way if they want to. In some cases, it may take quite a while, and we may have to use the method several times, but generally once children find that this mild but firm procedure is strictly enforced, they will pull themselves together and plan. When they do, we are back to step four, and maybe this time the plan will succeed. While this is hard to do with a screaming child at home, it will work. If a two- or three-year-old child is totally out of control, then the parent must act as the chair. Hold the child gently and firmly until he or she calms down and then make a little plan.

The last step of reality therapy, step eight, is *never give up.* Throughout this book the tenacity of the therapist is seen over and over again. One chapter is called "Never Give Up" because it demonstrates this step with a person whose problems were so severe that it was discouraging to many of those who were involved in trying to help her. The therapist in this instance worked not only with the client, but with the overwhelmed staff. Do not approach a person thinking, If things don't work, we're going to give up. Run the old John Paul Jones idea, "We've just begun to fight," through your head instead. People call me a Pollyanna, saying all I can see is the bright and hopeful side, but when you are attempting to help another person who is down and sometimes almost out, this is the only side of you worth presenting. Not giving up also goes right back to step one. It solidifies the idea that the client belongs, and if nothing else, at least right now there is closeness. But it also signifies that the therapist is not going to give up on the responsibility steps, two, three, and four.

As you read this book, you will become aware of these steps of reality therapy as they are used. As important as they are, you will also discover they are not a recipe to be followed in cookbook fashion. Simple as they are to describe, their use may be, and usually is, complex. Using the steps is analogous to painting a picture. You could go to an art store, and perhaps for a few dollars purchase better supplies than Rembrandt ever had access to, but you still have to paint the picture. The steps of reality therapy are like the brushes, canvas, paint, and turpentine—they make the picture possible, but they don't by themselves paint it. They give a structure upon which to help the client, but you have to use your own ingenuity, creativity, and imagination in putting them into use.

For example, how do I get involved with this person who doesn't want any part of me or what I stand for? Read how Melvin Goard got involved with Vincent, a very depressed and withdrawn fifteen-year-old, in "The Road Back." Imagine how much ingenuity it took and you will see how difficult and creative this process needs be just at step one. Try to put yourself in William Abbott's shoes in "Banking on Your Interest" as he struggled with an intelligent but somewhat disdainful drug-using high school girl, to get her to begin to believe that someone cared from the start about her life. It's not easy. Making friends is hardly cut and dried. You have to figure out how to do it, and often a client will not only not help you at first but will fight you.

Nowhere is the need for ingenuity seen more clearly than in step four, the planning phase. Here the therapist, always moving toward figuring out a better way, suggests, urges, cajoles, draws out, drags out, and somehow or other gets a client to begin moving in a better direction to fulfill his or her needs. It takes a lot of strength to continually reject the person's excuses and keep saying that if we have a plan, we have got to follow it through or make another one. It also takes some self-control to avoid becoming angry and retaliatory when a client tests, taunts, challenges, or berates you. Few therapists, of course, would react directly, but there are many subtle ways in which a therapist can express anger toward a client, all of which should be avoided.

Throughout this book, you will see that the therapist remains non-judgmental about the client's behavior. It is this stance that helps a client decide that he or she ought to try something else. When we judge people or criticize them, they are almost forced to keep up their inadequate behavior to justify it. What they are doing at the present time may be all the client is capable of in attempting to feel worthwhile. Putting it down will only make him or her tend to repeat what has been unsuccessful in the past. Therefore, while we want our clients to judge their behavior (step three), we must again stress that it's they, not we, who make the judgment. This becomes especially difficult when a client asks you to make a judgment. People want justification for both what they do and how they feel. They want you to side with them and tell them, "I think what you are doing is right," or "I think you have a right to do it." We continually say, instead, "It may be right, but it's up to you to determine that, it's not up to me. I can't live your life, I can only help you to live it better, but you've got to make some decisions." When we make judgments, when we criticize, we are in a sense attempting to live the clients' lives. In most cases, this is not new—parents as well as others have tried to do it many times before, and we must not fall into that pit.

The last group of cases in the book take place in a school setting. Because they do, I think it is important to say a few words about the concept of schools without failure, which is my attempt to apply the theory of reality therapy to schools. I do not view schools as hospitals or clinics; their job is to teach, not to do therapy. They are places where children need to learn the academic and social skills of living. For this to happen, children need to be motivated both to learn and follow the rules, and what I discovered over and over again, as I began to work in the schools, was that we cannot motivate a child with failure. Children have to see the school as a place where they can fulfill their needs. "In school I want to be taught by a teacher who cares for me, and I want to get a chance to learn something worthwhile." Therefore, what we have suggested is that schools be very careful about failing children. Children cannot cope with feelings of worthlessness and usually turn to disruptive behaviors. They'll reason, "Since I'm not cared for, I'll create a lot of problems and get attention or I'll hurt the school or teachers that failed me." They also reason, "If I'm not learning, then I'll give up and stop trying." It is these three behaviors—disruption, revenge, and lack of motivation—that teachers struggle with over and over again.

A school without failure is set up to help children avoid all of these problem behaviors. We instruct teachers at all levels to express reasonable care and concern for the children in their classrooms, to get them to feel they're in a warm, human place where they belong. To do this, we have specifically taught the concept of the classroom meeting, that is, the teacher grouping his or her class in a circle so the children can face each other and talk easily and then, through skillful questions, getting the class involved in a discussion they all believe is important.

These discussions are usually not personal or problem solving so far as individuals are concerned, but they may be problem solving for the group. For example, the whole group or a sizable part of it may be out of order on the playground, and the teacher may introduce the problem during a class meeting. Most often the discussions are thought provoking, giving individual children a chance to speak their mind and in so doing gain the strength that always accompanies expressing oneself well to a group. A child who believes "I'm important to the group" will want to follow the rules and do his or her schoolwork to maintain that importance. In the chapter "I Hate School," you will see how this happens. When these meetings are held regularly, children become motivated and discipline problems drop.

In a school without failure, children are given second and third chances, because the worst thing that can happen to a child is to begin to believe that he or she is a failure and because of this give up trying. We don't want the child to see himself or herself in a dead end. We look for successes and try to build on those, and over and over we urge teachers to recognize the destructiveness of failure. We recognize that if a child does not work, eventually the child will have to be failed, but what we believe is that the child who is threatened with failure too early, may give up and fail long before failure need be a fact.

In a school without failure, however, individual children do express problems and concerns and do cause disruptions. These children need to be counseled individually, and in this counseling we strongly urge that the steps of reality therapy be used.

Finally, I'd like to say a word about the use of drugs in psychotherapy. Because the therapists in this book are not medical doctors, they cannot use medication, a situation that undoubtedly works to their clients' benefit. I am a firm believer in the effectiveness of good psychotherapy, and I do not support the current wide use of psychiatric drugs. People with serious problems cannot be made whole by chemicals. While some situations might call for a short-term use of low doses of some drugs, my experience has taught me that in most instances drug use, legal or illegal, stands squarely in the way of effective therapy. This is illustrated clearly in the chapter "Be My Friend," in which Rebecca, who was handicapped by drug use for years, had no chance to do what she wanted to do with her life if she continued to take it. The drug immobilized both her mind and her body, and under its effect she was helpless to do anything but go through the motions of living. Reality therapy, as I practice and teach it, uses either no drugs or extremely few, and then only for short periods of time.

5

An Overwhelmed Single Parent

The Problems of a Divorced Parent

Edward E. Ford

Sometimes I think of the room where I meet my clients as an emergency room. There seems to me to be an analogy between the people who come to see me and those who go to an emergency room. Some of the people who show up in the emergency room have serious, chronic illnesses that have unexpectedly become critical; others are healthy people who have been involved in accidents. Some of the people who come to me have very few skills in living—they just never learned. Their external challenges might not be that great, but even small challenges are too much for them. Others, however, are people who do have many of the skills necessary to live a happy, satisfying life, but a temporary pile-up of external problems has paralyzed them. You might compare them to people who have superficial head wounds when they arrive in the emergency room. There's blood all over the place. They look terrible, and they're scared. But basically, if you can stop the bleeding and calm them down, they'll be all right. What I am doing with my clients is teaching them a better way to live—hoping that eventually they can become better organized in solving their problems, whether long term or immediate.

Joyce Garrett was a client in the second category. When she came to me, she was exhausted, overwhelmed by the very real difficulties she had to face in every area of her life. But even as she spoke about her exhaustion, I could tell by what she had been doing that she had some areas of strength or confidence. She needed someone to help her sort out what she was doing, to set priorities and gradually to make better and more appropriate plans for handling her life.

You know the old story about the optimist and the pessimist looking at a glass of water. The optimist says it is half full and the pessimist says it is half empty. I try to be like the optimist. I look for my clients' strengths and try to develop and enhance them rather than look at and analyze their weaknesses. After all, it's the same glass of water that is both half full and half empty. But it makes an enormous difference where you start. The counselor's perception of a problem can become the client's way of looking at it.

Joyce chose to start our conversation by talking about her son. Ben was seven, and he was, well, pick your words from hellion, dickens, scamp, brat, or rascal. If you want to sound more clinical, add hyperactive. You name it, Ben had done it, and if it was forbidden he had done it repeatedly. The list included pulling the fire alarm at school, throwing rolls of toilet paper out the lavatory window, writing on the blackboard in crayon and on the walls in chalk, and running around in class. He seemed to have a penchant for throwing things out the window, particularly if they were beautiful and the teacher and other students had worked hard on them—the Valentine box, the Christmas display, the carved Halloween pumpkin, and other kids' lunch pails. The list went on and on, but there had long ceased to be anything funny about it. The teachers were at their wits' end, and Joyce knew that something had to be done.

As I listened to her talk about Ben, I was thinking about her. I didn't yet know all the other problems she was facing, but I suspected that Ben's behavior was part of a situation in which there were other, unresolved problems.

In an attempt to try to learn how better to cope with her son, she had attended a seminar I was giving on my book *For the Love of Children.*[1] I was impressed that this woman had enough energy and organization to attend a lecture, buy a book, and arrange for an appointment with a man she had never met—all seemingly because of her son. These may seem like ordinary, everyday things, things that people do all the time, but many people lack the skills of knowing how to cope, and they cannot even do this much. Joyce was showing that she did have enough strength to seek help. As a counselor, I look to see what skills, if any, my clients do have, and this was an obvious one.

And so I said to her, "I'm sure Ben has some real problems, but

[1] Edward E. Ford and Steven Englund, *For the Love of Children* (New York: Doubleday and Co., 1977).

I'm also sure he has something important going for him—a mother who loves him and who isn't too proud to ask for help when she needs it." Well, that uncorked the bottle, and almost as though I had planned it that way, Joyce cried a little, then recovered her composure enough to start talking about the rest of her life.

I want to insert a remark here about what I look for when I speak to clients about their strengths and problems. Their strengths are what they can do or what they are doing that is helping them; their problems are created when they have difficulties achieving what they want. Since the clients lack confidence in their ability to handle their life well, my job is to build that confidence, to help them function better on their own. Thus the best place to begin is to look for the strengths in their lives, for it is where they are doing something even partially positive that we often find the best areas for change in behavior.

When I talk to them about what they are doing, I always have in the back of my mind the various strengths they need. These strengths reflect our basic human needs. First, I look at what they are doing to fulfill their need to love, to have other relationships and friends. Thus I look at their family life, their friends, and especially at their close, intimate relationships.[2] Second, I look at what they are doing that gives them worth, status, or recognition, such as jobs, hobbies, volunteer work and, especially, disciplined personal activities done regularly, such as running, biking, swimming, and yoga. Third, I look at what they are doing for fun in their lives, both alone and with others. This includes all types of play activity, which is so essential to strength, for from play comes the development of relationships, imagination, creativity plus relaxation.[3]

In Joyce's case, her relationship with her mother and father was a difficult area in which to build a sense of love and belonging, and that with her ex-husband, Steve, almost impossible—but the one with her child was comparatively easy. Although you do have to work with the difficult problems in a person's life, it is best to begin with the easiest ones (where some strength exists); this then builds the needed confidence to resolve the tougher problems (where there is much weakness). Bill Glasser taught me years ago to start with the easier ones—they are tough enough.

Notice, though, that when you recognize the strength, you have

[2] See Edward E. Ford and Steven Englund, *Permanent Love* (Minneapolis: Winston Press, 1979).
[3] See *For the Love of Children,* Chapter 7.

to acknowledge the problem almost in the same breath. Denying the problem does no good whatever. I call that the "Aren't you a big boy?" approach. Junior comes home crying because the big kids wouldn't let him in the game, and Dad says, "Aren't you a big boy to be crying about a thing like that?" Dad is acknowledging more strength than Junior really has—if Junior were really that big a boy, he wouldn't be crying. And at the same time, Dad is denying the painful reality of what has happened. The reality therapy approach is to say, "I can see you're upset. It's tough not to get into the game. But I've seen you play, and you're not that bad. You react quickly and you're a fast runner. Maybe there's another game you can get into, or even another sport. Let's talk about it." Sometimes parents who instinctively take this approach with their children need help in applying this good sense to their own lives, and this is a role the counselor takes.

After my initial acknowledgment of both her problem and her strength—at least *one* problem and *one* strength—Joyce began to talk about herself very freely, and I questioned her only for more information or slight clarifications. I didn't ask any probing questions; I wouldn't have known where to begin to probe. People vary considerably in their deportment with a counselor. Some always find it hard to talk, but many find it hard only at the very start. Not long after the start—and you never know quite when this moment will come—there often occurs that popping of the cork I mentioned a moment ago. Once that happens, you just let the bottle bubble over for a little while, but you have to direct its flow as much as you can. You don't yet know what's important and what isn't, but you try to remember as much as possible of what you are hearing. As soon as I can I try to direct my clients' thinking, to find their strengths, to get specific about various areas of their lives, and to make sure they don't wander in their thoughts.

What I heard about from Joyce first was the breakdown of her marriage. She had married Steve eight years earlier, when she was twenty-three and he was thirty. He was handsome, virile, and powerfully built—a construction worker she thought was sensitive. Joyce had been ecstatic on their wedding day, but things began to go wrong that very night. His "lovemaking" was physically painful to her then, and continued to be so abusive that one year after their marriage her doctor ordered them to stop having relations until she healed.

Shortly after they resumed relations, she became pregnant, and then came another disappointment. Steve, though claiming to be delighted that he was to be a father, found it impossible to be intimate with a pregnant woman. From the time her condition became apparent until Ben's birth, he never touched her, and after Ben's birth, his lovemaking was sporadic and sulky. He began to ignore his family and to drink heavily. In effect, Joyce was already raising Ben alone.

The situation began to worsen shortly after their fourth anniversary, when Steve fell forty-two feet from a scaffolding, landed on all fours, and bounced onto his left side. His wrists were horribly shattered, and during the next four years he was under constant medical care, unable to work and faced with a wearying round of surgery, therapy, and rehabilitation. During this period, his drinking problem turned into serious alcoholism. Joyce decided she had had it and filed for divorce, which was granted a few months before she came to see me.

To her credit, Joyce did not regard her divorce as a sign of failure on her part. She had married in love and good faith and had struggled to cope with problems that really were not of her making. But in the aftermath of the divorce, she was faced with several serious problems, one of which was Steve's continuing dependency on her. He would call her and play on her sympathy with long accounts of his loneliness, pain, and job and money problems. Many of there were problems that she faced, too, and she found her will to begin making a new life for herself sapped by these long and unwelcome sessions with him.

Joyce's financial problems were serious. The divorce had left her with legal debts. Steve was almost never able to put anything aside from his workmen's compensation, social security, and part-time employment to help with child support. Her job, as secretary for a law firm, paid little and offered little hope for advancement.

Under these circumstances, it was difficult for Joyce to house herself and Ben independently. She tried sharing a place with another divorced woman with a child, but that didn't work. She took an apartment at what appeared to be a bargain rate, but it turned out to have a dangerous gas leak, and she had to go to small-claims court to get back her deposit. A neighbor of her parents offered her his house rent-free for the period it was to be on the market in exchange for maintenance, but maintenance turned out to be twenty hours or more per week of hard work keeping a house, grounds, and pool in "open house" condition for a man who treated her as an employee.

She was happy to leave when the house was finally sold. Finally, Joyce had no alternative but to move in with her parents, with whom she had already stayed intermittently between the other arrangements she had tried.

Unhappily, Joyce's parents' circumstances were not particularly comfortable, either. Her father was senile and dying. Her mother resented the fact that at a time when she would willingly have turned to Joyce for financial aid, she instead had to provide a home for Joyce and Ben. For whatever reason, she berated Joyce continually for the expense she was causing her parents and commented on her social life as she might have on that of a sixteen-year-old—she disapproved of Joyce's late hours when she dated, her boyfriend's style of dressing, her choices of recreation. Joyce found it frustrating, not least because she did feel embarrassed at her inability to support her parents in their own quite real need.

Joyce's social life was at a low ebb when we first met. Her mother's carping hadn't helped matters but there were other inhibiting factors. Joyce was a rather attractive woman, whose good looks were much enhanced by a warm, solicitous, almost maternal attitude. One could well believe that she had cared for her husband through several years of convalescence. She was a good listener, too. After her separation from Steve, she was pursued by a variety of men. Unfortunately, all of these encounters seemed to her to become quickly sexual and then collapse. She became very apprehensive, particularly about going to bars where, as she saw it (thinking of Steve), a woman was likely to meet only desperately lonely, alcoholism-prone men. But if not in bars, where else? Not knowing anywhere else to go, she chose to spend her evenings watching television with Ben and her father.

However, the main concern Joyce expressed when she came in was for Ben. I felt that if we could create a happier, more loving home life, and bring her closer to her son, we would eventually calm him down at school. Ben's behavior at school was serious, but because of Joyce's easy access to the boy, since he was still young, I believed that strengthening her relationship with him was the way for her to see results—to see that something she was doing was helping. The quicker a client sees something happening for the better because of something he or she is doing, the sooner confidence or strength begins to build.

In this way, my kind of counseling is very *unlike* working in an emergency room. Medics working there or paramedics in an ambulance have to think first of respiration and circulation and loss of blood; a broken tooth may have to wait. But the soul doesn't work quite the way the body does. Sometimes doing the psychological equivalent of capping a broken tooth may give a person the strength to, as it were, set a broken bone, and then to administer artificial respiration, and then to get the heart beating, and finally to get up and walk away—right out of the counselor's office. What the counselor has to ask is not "What *should* this client do?" but "What *can* this client do?" If you can just get the client to do some small thing that he or she *can* do, then there is hope that later this person may do the larger thing that he or she *should* do.

Although it was because of Ben that Joyce had come to see me in the first place, she wouldn't have spoken so freely about herself if she hadn't wanted to work toward solving some of her other problems. We spent only about fifteen minutes of our first hour actually talking about Ben. But I did restate the problem—Joyce thought that Ben's problems were school related, and I was sure that they were only partially so. But to realize the benefit that I wanted Joyce to realize from working with her son, we had to set ourselves a task that was as completely as possible within the bounds of her life with him. I pointed out that she couldn't go to school with him. We had to confine ourselves to the things she did do—or could do—with him and see whether an improvement there could bring about an improvement at school, too. For a client just growing in self-confidence, a therapist must look for a task in which less can go wrong. I didn't want Joyce to take on the reform of her local school—not yet, anyway! It would be helpful if she could just enrich her home relationship with her own son.

Joyce was reading *For the Love of Children,* and this smoothed the way. In that book, I stress the importance of parents and children sharing activities, activities that ideally call for real effort from which flows natural conversation. Formal parent-to-child talks—if that's all the parent does with the child—can be awkward, often impossible. Indirect communication is much better, especially for a parent and child who may have begun with a fairly weak relationship and are starting to build. That indirect communication comes easiest when there is a meaningful, effortful activity to share. Television just isn't that, and Joyce took some of my harsh words about television in my book very much to heart.

Ben was really "hooked" on watching television. He would sit in front of the tube from five-thirty or six to nine each evening and often most of Saturday and Sunday. He even watched it for an hour or so before going to school. Even though television had been her best babysitter, Joyce was intrigued with my idea of television "dieting." Television "fasting" would be no television at all. "Dieting" means just a little television—and *a little more of some other, healthier activities.*

Joyce cut Ben's nightly watching to just one hour and weekend watchings to a total of three hours. Television sometimes seems to work almost like a drug. There were, in fact, some withdrawal pangs for both mother and child—they became a little nervous and upset during the first few days of this television "diet." Soon, as they found other activities, the symptoms went away. Both had to *decide* what they would watch and what they would not watch. They didn't just turn it on and stare at what lit up, or just flip channels until they found something that caught their attention. At its best, television is not much of a vehicle for mother-son interaction, but now they were at least making decisions about what to watch.

In the time opened up by television dieting, Joyce and Ben planned a number of activities, some of which were physically demanding. And here is where Joyce and Ben developed the skills of problem solving. First a list of all kinds of possibilities was developed. Then they set up mutually agreed-upon criteria, such as how much time they had, what expenses would be involved, and whether Joyce could keep up physically with her young, energetic son.

I hadn't realized what her son was like until I visited her at home once and met him. With his short hair and stocky build, he looked like a junior drill sergeant. Having taught school myself, I could well believe that he was guilty of all the schoolroom charges brought against him. But not to wrong him—a boy like Ben needs and will often respond eagerly to hard physical work. Fortunately, one of their first plans was to turn their attention to the yard. Ben turned out to be an amazingly hard worker in the yard—planting, transplanting, weeding, hoeing, irrigating—he would work for hours. At the end of that kind of Saturday, he would go to bed and fall asleep immediately. The too-frequent scenes, the tantrums, that had attended bedtime became a thing of the past.

Joyce and Ben both took pleasure in seeing the yard improve, and with my encouragement she came up with other activities they could share. They went to the zoo, they took hiking trips, and they climbed some of the local mountains—activities that seemed obvious enough, but they did take more effort than just watching television, and the increased effort invested produced a new relationship between mother and son. In school, although Ben is not and never will be a teacher's pet, the worst excesses of his misbehavior seem to be over. As we all know, a kid who acts up that way is usually looking for attention. What we forget is that the solution is not to deny him attention but to give him the right kind. When Ben started to get the right kind of attention at home, he demanded less of the wrong kind at school.

I felt a turning point in Joyce's and Ben's relationship when Joyce told me about Ben's fort. Not surprisingly, he loved war games, bombing, shooting, and violence of all sorts. He had built a kind of foxhole or fort, as he called it, in a corner of the back yard. One Sunday, after a long Saturday of yard work, Ben invited Joyce to the fort for provisions, or whatever he called it. He wanted to share a candy bar. The soldier who had been at war with Mom and with the world was ready to make a peace treaty. I thought it was a touching incident, but I tried not to make too much of it with Joyce. The last thing I wanted her to believe was that her troubles were over. The changes she had made in her life with her son had to be permanent or the old problems could easily return. Still, the meaning of Ben's invitation was not lost on either of us.

What I have described in a few paragraphs took several weeks to happen. Each week, Joyce would tell me what she had done with Ben, and I would then get her to evaluate what had worked and what hadn't. Then we would make a plan for the following week, adding a new idea and dropping something that hadn't worked. But basically things were going well, as I expected they would, and I used Joyce's small but growing confidence in her ability to make something go well for her son as we began to look at the rest of her life.

The most draining of her other problems seemed to be her relationship with her ex-husband. There was nothing she could do about Steve's problems, but hearing him talk on about them at such length, in unwanted phone calls, was exhausting her. We began to role-play: Joyce would be Steve, I would be Joyce. "Steve" would start to talk about what a rotten day he had had, and "Joyce" would say, "Steve, I don't mind talking to you, but I will only talk about your good news. When you've got something cheerful to say, you can call, but if all you have is problems, I'm going to hang up right away. I've got problems of my own, and listening to yours doesn't help me handle them." I'm telescoping, of course, but that was the gist of it. Not being allowed to whine to Joyce seemed to cut down the frequency of Steve's calls. The ones that did come began to seem more welcome. Their relationship became, little by little, a more friendly and slightly more distant one. Since there was absolutely no hope for a reconciliation, this is what Joyce needed and wanted.

We took the same tack, more or less, in trying to improve Joyce's relationship with her mother. When the mother started to whine, Joyce, with my encouragement, would say something like, "I know what our problems are. After all, I live in this house, too. I am willing to talk about what's going well for us or what we can try to improve, but I am not going to be just an audience for complaints." There were some very practical matters that had to be worked out, but once Joyce and her mother had agreed in principle about how Joyce and Ben would share the parents' (or grandparents') house, it was possible for Joyce to be firm. It was very clear at this point that Joyce's success with Ben and even, in a sense, with Steve made it possible for her to hold up her head in her mother's presence. Joyce was now a happier mother, a good ex-wife, and a responsible adult in her dealings with her ex-husband. The relationship with her mother was intrinsically a much trickier one. Among other things, she was the older woman's guest. But even guests should be treated courteously, and Joyce learned to claim this courtesy in an appropriate way.

Joyce's new control in the home life she shared with her mother had a noticeable impact on her social life. The mother's chief irritation was over the men Joyce saw, the hours she kept, and the places she went. The implication in the mother's criticism was that Joyce lacked judgment where men were concerned. She had made one mistake—she was likely to make another if she didn't listen to motherly advice. Fortunately, as she took charge of her relationships with Steve and Ben, Joyce began to see her "mistakes," if that is what they were, as part of a past that needn't affect her present, and at this point she read my book *Why Be Lonely,*[4] which suggests to single people a variety of ways to make friends. Joyce joined a ski club

[4] Edward E. Ford and Robert Zorn, *Why Be Lonely?* (Niles, Ill.: Argus Communications, 1975).

and seemed to enjoy it enormously. I don't really know if the mother continued her criticisms or not. The important thing is that Joyce no longer allowed such criticism to deter her from making new friends.

Finally, there was the very large and apparently "unpsychological" matter of Joyce's finances. She was receiving an inadequate salary as a secretary in a law firm. Apart from the salary, the job was unattractive for the meager opportunity for advancement that it offered. I took it as real evidence of new strength in Joyce that she chose to take a job at a lower salary in a bank where opportunities for advancement seemed to be better. With no encouragement from me, she also spoke to a credit counselor and arranged for the repayment of her legal expenses through a salary deduction.

Unfortunately, the bank job went sour very quickly. A vice-president at the bank began "putting the make" on her in a way that both ruined the otherwise pleasant work environment and seemed to cast a shadow over those prospects for advancement. If Joyce had to have a serious new setback in her life, it was better that it happen while she was still seeing me. If she could be resilient in handling this new setback, I thought, then her working confidence, her basic ability to cope, would be tested and ready for use.

At this point her membership in the ski club turned out to be very fortuitous. She met a very nice unmarried man who worked for the phone company and who urged her to apply for a job there. She was skeptical of her prospects, but with his encouragement she filled out an application, and to her delight she was offered a job at a salary as high as her initial law office salary and with prospects for advancement.

I am not seeing Joyce regularly now, and she has not called me in a few months. She is free to do so, of course, and if she does, I know it will be because she is having trouble with a decision. It will be my job to help her evaluate and clarify what she is doing and then ask her what she intends to do about it. I expect that if that happens, I will now have many areas of demonstrated strength in her life to which to point, and I will say, "Okay, you're upset. Let's talk about what you are doing. We'll figure out a better way. I know you can do it."

6

The Boy Who Wouldn't Talk

Elective Mutism in a Ten-Year-Old

Gerald B. Fuller

John, age ten, was referred by his parents at the request of the public school system where he had been a source of despair to authorities for his entire school career. His difficulty was a simple one: beginning with the first day of kindergarten, he refused to talk in school.

He had entered school at the age of four, and during the first few weeks he cried much of the time. Initially the teacher, who was described as quite warm and accepting, spent considerable time trying to work with John, but after a couple of weeks she placed him in the hall so he would not disturb the rest of the class. Finally, he was taken to the principal's office, where little was accomplished. The crying stopped after a month, but the silence remained. The teacher lost interest in John. He was, in fact, a relief compared to some of the noisy children. The other children, initially critical and teasing, soon became indifferent, an attitude that persisted for the remainder of the school year. But his kindergarten teacher did report that he did his work well.

Promoted to the first grade, John continued his silence. A school social worker saw John several times, and when she could not get him to talk, she contacted his mother—the first his mother was aware that he was not talking in school. She indicated that he did talk with family members at home and with relatives outside the immediate family, but only in a soft whisper. He did not talk to strangers or salespeople in stores.

The first-grade teacher, after a great deal of effort consisting mainly of bribery with special privileges, was able to get him to whisper to her on a few occasions, a response that apparently satisfied her. He was progressing in spelling, arithmetic, and writing, and she, too, found him rather a welcome relief from her noisy, unruly students.

When he passed into second grade, the new teacher was not so casual about John's behavior. She arranged a special conference with his mother and recommended he be taken to a child guidance clinic, where a psychiatrist followed his case for about six months. He was diagnosed as having elective mutism, manifesting anxiety, social withdrawal, and depression both at school and home. Using an analytic approach, the psychiatrist made no progress in eliciting any verbalizations. He advised the mother and school not to stress the lack of speech and suggested that John would eventually grow out of it. This produced no change, and the mother terminated John's treatment.

Going into third grade, John found the school's reaction becoming more intense. A school psychologist began working with the teacher, using a behavior modification approach. John was to get one point for each time he spoke to a peer or teacher and could redeem ten points for fifteen minutes of free time. This approach, too, was unsuccessful, and a response-cost procedure was instigated where ten points were subtracted from his total score if he did not speak a minimum of five times in each class. Seeing no improvement, the school attempted one final comprehensive behavior modification program. The teacher was to interact with John, using no rewards at first. Later she was instructed to encourage him to participate actively in class by reinforcing appropriate behavior with praise and reinforcing talking with a star. Some whispering did occur, but it lasted only about three days, and once again John became mute. By this time he had become a legend in the school system. A multitude of school personnel was eager to take up the challenge of getting John to talk.

At the end of the third grade, and after the mental health center had failed to help, the family was referred to the psychology center of a university, where the present therapist became involved with the case. In the initial interview the parents indicated their extreme frustration and anger with the therapeutic techniques used up to that time. I told them that a reality therapy approach would be employed and explained the general principles of this technique to them.

They seemed interested, and therapy began in June 1976. It was decided John would be seen once a week for a one-hour session.

John's mother had told me she felt the mutism was the result in part to family dynamics. He was the second of five children, having an older brother, two younger sisters and a younger brother. The other two boys had strong, outgoing personalities and were very verbal, and John seemed particularly intimidated by the older brother and had trouble relating to him. Instead of jockeying for any kind of status or position, John would retreat and play by himself. He never showed overt signs of anger or upset but preferred to withdraw from any situation that seemed troublesome. He seldom asked for help in resolving difficulties and seldom required disciplining. His mother saw him as a good boy who was quiet and reserved, entertained himself well, and enjoyed being alone. In his preschool days he had played occasionally with other neighborhood children but had seldom spoken to them, contributed little to the play, and eventually stopped.

John's father played with his children a good deal and seemed to enjoy them, but his relationship with John is unclear. The mother implied that her husband was upset with John's limited talking but had not involved himself with the problem. This might be attributed, she thought, to the fact that although the father spoke now without difficulty, he had had a severe stutter until he reached adulthood.

John was having difficulty with periodic bedwetting. He had been fully trained at two years of age but reverted at about three. His parents employed a number of techniques—forcing him to sleep in his wet bed, making him wash the sheets, or getting him up in the middle of the night to change his sheets and take a cold shower—but nothing had helped much. He is now on medication that prevents him from sleeping too soundly, and this has helped him to gain some control, but some bedwetting continues. The mother reports that this has been a big embarrassment for John.

During the first few weeks that I saw him, John was tense, stiff, immature, and sensitive. He lowered his head to avoid eye contact, and if the situation became too stressful for him, he began scratching his left arm and right cheek. He was fearfully shy and refused to speak. I formed a beginning relationship with him through playing games, going for walks, or getting some candy at a nearby store. He showed little initiative and remained mute. As he gradually relaxed, however, he began to smile and laugh a bit during the sessions.

When asked a question, he would shake his head or on occasion write his answer on a piece of paper.

As the relationship became stronger, I told him that we would no longer play for the entire hour. Instead, we would talk or sit together first for fifteen minutes. When he came for the next session, this plan was begun. I began asking questions dealing with such topics as his happiness and unhappiness, and events at home and at school. Although he didn't speak, he nodded yes, that he was unhappy at home and at school. Since he wouldn't talk, I repeated to him what his parents and the school were saying about his behaviors and asked for his opinion. The behaviors included not talking in school, having no friends, crying a lot, and receiving poor grades. I put these on a piece of paper and asked him to check the ones that made sense and that he agreed with. He checked the first two, not talking in school and having no friends. With several of his problem behaviors out in the open, I asked him if these were making him unhappy and if he wanted to do something about them. He nodded.

But although some behaviors had been identified and a value judgment made, John was not yet ready to do something about them. Attempts to elicit a plan resulted only in a lowered head and a shrug of the shoulders. At this point, more strengthening of the relationship was needed, since he would tighten up and withdraw from me when pressured further to generate ideas on his own.

The sessions continued with the fifteen minutes of sitting and my talking. Initially I would talk and he would nod when possible, or else we sat in silence. On occasions I would ask a question and then answer it for him in a manner he didn't like. This made him uncomfortable but did not elicit any speech. I began talking about his refusal to speak at school. He indicated that he wanted to talk, that he understood that it was important to do so, that he realized his not talking might result in his failing for the year, and yet he refused to speak.

At the same time that our relationship grew stronger, it became more threatening to John. He had begun to initiate some silent mouthing that indicated at least some desire to talk and was now faced with giving up his symptoms. A chance call I made to his parents' home added to this pressure. Expecting his mother to answer, I was surprised to be greeted by a loud male child's voice. It was John's. At the next session I confronted John with the phone call. He smiled but did not respond.

At this point I felt that pulling on our relationship might motivate him to speak. I said that he had been coming for a long time now (two months) and that it was I who was doing all the work, that he had contributed very little, especially in terms of doing something. I went on to say that it didn't make much sense to continue, as it was now becoming a waste of time for both of us. I suggested we consider termination. He was told to think about this and that it would be pursued at his next session. He agreed to this with a nod of his head.

On his next visit he appeared more uneasy than usual. He started the session by indicating he wanted to play. I countered by saying we needed to discuss what had been agreed to in our last session. After a brief review of the problem and a reconfirmation of his value judgment, I asked him to talk. Again he refused. In an attempt to force the issue, I suggested I call his mother and tell her we were terminating. He sat still for several minutes before indicating consent. I immediately said I had decided against it, changed the subject, and we went to play.

The rationale behind taking such a chance was the risk that our involvement was great enough that he wouldn't terminate. Strong as it was, however, it was not yet sufficient to replace his old behavior.

With this in mind, I backed off and continued to be friendly and interested in John. Therapy is based on a relationship, and there are times in every relationship where one loses face or gives ground. Frightening as it may be for the therapist, it demonstrates to the client the important lesson that one can be strong without always being in control. For the next month I avoided the problem and focused on the involvement. His nonverbal interaction increased and he was more relaxed, laughing and appearing content.

At the end of this month, I once again asked him what he was doing and whether it was doing him any good. He seemed quicker to recognize his symptoms and to indicate he was not pleased with them. While joking with him about my hearing his voice on the phone, it occurred to me that he might talk into a tape recorder. He indicated he would not. I asked him if he would take the recorder home, talk into it there, and then bring it back the next time. He agreed to this, and we shook hands on the plan. But he didn't follow through.

Instead of preaching, I simply told him he hadn't carried out our agreement and asked if he wanted to try again. He indicated that he did, and the following week when he arrived bringing back the tape and recorder, he gestured to me to put the tape in the recorder.

This I did, and I heard, in a whispered tone, the word "hello." I praised him for this feat and put my arm around him.

Over the next several sessions, John's responses on tape were enlarged into whispered sentences. Each of these responses was reinforced with praise, and I asked him often if it felt good to have made this accomplishment. He would always smile and nod yes.

But it was time to move on, and during the next session I again told him that for us to work together more effectively he would have to start talking aloud to me, that using the tapes was a good start and an indication that it wasn't so bad to talk. I emphasized that it was time for him to demonstrate his contribution to our relationship and to talk, since I had been doing most of the work. "Please say 'hi' to me," I said. There were several minutes of silence, and finally, with great effort and initial mouthing behavior, he said, "Hi," in an audible whisper. This was a special moment for both of us and was followed on my part by much praise. And on leaving, he whispered, "Good-bye."

I was impressed again with what a strong involvement means in therapy, and its critical importance in effecting change. How much it must have taken for him to say those words for me!

My expectations for the next session were quickly lowered when John again sat and said nothing during the beginning of the hour. I asked if he would talk out loud, and he shook his head. Reminding him of the progress in our last session and the triumph of his success, I asked if he would talk to me with my back to him. He nodded and we shook on it. I turned my back and looked out the window. About five minutes had passed before he spoke loudly enough for me to hear him. I asked him several simple questions, and he gave me the answers. We then talked about his success during the session, with a lot of praise from me. We made a plan to continue this approach for the next couple of sessions, to which he made a written commitment. The plan was carried out, he talking to me in a whisper while I sat with my back to him.

After this, I made a plan with him that we would talk face to face. When he arrived for the session, he was more uneasy than usual. He sat down, and I said, "Hello." About two minutes of silence followed before he whispered, "Hi." We talked about what he watched on television, did on the weekend and in school. This continued for several sessions, then I asked him what could be done to help him talk in his normal voice. At first he shrugged his shoulders, but then he said, "Talk louder." This became his responsibility for the next session. At the next meeting he fulfilled his commitment and we talked for approximately thirty minutes. After this, each session lasted for about forty-five minutes, and we were able to talk for the entire time.

Up until this point I hadn't taken on his refusal to talk in school, since I wanted him first to get used to talking in his loud voice with me over a period of time. Now, however, I asked John if I could call his teacher to check on his school progress. I hoped to get some generalization effects from his success. He agreed.

I learned from his teacher that John was not talking in the classroom, and at the next session I asked him if this was true. He said it was. When I pursued the matter, he said he didn't want to continue his old way. I asked him what his plan would be, and he said he would talk to his teacher. I indicated the plan wasn't quite clear to me in terms of "how, when, and where." After some discussion we decided that he would talk to the teacher on Tuesday and Friday mornings. When asked what he would say, he indicated that he would say, "Hello," and ask to go to the bathroom instead of just raising his hand. I wrote this plan on a piece of paper and we both signed it, with each of us receiving a copy.

When he came back the following week, he indicated that he had carried out the plan, and over the next several sessions we worked on increasing the number of days he would talk and the things he would say. Everything seemed to be progressing even better than I had hoped. Each time a plan was formulated, a commitment was made and executed. But then a phone call changed all that.

John's mother called and said that she had just returned from a parent-teacher conference, where she had been told that John was not talking at school. Since she had told me previously that John was talking more in the neighborhood and in the local stores, this was an eye-opener for her as well as me. John had been telling both of us that he was talking at school when, in fact, he wasn't. This was a lesson for me. I had taken his word, which on the surface appeared to be the thing to do, since a good relationship existed between us. However, he had learned to keep me off his back by setting up a plan and then indicating that he had carried it out.

The next time John came to see me and indicated he had completed his plan, I asked him if he had any objections to my calling his teacher and checking on how he was doing. He said yes, and I asked him what the objection was. His reply was that it wasn't necessary, that he was telling me everything that was happening. I said I wasn't sure of this, since his mother had recently called me and told me he wasn't talking in school. He admitted this, and started making excuses for his lack of success. I interrupted immediately, asking him if he wanted to talk in school; he said he did. Similar plans to the ones he'd used before were formulated, with the stipulation that I would call the teacher each week to check on how the plans were working. I told him I was very interested in his progress with talking in school, and in knowing whether the teacher felt it was going the way he did. He agreed to this additional plan.

In an attempt to coordinate our efforts, I saw the teacher before our next session. She was cooperative and interested in helping in any way possible. I told her of John's progress with me and of some of the techniques that I was using with him. She agreed to read up on reality therapy and to carry out some of my suggestions. I particularly emphasized the need to praise his talking and the consequences to be used if the rules were not followed.

I told John what had taken place at this meeting and what could be expected. It became evident that he was much more likely to talk if he went up to the teacher's desk and whispered than if he attempted to speak from his desk. We started with this approach, and shortly he was doing this at least once a day. The approach included asking a question when he had one, followed by answering the teacher's questions for him. He also made and carried out plans to talk to his gym and music teachers. Again he was able to communicate with them in a whisper. During this period he was strongly rewarded for his successes, which did appear to increase his feelings of self-worth. He would now admit that school was a better place than before and he enjoyed it more. We discussed talking louder and from his desk, but he was still not willing to make a commitment to either of these plans.

At this point the school year ended, and because of a number of scheduling problems and summer programs, it was decided that there would be no therapy sessions during the summer. John's mother would contact me in the fall if things were not going well for him.

In the beginning of October his mother called and told me that he had regressed again in school and that he wanted to come and see me. His mother attributed this in part to his new teacher, who was older and more authoritarian than the previous one. She reported that he had had a good summer, that he had talked to others outside the home and was less shy and more outgoing.

After talking to the new teacher and John, we were able to pick up and begin pretty much where we ended in the spring. He was still talking in a loud voice to me, and in no time at all he was whispering again to the teachers. Shortly after this he was able to give me a value judgment and commitment that he wanted to talk out loud at school. We agreed that this would occur with the teacher alone at her desk and established as well that if it was not carried out, he would have to miss recess. Because he understood and agreed to the outcome before he engaged in the activity, this was seen as a logical consequence of his behavior, not as punishment. Punishment is any treatment that is inappropriate for the act—physical or psychological pain. Reasonably agreed-upon consequences are not punishment.

John did not talk out loud to his teacher at her desk the first time and missed recess. We agreed upon the stipulation that he would have to come up with a plan so it wouldn't happen again. His plan was to try it once more with a specific sentence, which turned out to be, "Can I have my math assignment?" This time it worked for him. At this point, he and his teacher agreed to his doing this at least three times a week, the days being his choice. This worked, and shortly he was saying something at least once a day out loud. Since the teacher was working so well with him, John and I agreed to meet only twice a month.

There were ups and downs during that school year, but overall he continued to improve. Toward the end of the school year he was beginning to talk out loud from his desk, but this remained somewhat of a problem area for him. I agreed to continue to see him once a month during the summer to help him prepare for a new teacher and grade.

In the last several sessions, he has been talking "a blue streak." He has been spontaneous, showing no shyness and being much more confident in his own ability to perform. We went to the store to buy candy, and there he asked the clerk several questions and responded to a question asked of him. We have also talked about alternative strategies and choices—he has to talk out loud from his desk when school begins this fall. He appears confident about this and so do I.

During the course of the therapy, I repeatedly emphasized that I was interested in John and in dealing with the present, particularly in his attempts to succeed and deal with his problems in an effective and responsible manner. It was necessary to assure this boy that I would stick with him until his problem was resolved, so to this extent the relationship played a major role. When he resorted to "I can't" in discussing certain situations, I converted that to "you mean you don't want to or you won't—let's explore the choices you have." Until we were involved and he realized that he was responsible for his own behavior and that something could be done about it, we made little progress. But through the involvement he finally realized he was responsible for talking and understood his capacity for more worthwhile behavior in his immediate environment. His decision to become involved, to change his behavior and to continue talking, was the essence of the therapy.

7

A "Together" Lady Falls Apart

The Relationship of a Middle-Aged Couple Breaks Up

D. Barnes Boffey

Mary's call had come in a week earlier, saying "she needed someone to talk to." I had known her slightly as a fellow member of a local youth council. She seemed to be intelligent, honest, and open with others. Watching her play a secondary leadership role in this group, one might have classified her as a quite "together" lady. She had attended youth council functions several times lately with a man unfamiliar to me, and I guessed our visit might focus on that relationship in some way. I supposed she might even be contemplating marrying him and just wanted to check some things out with an unbiased person before she did.

When Mary walked into my office, it was very obvious that she was not considering, at least at that moment, anything so prospectively enjoyable as marriage. She was in tears, but obviously holding in her anguish until she was safely within the confines of my office. As she sat down she said, "He dumped me—he broke it off." She took awhile to become "composed," then explained that two weeks ago she had decided to come for help because she felt her relationship with this man, Robert, was not going well. What concerned her was that she thought she might be making the same mistakes with Robert that she had made in a previous marriage. She had begun to feel uncomfortable, even to the point of considering breaking off the relationship. What had happened earlier on this day of our first session, however, was that *he* had called *her* and broken it off suddenly. She had been caught up short and her pride was hurt, but more than that, she was feeling the real pain of a broken relationship. They had been living together for a few months, and that hurt even more.

Many of Mary's first thoughts were basically self-pitying, and she shared her thoughts of how scared she was of finding another relationship at her age (she'd recently reached fifty), how much of a "bastard" this guy had been to let her down the way he had, and how stupid she was to let him do it to her. What made it worse, we decided in kind of a joking way, was that she hadn't had the chance to decide on ending the relationship—she had been the "dumpee" rather than the "dumper." Mary's emotions, especially her fear of the future and her anger in the present, really had her down.

After getting the general picture of "what was happening," I felt we needed to clarify a direction to go in. Mary needed to begin to make changes in her life that would bring about a workable solution to her current crisis. Then she needed to focus on moving forward. We did not need to describe and understand all the aspects of the problem. This would have kept us at ground zero and delayed creating the answers Mary needed. We needed positive action now.

Sensing that she herself had been ambiguous about the relationship, I asked, "Would you have chosen for the relationship to continue? Do you want to see it end?" It was important to state whether we would be trying to (a) put the relationship back together or (b) recover from it. This was an important step because it was, I felt, the first time Mary sensed she had a choice in the matter. She was acting as though she were a helpless drifter waiting for the fates to buffet her around, but here she had her first choice.

Mary responded quickly, almost startled to realize that she really wanted to be out of the relationship—she wanted to get it behind her and start feeling better. She had made an important value judgment, and by doing so could now begin to take an *active* part in finishing the relationship and making choices about how things turned out. Mary, by coming for help at the very beginning of this stressful time, was able to make rational choices right away and save herself a lot of pain. Had she reacted to the situation with a series of punitive, emotionally motivated responses, she could have made many regrettable decisions in the first five or six days of the break-up, and done many things that could have adversely affected her emotionally for months to come.

Mary talked about her anger and how she wanted to get back at Robert, and she talked about not being able to face him when he called again about what he wanted her to do with his clothes and other things. At this point we talked a little about reality therapy, and I mentioned that reality therapy states that what one does will determine how one feels. If she wanted to feel better, she would have to determine how she would like to handle the situation, endure feelings of fear and apprehension while she carried out her decision, and wait for new feelings, like satisfaction, to take the place of the old ones. She was receptive to this idea because it meant she would not be experiencing as much pain in the near future.

In many ways Mary had strength before she came to see me, and this helped her to begin her "recovery." She was open to the realization that her anger at Robert had a backlash that would keep her weak and vulnerable. She knew that if she acted on her anger it would only increase.

Crucial to Mary's growth over the next five days was the fact that she accepted, in some ways on faith, that *acting* on negative feelings was self-destructive. If she felt frightened, for example, and then acted on that fear, the fear would increase along with her pain.

She had especially wanted to curse Robert out for leaving so suddenly and not telling her daughters, who had grown very fond of him, that he was leaving. She had already told her daughters that Robert had left, but—refusing to allow him to escape the consequences of his behavior—she had also told them that he would have to tell them why. God knows she wanted him to hurt, but she also saw herself calling him up and starting to curse him out, then yelling and losing control of herself over the phone—something she really didn't want to do. We explored this, to see whether the phone call would help either her or the situation, and she agreed it wouldn't— but she wanted him to feel a lot of pain.

I asked her, if she could arrange it ideally, how she would like the situation to end. How would she handle it? In other words, if it were to become a success for her, what would have to happen? At first she had trouble visualizing her choices, but eventually she was able to come up with the suggestion that she send him a note, a simple statement telling him where she had left the situation with the girls, a note that avoided preaching or the laying on of guilt. It was important that she underplay her emotionality. She wanted to get the message across without doing something she would feel bad about at any point in the future. She didn't want to give Robert any "ammunition" to use against her, in calling her irrational or anything else. She also agreed to write the note that day, and in this she took her first step toward action.

I said now, "Okay, you have some other choices—how would you like to handle them?" She could choose when his things would be out of the house; she had a say in how their few joint possessions were to be distributed. Every time she *(a)* saw options in how she would like to handle a situation, *(b)* chose a way that would help her, and *(c)* acted on it, her world got larger and she got stronger. All the choices put her in a state of semi-shock, but as she chose she gained more strength.

Mary had to accept the fact that breaking up would create pain—and had to commit herself to accepting that pain in the short run. It hurts when you take a splinter out, but not as much, all told, as if you leave it in. She also bought into the idea that she did not have to play out the little drama in any preconceived way, and this was exciting to think about. As part of my role, I laid out several scenarios for her, from "the fearful fifty-year-old lady begging for her lover's return," to "the really together lady who would take charge and keep cool," to "the embittered lover who would swear off men and relationships forever." We generated several more, and after that she could choose one she liked. My descriptions were not as important in their content as in the fact that I believed there were endless ways to handle the situation, and that she did have a choice.

As we talked during that first meeting, our relationship gained strength, and constant focus on "how things could get better" and "ways for her to get strength" made the atmosphere very hopeful. And when the visit ended, she had made several plans for ways to handle situations that would arise in the next few days, and had made a commitment to attempt them *even if she felt scared and felt as though she couldn't.* She knew she was able to, and I was trading on our mutual involvement and my caring that she would have the strength to do it.

The most specific decision she made concerned the things of Robert's that were in the house. She decided she would specify when and where he could pick them up (when she wasn't there) and what would happen if the things were not gone by her deadline.

THERAPIST: Okay, Mary, do you think it would help to decide how you would like his things dealt with?

MARY: What do you mean?

THERAPIST: Well, he's calling the shots about when he's going to pick up his things, right? He said he'd pick them up next week. Are you comfortable with that?

MARY: No, I really want his things out of the house, especially in the bedroom . . .

THERAPIST: Okay, how would you like to handle it? What would you do if you really had your act together?

MARY: I'd clear everything out of the bedroom tonight and tell him to pick it up soon.

THERAPIST: What do you call soon?

MARY: I don't know—say by Friday?

THERAPIST: Is there anything to stop you from doing that?

MARY: No, I guess not, but I don't want to be there when he shows up. . . . It would be too hard.

THERAPIST: So, it's by Friday and when you're not there? What time should he come?

MARY: Wednesday or Thursday morning would be good.

THERAPIST: Okay, and what can you do with the things if he doesn't pick them up?

MARY: I feel like leaving them on the front lawn.

THERAPIST: Would that help you?

MARY: No, but I'd hate to be too well adjusted about this whole thing. [Laughter]

THERAPIST: So, what's the decision?

MARY: I could leave them at the church. . . . He'd be embarrassed if he had to pick them up there.

THERAPIST: You feel comfortable with that?

MARY: Yup . . .

She also decided to do this without losing her cool. To have control over her life in even very small ways was incredibly important at this time. She was moving forward.

Before she left, we talked further about the concepts of reality therapy, and I mentioned the four success pathways: love, worth/recognition, fun, and self-discipline. I mentioned that at this time, when she was feeling great stress, it was especially important to do good things for herself in each of these areas. She said she could get more active in youth council activities, and do other things that might bring her some fun.

Mary left after having worked hard and accomplished in one session what might have taken other people with less strength a much longer time. The number of visits is not important—it's the concepts and how they are applied and acted on that determine success.

Mary might have spent time "finding out *why* the relationship failed" or "understanding her feelings" or "gaining insight into her patterns of being married." Instead, she had taken action and changed her life for the better. Mary decided we should get together again in five days to check her progress and give her a boost. We agreed that she could call me anytime in the next five days if she felt really down (which we both agreed she probably wouldn't, but at least we could leave it as an option), reviewed her plans, and said good-bye.

Mary returned only one more time. During the five days after we first met, she was able to work on the choices she had made for herself and gained a great deal of confidence. Her pain did not disappear over the days she was gone, but things were definitely better. It had taken months to build the relationship—it would take a while to diminish the feelings of involvement. The hurt continued, but with Mary's actions and our strength in the therapeutic relationship, she had the strength to cope with the pain until her accumulated actions built up new long-term feelings.

In the five days, she had ended the relationship the way she wanted to, and could now walk away feeling good about the way she was handling it. Most of the plans she had made turned out well. Mary had written a good note, Robert had picked up his clothes as requested, and there were rules, established by Mary, about any future communication. Robert did not contact the girls as requested, but Mary was able to handle this denial of responsibility on his part as she saw that she was able to act more successfully on her own. In reviewing the successes of one week, Mary was astounded by how well things had actually gone and began to get a feel for the power that lay in her choices and her action. Her week was not all roses, and mixed in with her courage were crying times, angry "thing-throwing" times, and lonely times when there was no one to talk to, but by acting on what she had decided would be best for her, she had gotten over the rough spots.

Mary felt she had the idea of what she needed to do now—the important part was doing it, and she felt good about our time together.

We made a third appointment, cancelable if things were going well, just to make sure she had a point in time to aim for if things started to slide backwards. She did cancel that appointment, and the next time I saw her she was wearing a "women's movement" T-shirt and enjoying her strength.

8

"I Don't Have to Be Sick to Be Somebody"

An Older Woman Gives Up Being Depressed

Ronald C. Harshman

When I first met Viola, she was a sixty-four-year-old woman who had been severely depressed for approximately two years. She had previously been admitted to the psychiatric ward of one of the general hospitals, and at that time had received five electro-convulsive-therapy treatments (shock therapy). Viola was still under the care of a local psychiatrist, but his primary concern with her was keeping a check on her current medications. He had prescribed Stelazine, Valium, and Tofranil, and Viola appeared to be very much involved in the routine of taking these psychotropic medications.

During our first visit, Viola seemed eager to convince me that she was extremely depressed and that I would not be able to help her. She had been referred to me by the chief psychologist at the university hospital, but she viewed seeing me as just one more in a long series of what had been disappointing psychotherapeutic experiences.

Before the onset of this depression, Viola had been a very attractive and involved woman. She talked about having been very active socially and prided herself on her previous abilities as a homemaker and hostess. She now presented quite a different picture, appearing in my office looking haggard and unkempt.

Viola told me that she had been happily married for thirty-nine years and that she and her husband, Ralph, had one adopted daughter, now thirty-five years old. Ralph held a senior-level position with one of the major oil companies, which enabled them to live very comfortably.

Viola linked the onset of her depression temporally with a situation that involved Ralph. Three years earlier, Ralph had been assigned a new secretary, whom Viola described as being "very pushy and sexually provocative." Some of his colleagues had joked with him about the secretary, and Ralph had become concerned that some of the "stories" might get back to Viola. He discussed this concern with one of his former psychology professors; unfortunately, this professor advised Ralph to tell Viola everything about the new secretary. He further advised that it would be a good idea for Ralph to arrange for Viola and him to go out socially with his secretary and her husband. The apparent rationale behind this advice was that it would prove to Viola that there was really nothing going on between Ralph and his secretary.

Although there may have been good intentions behind the advice, the situation backfired, and Viola became increasingly depressed. Some of Ralph's "buddies" had apparently made anonymous telephone calls to Viola, advising her that a "relationship" was going on between the secretary and Ralph. Although Viola tried to ignore the calls, she wondered why Ralph was pushing her more and more into the secretary's presence. Viola, confused, was not able to handle the situation in an appropriate manner and began to misinterpret Ralph's motivations. She convinced herself that Ralph was arranging the social interactions to enable him to spend more time with his secretary. According to Viola, as her depression became more and more intense, she began to withdraw from all her usual social activities. She approached Ralph with her insecure feelings, but the more she attempted to do what she hoped would solidify her position, the more things began to crumble around her. For one thing, Ralph and Viola were experiencing sexual difficulties—he was not able to maintain an erection—and Viola made the assumption that this was related to "the other woman."

Ralph's supervisor had become aware of the situation and, or so Viola thought, fired the secretary because of it. Unfortunately, Viola was already well on her way to locking herself into a failure identity. She became more and more depressed, and although Ralph continued to reassure Viola about his positive feelings for her, Viola kept on with her "give-up" pattern.

At our initial session, I learned that Viola accepted her identity of being "the most depressed." She refused to see any other perceptions of herself and negated any possibility of change. She had seen "the best doctors," had been taking all kinds of medication, had gone through shock treatments, had been hospitalized, and nothing had helped. With all this "sick" history, how could I really expect that she could get any better?

I felt that her continuing use of the psychotropic medication was helping to perpetuate the unhealthy state of affairs. I discussed my assessment of the situation with Viola and told her that I honestly believed we would be able to improve it if we were prepared to become really involved with each other and work hard together. I indicated that it would be important for Viola to advise her physician and psychiatrist of her involvement with me and tell them that I would be attempting to help her discontinue the use of medication. Viola agreed to stop taking the Tofranil that weekend and take the Stelazine every other night. As her first homework assignment, I asked Viola to put on paper honest evaluations of how she saw herself in the three major roles of her life—her roles as woman, mother, and wife.

At the second session, Viola told me that she had taken the Stelazine every night but had stopped taking the Valium and Tofranil altogether. She was very proud of herself for having been able to do this, even though she had misunderstood my directions. We were able to clarify the original instructions, however, and Viola began to reduce the Stelazine but resumed the Valium. Later on we were able to discontinue the Stelazine and reduce the Valium gradually until she was no longer taking any medication.

The role descriptions Viola had written indicated just how much she had given up any positive perceptions of herself. She related to things that she had previously been able to do, but saw herself now in terms of those things she was not doing. As a wife, Viola wrote: "I always did everything that I could to please my husband, but I don't feel up to doing anything now like I used to. . . . I care what I look like, but can't seem to enjoy dressing up like I used to." As a mother: "I would like to be well enough to babysit with the grandchildren, but they are so active I couldn't do it at this time. . . . My daughter and family have just moved back here, and they have been very busy. When they come over, I enjoy seeing them, but after a while I get very weary and very nervous, but they are very good to me and seem to understand."

Finally, as a woman: "I get very confused and want to lie down all of the time, but then I can't rest and get up and down a lot, don't seem to know what I want to do and it seems so lonesome, but if anyone would come to visit me I would enjoy it for a little while, then in my mind I would want them to go. . . . I don't seem to be as interested in keeping myself as clean as I should, I used to love taking baths and always have my hair look nice and tidy. I plan meals that are as easy as can be."

Clinging to her negative self-concept, Viola repeatedly asked me if I had ever worked with anybody who had been quite as depressed as she was. I assured her that I had, but I also began to confront her with the need to start doing something if she wanted to see any improvements. We talked about many of the activities that Viola had enjoyed before her depression. She indicated that she had enjoyed visiting friends, giving formal dinner parties, planting her garden, baking, cooking good meals for Ralph, and participating in many recreational activities. I told Viola that there was no magic in getting better. We would work on her doing things that would allow her to feel worthwhile and cared for. We discussed the written role perceptions, and I tried to impress upon Viola the need for her to start being accountable for her own behavior.

During the next several weeks, I saw Viola on a weekly basis, and each time that we met I assigned her more and more "homework." These assignments related primarily to her "doing something." Viola appeared to respond well to taking a maternal outlook toward me, an aspect of her personality I was able to use by getting her to do things like bake cookies and bring some to me. Viola followed through with the assignments but continued to come prepared to tell me how poorly she had done. She still compared her present functioning with her previous levels of achievement, trying to convince me that she really was "quite sick." I began confronting Viola about her appearance and suggested that she start taking more care in how she dressed for our sessions. Each time that Viola started to wallow in her misery, I attempted to use the building strength in our relationship to confront her with a "why don't *you* do something about it?" type of approach.

Viola had the benefit of another person being interested in her getting better. Ralph's supervisor's wife had previously been depressed and was now taking a personal interest in helping Viola. She drove Viola to my office for the first several sessions and repeatedly asked me for advice. As therapy progressed, Viola's friend felt more and more comfortable in setting higher expectations for Viola, and as a result Viola had two people that she knew cared about her, both telling her that she could do better. Viola respected this interested and well-functioning woman and appreciated her friendship, and because of it she began to feel more worthwhile.

Unfortunately, Ralph had become very wrapped up in what he perceived as his own responsibility for Viola's condition. He was inadvertently supporting her failure identity by not letting her know he expected her to change her behavior. I met with him, explained the situation, and solicited his assistance. Ralph found it difficult to set expectations for Viola but when he saw the positive results as her friend took the same approach I did, he was able to become more involved in the therapeutic process.

During our seventh session, Viola was able to verbalize the most significant changes that had taken place in her total outlook. Whereas she had been trying initially to establish herself as the most depressed patient I had ever seen, Viola now started asking me if I had ever had any patients who were able to get better any more quickly than she was. But she still maintained some safety in taking this position, continually reassuring me that she had been and still was really "quite sick." She was having a difficult time in abandoning her failure identity, but at the same time she wanted to invest effort in developing the success identity we had begun to create.

Viola was now beginning to trust the degree of caring that was inherent in our relationship. She knew she didn't have to remain locked into a failure identity, but she still needed some justification to move out of it. She was faced with heavy pressure from me to get herself moving. I was using the strength of the relationship we had built in a constructive manner, forcing her to look at what she was doing to herself. Because of the trust in me (and us) she became more prepared to abandon the negative self-concept. Viola was starting to get involved in some of the social activities from which she had previously backed away, and although she was still struggling with this process, she was able to admit that she did enjoy doing these things again.

As Viola became more secure in her healthier self-image, we were able to start looking realistically at her marriage. She and Ralph had never reconciled some of the traumatic experiences they had lived through together. When Viola was forty-three years old, she had been seven months pregnant before the pregnancy was confirmed. Her physician had been lecturing her about the weight she had been putting on when one day she asked him about the unfamiliar lump in her abdomen. She was referred to a gynecologist, who determined that she was indeed pregnant. It had been the first pregnancy after eighteen years of marriage, and although they tried to save the baby, the efforts were in vain—Viola was suffering from high blood pressure and was toxic as well. Although she carried the baby for a full nine months, it was stillborn. Ralph and Viola appeared to accept this situation in a very philosophical and stoical manner, but they had never been able to talk much with each other about their loss.

Although Viola and I recognized that we could not do anything about altering this unfortunate experience, I felt it was important for us to be able to identify the way in which Viola and Ralph had failed to communicate honestly with each other over a long period of time. Viola realized that it would be important for her to begin to break the impasse now, to resolve some of these issues with Ralph rather than just pretend that since they loved each other everything would work out okay. Viola began to understand that she had to accept responsibility for what happened in the relationship with her husband.

We spent the next several sessions discussing ways in which Viola could approach Ralph and even engage in brief, meaningful discussions about their previously hidden concerns. She did approach him, and even though as they talked the subject quickly turned to Viola's depression, they didn't take the direction of "Oh, woe is us," but were able to talk openly about healthy ways of altering the present situation.

They began to feel good about the way they were finally resolving some of these lingering issues. Each was able to acknowledge a willingness and commitment from the other to make things better. Viola began to recognize that the sexual difficulties were, in part, being perpetuated by her own behavior and attitude. By the same token, Ralph was able to see how, inadvertently, he had been perpetuating and supporting Viola's depression.

Ralph was looking seriously at the possibility of retiring, and Viola was able to assist him in realistically assessing his future with the company. Both felt that Ralph was not going to move any further up the organizational ladder, and he was beginning to feel that his usefulness to the company was declining. For the first time Viola was able to discuss this matter with him without "putting him down," either for his feelings or for the reality of the situation. Instead she encouraged him to look at his previous accomplishments with and contributions to the company, and together they were able to examine other possibilities for their future with a much healthier outlook.

As Viola and Ralph were able to resolve more and more issues, and as Viola began to feel better about herself, her dependency upon our relationship and the need for our involvement began to decline. Viola and I talked about this, and she recognized how much more comfortable she was feeling with her new success identity.

We saw each other less often. We joked about Viola's not coming to see me the next week on the condition that she use the money either to buy herself a new dress or play golf. Viola did this a few times and felt good about it. She looked better, felt much better, and continued to become more involved in meaningful discussions with Ralph.

I saw Viola for fifteen sessions over a period of six months. She was able to abandon any use of psychotropic medication and, more importantly, was able to reestablish herself with a much healthier and more productive self-concept. It has now been several months since our last therapy session, but I still hear from Viola occasionally. Ralph has retired, and they are enjoying their leisure time together.

9

Doing Makes the Difference

A Twenty-Year-Old Woman Begins to Take Control of Her Life

Douglas D. Walker

It was cool out. One of those gray days, too cold for shirt sleeves, too mild for a jacket. The sweater she wore made sense. Her hair was expensively cared for, though it fell loosely about her face when she looked down, something she seemed to do a lot. Other than what I saw, I knew nothing about her. Nothing unusual about that. After all, that's usually the case the first time you meet someone.

I found out that she had been referred by HELPLINE in Los Angeles and she couldn't afford to pay anything, which seems to be true of many of my clients—you don't have to have money to have problems. Other than that, all I knew was that Wren Holland was a young woman seeking counseling.

She told me that she had asked HELPLINE to refer her to "a realist." Wren said that in the past she had sought good psychiatric help and, in her words:

to no avail, I might add. The problem I encountered was that at the end of one session with an analyst I came out with problems I never knew I had. After lengthy elaboration on my inabilities, hostilities, fears, and various other negative feelings, my therapist asked, "Do you know you have this facial twitch?" I just got more depressed.

Wren continues the narration:

If my memory serves me well, I started reality therapy at what might be called a low point in my life. This is not to say that everyone doesn't get depressed at some point in their lives, but I was beginning to see it as a lifestyle, making a real habit out of feeling down. Moreover, I was running out of people to blame for my misfortunes. That was the worst part of all. I had had the standard set of excuses as to why my life lacked mirth and merriment—it was my boyfriend's fault, my parents' fault, my job's fault, et cetera, et cetera—and it was a great comfort to know that *I* had nothing to do with it. Whatever, the fact still remained that I was feeling miserable and some change had to be made.

So she called HELPLINE, they referred her to the Institute for Reality Therapy, and she came in. The first session we spent chatting generally about what was going on in Wren's life that had caused her to seek help. She was twenty-two years old and she was working, but in a branch office that was about to be closed by the parent company from back East. She was pregnant for the second time, knew she didn't want kids, and had lined up her second abortion. She had been to college, done quite well, but quit before finishing. The problems continued to pour out. Her parents refused to talk to her, in fact, would not have anything to do with her because they didn't like the man she was living with. Ah, yes. The man she was living with. He wasn't doing much. He loved smoking dope and being with his friends. He wasn't working. He didn't talk with Wren much, in fact he avoided her, and she found herself spending increasing amounts of time alone. Her weight had been fluctuating for years, and as her problems got heavier, so did she.

It's amazing how much time you can spend elaborating on the problems. We spent all of the first session and most of the second session unfolding all the troubles. I'll let Wren pick up the story here.

Doug let me pour my heart out about my problems—parents, living situation, how I couldn't do this or that. Then, toward the end of the second session, he asked, "Well, what are you going to do about it?" That really surprised me! "What do you mean *me?* I *am* doing something! I'm here!"

You see, everyone else always asked me how I *felt* about my problems. I had those answers down pat, but when he asked me what I was going to *do* about my problems . . . I was surprised by that question, I didn't know what to do, so I asked him to give me some multiple choices. He did. Doug said I could do nothing, continue just the way I was. Second, I could make some radical changes, move out, quit the job, move to the East coast, et cetera. Third, I could start small, start with one thing I really could manage to change that might make life a little better for one hour out of the day or week.

Wren told me she liked to spend time alone. I told her I thought that was basically good, but within reason. Twenty-four hours a day of alone-time seemed to be a bit excessive. She agreed. In terms of multiple choice, she picked number three, so I asked what little thing she thought she could do between now and next week.

"I could give Darlene a call."

"That's fine. Do you think you will?" I've learned to ask questions like that to follow through. Sometimes that extra question, "Will you do it?" is the nudge people need to move them from having the idea or plan into performing or executing the plan. It is the doing that makes the difference. The planning just helps you get there with the most efficiency. If you don't *do* something different, things aren't likely to *be* any different. That's one of the reasons why after the plan is made in reality therapy, the next step is to get a commitment that the person will follow through on the plan. So I always ask that question.

Answering, Wren said, "Yeah, well okay, but I'll just be doing it for you, not for myself."

"That's all right," I told her. "As long as you're doing something healthy, I'm not particular about who it is you do it for."

Wren told me later, "I was running out of excuses fast. I kept trying to avoid action, I just wanted to talk about it, not do anything about it, but at that point it was easier to complete the task than to try to maneuver my way out of it. So I did call Darlene, we made plans to get together, and to my surprise, really, we did have a good time."

As the sessions continued, we talked about things Wren used to do that she enjoyed but for one reason or another had given up. She used to do more in the way of hobbies, including painting and sculpture. She composed humorous letters to her sister. Her sister loved them, showed them to all her friends, even responded with funny letters of her own. I asked Wren whether she could start doing either or both of those things again. Wren said her friend Darlene enjoyed painting, too, so she called her up and the two of them started painting together once a week. She wrote to her sister, too, although that never became the routine that the painting did. "Still," she says, "I was spending about one day a week making a plan and following through on it, which is something that didn't come very easily to me.

"The best part about it was the expression of delight on Doug's face when I would come back in and report, even if I had had a lousy time."

Actually that look was probably as much surprise as delight. I was fairly new as a reality therapist, and I wasn't sure people really would do the things they planned to do. Nowadays I'm delighted when people follow through on plans, whether they had a "good time" or not, because I know that following through on something is often its own reward. Wren at that time was feeling very much out of control, not at all sure that she could do anything worthwhile. It took encouragement from me to get her going. She needed to start getting control of what she was doing, and knowing she could follow through on a simple plan was getting her started toward the good feelings she needed to have about herself.

When Wren remembers this early stage of therapy, it's:

I'd say "Guess what I did? Blah, blah, blah," and he'd say, "That's great!" Coming in and telling somebody about an experience adds to the experience itself. Kind of like pictures from a vacation. Sharing a good time makes it better, sometimes sharing a bad time makes that seem better, too. At least, it can help put the experience in perspective so it doesn't seem so overpoweringly bad. Plus, it felt good to know that I did have enough control over my life that I could follow through on plans, even though not all of them worked out.

To a person whose life is going well, whose self-esteem is high, these plans may not seem like much and the successes may seem relatively minor. To someone like Wren, whose self-esteem was very low, a little success went a long way—a little bread to a hungry person can taste very, very good.

As Wren succeeded in the seemingly small things, she felt strong enough to deal with some of the weightier problems:

In terms of my boyfriend, I tried a few times to talk with him, but I sort of gave up working on that. My relationship with him was a futile situation. In other words, not everything in my life was good, but the point, to me, was that there were some parts that I could work with that would make more of my day happy. I felt proud of myself afterwards for doing some productive things. Not only did I feel proud privately, but reporting back to someone that I did do something helped, too. I felt I was being reinforced.

I asked her, "Was it ever fun just doing some of those things, apart from getting any reaction for having done them?"

"Sometimes," she said. "It depended on what I was doing. I don't remember all the things I was doing other than going out with Darlene, the painting, and the letter writing. I just remember feeling better."

Wren may not remember, but I remember at least some of the things that were happening about that time, and they weren't all positive. Her job did terminate. It was no reflection on the quality of Wren's work, the company just folded. Nevertheless, here she was without a job and still without the college degree she really needed to get the kind of job she wanted. Joblessness leads to other problems. Who pays the rent?

She was living with Jim, but this relationship had never been close. He had been nice at the beginning, but almost as soon as Wren moved in, as soon as the challenge was over, his attitude began to change. So did his behavior. He spent more and more time getting high with other friends. (Wren never liked getting high very much—drugs were not a problem for her.) He spent a lot of time working on his car and less and less time with Wren. Perhaps she needed more than he could give. The relationship, which seemed to have been built more on expediency than commitment, was fading rapidly. Wren could not depend on Jim to support or even help support her. She had been paying him rent since she moved in and had to continue doing so.

Her parents, who still weren't talking to her, had stopped when she moved in with Jim. They had tried to break up the relationship from the beginning, and no doubt the pressure they put on her had been a major factor in Wren's decision to move in with him. She was running from the hassles of home probably more than toward the promise of a sound relationship.

In any case, here she was facing the reality of being unemployed, having no money to support herself, and having no one to help her pay her bills. She was feeling overwhelmed again, upset. It's hard to think rationally when the emotions are so powerfully activated. "What am I going to do now? I don't have a job, I know my boyfriend is going to kick me out. I could get some crummy job, but I could never support myself."

"Well," I told her, "there are still choices."

"Oh yeah? What?"

"Well, for one thing you could fall apart." We both laughed. That seemed to help us relax and get us down to the business of figuring out just what the options were at this point.

School is something in which she had done well, had enjoyed, and had almost completed. I asked her about finishing the work for her degree.

"But where would I live?" No matter what road you start to walk down, there are always problems to be worked out. "How would I pay for school and food and all that? I just don't think I'm cut out for working at some lousy job eight hours a day, living in the dorms, and studying hard the rest of the time. I just couldn't do it."

"What about your parents? I mean, I'm getting the impression that you're thinking about leaving your boyfriend anyway. . . ."

"I may not have any choice."

"Right! You told me you thought he was about to ask you to move out. So what about your parents? Would they talk to you if you were no longer with this guy they don't like?"

"I don't know, but I think they might. I've been thinking about them a lot lately and wondering how they'd feel. I just don't want to have to hear 'I told you so' from them."

"Are they likely to do that? I know some parents would, but some parents would just be so happy to have their daughter out of what they thought was a bad situation that they'd leave the past alone. What do you think?"

"I don't really know, but they felt so strong about it. . . . I think they'd be glad to see me back, but I also think they'd do the 'I told you so' bit."

"So what are you going to do?"

"My parents have a boarder living with them. I could call her and ask her to feel them out."

"Do you think this person would do that for you?"

"I think so. She and I have been talking lately, and she wants me to move home. I think she'd be willing to talk to my folks."

"It's certainly worth a try. When could you call her?"

"Today, I guess."

"Sounds good to me. Now, what will you do if your parents say no or if they do get into a lecture about how wrong you were?"

"The lecture part I think I can handle. After all, I've had those from them all my life. If they won't take me back, I don't know what I'll do. I suppose I could stay with Darlene for a while. . . . I just don't know."

"If they say no, would you call me and let me know what you are going to do?"

"Yeah, thanks."

I didn't hear from her until the following week. She came in beaming. She had called her folks and they were more than glad to have her back. They needed someone to watch the house while they would be away on a trip, but it did seem they were genuinely glad to have her back. The most surprising thing to Wren was that they hadn't even given her the lecture she was expecting. Things were off to a good start. They even agreed to support her while she finished the work for her degree.

We were still moving up the ladder. The job was no longer there, but school was a realistic possibility. The boyfriend had faded, but her parents' doors had reopened. Life wasn't all winning, but it wasn't always losing, either, and there seemed to be some gain in the exchange. We both felt we were going in the right direction, but we weren't "home free."

There had been problems relating to home before. Wren was the youngest of three children. The older two had disappointed their parents, and Wren felt that her mother and father were working overtime to get her to fulfill their expectations of what a good daughter should be. They had criticized her a lot. She was a young adult in her early twenties, but they had assigned her all kinds of errands, hassled her about when she came home, and gave unsolicited opinions, mostly negative, about her friends. As Wren saw the relationship with her parents, they rarely spoke except to argue. That was why she had run to Jim in the first place, and this temporary good feeling about the reconciliation wouldn't last unless some changes in relating occurred.

Wren liked her privacy. That's what she said, anyway. I think she liked avoiding upsetting encounters. Her parents' home was big, and she thought she could live there rather autonomously. It rarely works that way. There is usually a trade-off for not living alone. If you like people around, you need to adjust to them. "There's no free lunch," as the saying goes. In Wren's case, the price for "lunch" was that her parents expected her to run errands for them, watch the house for them when they left town, and generally be around when they needed something done. That was the advertised price, anyway. The hidden costs had to do with criticism, bickering, and arguments, both petty and major. Wren found herself trying to avoid her parents more and more. "Every time I see them, we get into an argument. This morning they got on my case about the hour I got home last night. Yesterday we argued about some politician on television. If we're not arguing, they're criticizing me for something. Why can't they leave me alone?"

Now that's a tough question. I'm always tempted to say, "Because you're there!" That's probably only part of the truth. I think that in their heads they have an idea about what a "good daughter" is and they are just trying to get Wren to fit that mold, that idea.

"I know there seem to be a lot of hassles with your parents but are there ever any conversations that don't have an element of contention?" I was looking for strength on which to build.

"No. The only time we talk is when Mom tells me something I did wrong or when Dad complains about me or Mom or something."

"Who initiates the conversations?"

"They do. I just try to stay in my room until they're gone."

"What would you think about the possibility of your initiating a conversation on some nonvolatile subject? Ask your folks what they're doing in terms of their work, something like that."

"It would just lead to an argument sooner or later."

"What if you kept the conversation short?"

"What do you mean?"

"I mean, what if you approached them when there was no current problem, at a time of the day when they're least likely to be tired, irritable, upset . . . in other words, right after work and before dinner would probably not be the best time. You live with them, you know them, you pick the time you think would work the best, and take a few moments to ask them something about their day or share something about yours that is completely benign. The other thing I would suggest is that you keep it short, cut it off after about ten or fifteen minutes. Sometimes long conversations have a way of working themselves around to unsettled touchy subjects. What do you think? Do you think you could do that?"

"What would we talk about?"

"I don't know. I was hoping you'd have an idea."

"Hmmm. I suppose I could ask Mom about her class. She's a teacher, you know, and she really likes her work. She'd probably think it was phony, though, if I just asked her about her class out of the blue."

"She might. All I know is that if you continue hiding in your room, things are likely to remain the way they are now. The only hope for change is if you initiate it, and one of the areas where change is needed right now is the realm of conversations in the home. What's the worst that could happen?"

"Yeah. I see what you mean. The worst that could happen would be another argument, but that's what we have now anyway. I suppose I could try it. Just cut it off after ten or fifteen minutes, though, right?"

"Right."

She tried it, and she made it work. Sometimes you can't get rid of the bad, but you can usually add a little good. We didn't get rid of all the arguments, but we did reduce the percentage of conversation time that was taken up arguing. That made home a better place to be, and Wren didn't feel like she had to hide there all the time.

Wren had come a long way since our first visit. She had reinvolved herself with friends, she was working on her art again, she had dealt effectively with a relationship that had ended, and she had not only reopened the relationship with her folks but had made it a much more positive relationship than it had been before. These were all issues that we had dealt with in therapy. We had looked at what was happening and then figured out how we could make things happen in more productive ways. As the therapist, I had been active in helping Wren come up with plans. Sometimes I had suggested general areas, such as the nonvolatile conversation with her folks. In the beginning I had been even more specific, as when I had pushed her to get involved in her painting and to write to her sister. But now Wren had gained strength and was capable of more responsibility in terms of the plans she was making.

One day she came into the office and said she was enrolled in school. We had talked about her finishing the work necessary to get her degree, but had not made any specific plans. She had done this on her own, and her beaming face told me how proud she was. This was a turning point. Therapy had progressed from my making the plans to our making the plans and now to her making the plan.

Now our sessions were more for reinforcement or for checking out Wren's plans. There was still some upset with her parents from time to time, but Wren was feeling very comfortable living with them, and there were also some very good times—dinners out, casual chats (most of them initiated by Wren), even occasional shopping trips with her mother.

School turned out to be very good. Wren had always done well academically, and the stimulation of being around other young people was almost inspirational. Wren decided she wanted to get involved socially with other students, but was self-conscious about her weight. We made a diet plan that included activities and alternatives to eating and listed specific foods to eat that were not fattening. I had a scale at the office, so we kept a chart of her weekly weigh-ins. She lost weight—enough to justify some new clothes. She was feeling really good about herself now. Her sense of humor had always been good, but now it was great. She has a quick wit and is quick to respond to someone else's wit. Her laughter is infectious, and she was using it more and more.

Wren had a professor who was young, attractive, and single. She started asking a lot of questions in class, being the last one to leave class, and leaving her car in the same general area as his so she'd be walking in the same direction he would be after class. She really had figured the whole thing out very well. They talked some; he asked her out.

Wren was doing everything just right. She was feeling quite good about herself, doing well in school, looking well, enjoying some of her old friends, but she wanted more. Most people do. I suppose the formula for security for such people is something like "security equals the amount of caring we think we are getting over amount of caring we think we need." Wren was experiencing some caring, but she wanted to feel she belonged with someone special.

I knew she was vulnerable, that her wants and needs were greater than her fulfillment, so I asked her a lot about this young man. He seemed to pass the tests. He was kind, considerate, caring, had a great sense of humor, "especially in bed," she told me.

"Oh," I said, "that's a terrific place for humor. What do you do, climb into bed and point? Sounds like a great relationship."

She roared with laughter. She was feeling so good that everything was funny, everything made her giddy, everything was finally working out after months and months of being down.

He was completing his Ph.D. while she was completing her B.S., and they would study together. During the week she continued to stay with her parents, but on weekends she stayed in his apartment. They studied, played, went out, and fell in love.

Their courtship went fairly smoothly. The parents criticized her for the hours she kept. Wren's sister wasn't wild about him, but she lived up north, so her opinion wasn't that important to Wren. Wren's parents did think he was nice, and they were impressed by his ambition. The four of them even went to dinner together. Some of the old negatives Wren had experienced with her parents were still there, but so was a new tolerance.

Wren's new relationship progressed as nicely as her grades and as rapidly as the semester. At the end of the first term she had A's and a ring. By the end of the second semester she had finished her degree, he had acquired a teaching position back East, and they had set the wedding date.

"Do you think it's too fast?" she asked one day.

"I don't know. Certainly things have happened rather quickly. No doubt problems will arise, the question is . . ."

"I know. What am I going to do about it?"

10

"I Won't—I Can't—Maybe I Can"

An Alcoholic Finds a New Life

Lee M. Silverstein

A recent trip I made to the West allowed time for a stopover in Phoenix for a business-mixed-with-pleasure reunion with Kit. Between workshops and conferences we caught up on happenings since our last visit. The meeting contrasted sharply with our first, eight years earlier, at Blue Hills Hospital.

Kit had been in a group session at that hospital, a state hospital for alcohol- and drug-dependent persons where she was a patient and I a counselor, and our initial encounter is perhaps a sharper memory for her than it is for me. Gradually, however, she became a distinct, important figure in my life. My immediate recollection is of a bloated, cynical alcoholic, verbal and sophisticated even in her most intense pain. She was stuck. Things were not as she wanted them to be. Her life was not working out as she wished. We began to talk about it. We talked about where she was at that moment, about the most hurting areas, about where her pattern might lead if she didn't change, about her values and about the gaps between her creeds and her deeds. We talked about what we could do together to clear up the inconsistency in her life.

As we talked we became friends, and as we became friends we began to trust each other. Involvement—manifested in loving, nurturing caring, and unconditional, nonjudgmental sharing—was born and began to grow. Together we initiated Kit's process of learning to reject irresponsibility and to accept responsibility for the consequences of her behavior. Eventually, better ways of operating would

.surface or be painfully extracted and accepted. Kit would discover options and alternatives that were available, if not always initially appealing.

As is true of most people who seek help, Kit was willing to admit interest in at least examining the possibility of making changes in her life. She had reached the level of pain, felt through loneliness, depression, and negative self-image, that offered the anything-is-better-than-this opportunity for change. Though such a time holds the hope and excitement of discovery, both of alternatives and of the realization that old resources could be converted to new ways, Kit—as others, as all of us—resisted change, knowing instinctively that old ways and patterns are easier and more comfortable and less threatening. The effectiveness of my effort to help her look at new ways and to walk into new worlds, tentatively and falteringly, was increased to the degree that we walked together, step by step. Kit progressed through the hospital program, contributing more and more in group. Eventually she would depart to face the reality of her home situation without the crutch of alcohol, to form new relationships, join AA, go on to school and to work, pass on the help she had received by leading a support group herself, and to create a new life for herself. Slowly, deliberately, hesitatingly, painfully, beautifully, she progressed, one step at a time. I offered support and encouragement, sometimes abrasively.

Kit's frequent calls and visits to my office during her first months and years of growth and discovery varied greatly in content but were quite uniform in the concreteness of our approach. Simplicity was the keynote. In the experience of redirecting my own life, as well as in that of those who have come to me for help, it has been the essential element. A person has a problem. It may manifest itself in drinking, as it did in Kit's case. It may involve overeating, gambling, drugs, or emotional upset. It is really never just any of these. It is a problem of living. The person's coping mechanism has produced results that inflict extreme pain.

Thus the first task for counselor and client, after establishing a rapport, is together to recognize and accept the reality that situations exist that are disliked more than liked, and to admit that it is possible to change these. Eventually Kit and I agreed on what that change might be, and identified the possibilities and options. We made a plan and commitment to the study and work demanded, but not until she was well grounded in two other concepts did the plan become optimally effective.

It was vital that Kit decide who was responsible for her critical situation. She had to figure out who the victim was in the chaos that was her life; she needed to decide whether she was the victim of external forces or whether, in fact, she was composing much of her own misery. It was not easy for her to come to admit the latter. She had long felt comfortable believing herself victimized by her mother, her husband, her daughter, and society. However, recognition of her own responsibility was essential before she could get in touch with the idea that she was what she did. Acceptance of this truth leads to another truth, the exciting, liberating one that we, Kit or any of us, can do what we choose to do. Kit's eventual consciousness of this freedom to choose led to an awareness of alternatives and ultimately to the ability to choose.

But the awareness and the ability to choose are not synonymous. Insight does not produce change. Often important and instrumental, it is not magic. The magic of the process of changing by choice in Kit's case was the result of, first, the dissatisfaction that Kit felt with herself. Her history of preoccupation with alcohol, her use of alcohol, her misuse of alcohol, her problem with alcohol all indicated that she had long known that things could be better than they were. She had long sensed that there was more to life than she had been experiencing. This was explicitly manifested in her difficulty with problem solving, entertaining herself, and getting along with other people. What she had found out over a long period of time was that while initially alcohol seemed to solve these problems, eventually it produced painful effects rather than positive results.

The second element in the magic of Kit's process of changing was her decision to change. Having established her dissatisfaction with the void she felt that alcohol no longer satisfied, she was able to make this decision—she was able to fill the void or need and finally dedicate herself to growth. She learned better ways and learned to respect her new behavior over and over again. Identity, which is our sense of meaning or self-worth, is the integration of behavior by doing things repeatedly plus the feedback we receive from others and ourselves. As she took that small, repetitious step in the plan, she began to change. As she began to change, she began to increase her trust in herself and in me. She began to believe in her capability to change in the freedom of choice that she had and in the successful results as each step toward self-control led to more self-respect.

My memory of the details of the plan that Kit worked out with me for herself has faded. Ninety meetings in ninety days was a base, however, and Kit's value judgment regarding the state of her life made her realize the urgency of exact compliance. She proved herself extremely capable of that discipline—but not without considerable difficulty, particularly with AA. The spiritual concepts implicit in the program repelled her, a feeling she expressed vehemently and frequently in our sessions. But her trust in me had been established, and she was willing to take my word for the value of the meetings and develop a flexibility regarding the spiritual aspects. The fellowship and comfort of the sharing and support outweighed her intellectual inability to accept all facets without question. After each tirade against the program, she admitted its beneficial effects for her personally. A less complicated, more novel part of Kit's plan involved a daily session of silver polishing each afternoon from four to six, during what for years had been the "cocktail hour!"

Kit and I became more and more skilled in listening accurately to one another and in speaking relevantly. I helped her to start asking herself some questions, to look at options and alternatives that would increase her feelings of being alive. I challenged and contradicted, as well, and got her to question, challenge, and contradict her previous belief system. Much of the time I played the devil's advocate, forcing Kit to define and redefine the words she used. Words people tell themselves enter into their view of the world. When they begin telling themselves that they must or they should or they ought, or that you must or you should or you ought, or that the world must or should or ought, they constrict their ability to change reality. I constantly asked Kit to listen to what she was telling herself about her mistakes and failures, about unpleasant experiences with other people, about every facet of her life situation. I wanted her to hear what she was telling herself about how she "should" feel or perform, how other people "should" treat her, how society "should" respond to her. As she listened, I listened, and we challenged the "self" talk. Who says? Where is it written? Where is the evidence? These demands, as long as they have force, are immobilizing. Minus such constrictions, Kit could open up her view of the world, thus enhancing her freedom and receptivity to choose alternatives in her own world.

As I walked with Kit into the changing world that she was deliberately, painfully constructing, I was, I hope, constantly supportive. This supportiveness took the form of validating, of frequently, honestly noticing and expressing appreciation of the steps that she had accomplished—successes, however small. Sometimes these were related to the homework assignments for which we made out a contract at each session. Whether it was reading an article or a section of a book, making a journal entry, experimenting with new behavior in a specific setting, checking on a school or job opportunity, or making a new acquaintance, the task was an integral part of our evolving plan. Sharing it at the next session, without excuses if it had not been accomplished, was an effective connector—a transition into a new point in the contract.

Kit's intense energy and compulsion in carrying out the plan, general and specific, reminded me of my own push out of the chaos of drugs and alcohol. I told her so, elaborated, and in our time together we exchanged reflections. Sharing was spontaneous and eager, narrowing the psychological distance between us, thereby enhancing the effectiveness of our relationship. How could I expect Kit to trust me if I were to refuse to let her know me? Often we fail our clients because we want to cure without daring to care. Human communication is impossible without caring; control and manipulation become ineffective substitutes. Exchanging confidences, weaknesses, and strengths, on the other hand, as well as offering and accepting tangible help and favors from time to time, are affirming and life giving. I did not treat Kit as an alcoholic or with a label or classification. We interacted as unique human beings engaged in a continual effort toward a more and more productive and satisfying life, a day at a time, searching for reasonable happiness and comfort.

When Kit came to me she was in pain. With remarkable energy and wit and commitment she redirected her life. In a dynamic world she is a dynamic person. Through her new patterns, and with the support of others, she has reached her goal of a subjective sense of well-being, the ability to interact with her environment in a mutually satisfying, respectful manner. She has chosen life. I look forward to my next visit with her.

KIT'S STORY

I often wake up in my apartment here in Phoenix, Arizona, sniff the dry desert air, and think to myself, What a strange place for me to be. Sometimes this strangeness is exciting. I look forward to the challenge of another working day and the beauty of a spectacular Arizona sunset.

Sometimes the strangeness saddens me—I long for my New England hills and my friends back East. But the point is that I do know how I got here. At fifty, I understand the seven-year process of personal changes that brought me all these miles to this new space. I understand it because at age forty-three, with help from a lot of people, I began to make choices and take charge of my life.

I grew up a painfully shy only child. I was given everything material to make up for my parents' inability to give me what I needed emotionally. I was given "lessons" in everything but living. I was taught to ride horseback, dance, swim, and speak. I was never allowed in the kitchen, nor was I allowed to get a job after school. Like many only children, I was terrified of being the center of attention and yet I always seemed to seek center stage. My parents both had high expectations of me. My mother wanted me to be a social butterfly. My father's dream was to have me graduate from a good college—education was very important to him. I didn't know what I wanted to be. I lived in fantasy.

In high school I did reasonably well. I was bright enough to get fairly good grades in courses that challenged me. The work I didn't want to do, I ignored. I remember flunking Spanish. Terrified of my father's reaction, I went to the Spanish teacher's home, where I cried until she agreed to give me a C. I became involved in dramatics, as it was more comfortable for me to play another person's role than my own.

I did get into a good Eastern college and was immediately over my head both academically and socially. After squeaking by for two years, I flunked out.

Six months later I was married. It was a large, formal wedding planned by my mother. My dress belonged to a friend of my mother's whom I didn't know. At twenty, I didn't have a clue as to who I was. Jack and I were inseparable. I cried if he needed to be away overnight.

Eighteen months after the wedding, my son was born, and my daughter followed in another year. I plunged into the roles of wife and mother. If things were wrong with my marriage to begin with, if Jack and I could not communicate about the things that mattered, it was no problem because I had found another friend. Early in my marriage I discovered alcohol. When drinking, I became another person—sophisticated, sensuous, witty, learned, and very, very grown up.

The first ten years of my marriage were spent doing normal, suburban housewife-type things. I drove my children to and from their various meetings, became involved in town politics, worked as a den mother, belonged to the local women's organizations. At five o'clock every night the cocktail hour began. Weekends were spent with friends, and every occasion was a drinking occasion. All my activities were done as "Jack's wife" or "John's mother." I did not consider myself an unhappy person, but I often wondered if there wasn't something else.

When I was thirty, we went to live for a year in Naples, Italy. That summer we traveled around much of Europe, camping. The traveling was very exciting to me. The life style—and drinking style—in Europe suited me well. When we came back to the United States, Jack and I organized a travel business. For the next eleven summers we took groups of teenagers camping in Europe. Looking back on it, my thirties were ten summers long. Summers were the only time that really had meaning for me. During the winter it was the same old routine, and my drinking increased more and more.

Jack and I had no real adult communication. We were in a continual power struggle. We competed for the children, competed in our travel business, and competed at home. I was stuck to him. Since I did not know what to do with my own life, I used my strength to try to make him change the way he lived his. We often reversed roles. First I would be the little girl and he would be Daddy. Then, for a time, I would be Mommy. It was seldom an adult relationship. Being a tour guide became something I could do well, but even that was my husband's creation.

In 1971, when I returned from our summer trip, I knew I would not be able to go again. I realized that my drinking had gotten out of hand. Both of the children had gone off to college, and the summer was the only thing left with meaning in my life. I was no longer suffering from unresolved discontent. At this point, in some sick, hopeless place inside me, I knew that both my drinking and my life were out of control.

I gave up that September and drank more than ever. I was terrified, angry, and isolated, even though my family and my friends still loved me. The fear became paralyzing. All I could do was sit at home, waiting for five o'clock, that magic drink time that brought temporary release. In this desperate state it did not occur to me to stop drinking. I was an organizer, a manipulator, someone who could give orders well and get things moving, but I still had absolutely no idea what it meant to take responsibility for myself. I could take care of others, and I was very good at getting others to take care of me. I wanted to run, but I was too financially and emotionally dependent to move. I wanted to die, and I almost did.

That fall, it became impossible to hide my drinking. I began to fall down a lot. My daughter came home from college, observed me for a bit, and then she and my husband managed to get me to agree to stay at a state alcoholism clinic. The moment I arrived there, I knew I was in the wrong place. My fellow patients had nothing to do with me. I became hostile, defensive, and brittle. At this point I believed that my future was in a precarious balance. I felt that life as I knew it was over. And it was. The problem was that I did not see anything ahead. The only friend I had, alcohol, was being taken away from me.

In the hospital I tried to stay in my room and edit travel pictures, but that was called isolating myself, so I angrily allowed myself to be drawn into groups. There I met two significant people. One was a woman therapist who validated my feelings and helped me explore the whys in my life. I continued in therapy with her for some time after that. It was very helpful to me in terms of understanding myself. But the first significant person I met there was my friend, mentor, and AA sponsor, Lee Silverstein. Lee laughed at me. This made me very angry, but his humor was so sharp and to the point that soon I was laughing myself. He called himself "the ex-drunk on the staff" and said that he was a reality therapist.

As the days went on in the hospital, I began seeking Lee out—first because he seemed to be the only intelligent person there, and because he really listened to me, and later because he always made me either laugh or think. I was determined to return to social drinking. Lee asked me to look at whether that was really working for me. Lee asked very direct questions. He always wanted to know what I was doing and what my plans were. Of course I had none.

In the course of my meetings with him, he suggested that I try AA. I listened politely with absolutely no intention of taking his advice. I left the hospital determined that I would not drink for "a while"—until I got my life straightened out. I was angry with my husband—we could barely speak. I didn't know what I was going to do about my marriage. Lee never pushed. When he said good-bye, he reminded me of AA and asked me to drop back to see him once a week. I agreed to do that.

When I got home, I wanted to do nothing but sit. I was very depressed and still very, very angry. However, I had made a commitment to Lee, and he had been fair with me in the hospital, so I want back to see him. He got me moving. He made me recognize that my loneliness and depression were not going to be cured by sitting. One Wednesday morning, feeling very sorry for myself, I got out the book with AA meetings listed that he had slipped me, turned to Wednesday morning, and went.

When I arrived at the door of the schoolroom where the meeting was being held, a woman, bright eyed, welcomed me in. It was incredible how starved I was for that kind of welcome. I had found a home. I began going to one or two meetings a week, then three or four meetings a week, and finally for a period of three or four months I went to a meeting every day. AA gave me continual reinforcement for not drinking. I began to learn about alcoholism and realize that (a) I could stay sober, and (b) there was no such thing as social drinking for me.

My relationship with Alcoholics Anonymous was not an instant love affair. Although I went to meetings compulsively to cut my loneliness and isolation, I was furious with the organization, its rules and regulations, as I saw them, and its "steps." I was particularly angry with the "God" bit. I doubt that I ever would have made it except that I was going to see Lee on a weekly basis. I ranted and raved to him each time I saw him, telling him how the organization should be changed. Again, he listened and repeated simple phrases, such as, "It seems to work." He gave me material to read that appealed to my intellectualizing self—articles about AA by Carl Jung, articles by atheists. With a smile Lee allowed me to take the organization apart—simply telling me to keep going back.

AA, my individual therapy, and my visits with Lee started me on a hair-raising roller coaster of exploration and growth. The sessions with Lee were exciting in and of themself—I never knew what was going to happen. Some days we would have lunch, some days Lee would involve me with some of the paperwork he was doing in the office, and we would talk while I was working. Some days we would get in his car and ride to a record shop or bookstore. He then shared the record or the book that he had bought, telling me I must get a copy also. He always gave me something to take home to read, articles about AA, about the human potential movement, about reality therapy—anything that would keep me interested. And each week Lee gave me an assignment to do something. He sent me to the movies, he sent me to lectures. After I had been sober about six months, he suggested that I take the two-hour trip to Beacon, New York, to watch a psychodrama. Lee was aware of my interest in theater and thought that I would enjoy this.

From that first trip to the Moreno Institute, my interest in psychodrama developed. Since psychodrama is the reason why I first came to Phoenix, it is easy to see why I still say that Lee is the person who truly got me "moving."

Shortly after I was discharged from the hospital, Lee invited me to join an outpatient group that he was forming. My protected suburban world view began to disintegrate as I got to know and understand people from all walks of life. In these groups of Lee's there were skid-row alcoholics, ex-cons, blue-collar workers, white-collar workers, men and women. His continual stress was on involvement, and we became involved with one another both in group and as friends on the outside. I got so interested in group process that I asked Lee if he thought I could ever have a group of my own. Always positive and affirming, he said, "Of course," and when I had been sober for eight months, I formed my own group of alcoholic people.

This group supported me throughout my learning the next two and a half years. With the group's permission, I practiced all my new skills. The group gave me feedback and cheered by progress, in school and in my emerging self-sufficiency. I was beginning to feel like a human being in my own right. The group was begun under Lee's supervision. Gradually he weaned himself away and left me on my own.

Lee also supported my "twelfth step work" in AA, which I began almost immediately. It was easy for me to fill the role of helper of others. As I began to help my new friends stop drinking and reinforce the need for them to stay sober, it became more and more difficult for me to keep my reservation that one day I would again drink socially. As I spoke with others about their drinking, I began to see the true consequences of mine. I began to realize that I was now living my life as opposed to having it happen to me, and that if I were to return to drinking, I would lose that.

I used Lee as a role model. He had given me his home phone number; I gave my people mine. I told them that I never minded being called after eleven at night and before seven in the morning, and I found that they wouldn't abuse this. Gradually I became the sponsor of a number of newer AA members. Many of these are sober today. Several are not. Four months after I stopped drinking one of the women with whom I was working killed herself. I went to her funeral and made a contract with her. "I will learn more about this," I said, "so I will be better prepared to help the next person who is feeling as badly as you were."

With my new busy schedule of AA meetings, group meetings, and counseling sessions, I began to have to give up some of my old habits. I started getting up in the morning. I began to be on time. My life became more organized as I took more responsibility for doing the things for myself that I should have been doing all along. I played with the word "responsibility." I liked the definition "response to myself." Later I began to examine my responsibility to others.

Curiously, as I became more responsible, my daughter, who had assumed the role of mother in the last months of my drinking, became quite hostile. I really thought I had lost her, but at Lee's suggestion we began to use the book *Born to Win*,[1] going through the exercises in it slowly and painfully at first and then with growing enthusiasm. My daughter and I took several trips together, one of them to see a psychodrama, one of them to an outdoor concert in the Berkshires. We became friends—closer than we had ever been before.

Growth was very painful in these first months, but I certainly was never bored. Jack and I still weren't getting along very well, and my financial dependence on him made me feel trapped—yet I could see no way out. My lack of experience plus my old college failure made me feel that the only working-world task I could possibly manage would be the checkout counter at the local supermarket. Going back to school seemed like an impossibility. In the first place, I felt as though I was too old to walk across the college campus to the classrooms. Secondly, we had no money—we were very broke. In spite of this, however, I became more and more interested in further education. The promise I had made to the woman who killed herself made me realize that I needed to know more in order to help people better. I began to see my future in one of the helping professions.

Again, Lee was encouraging. He mentioned a community college course in counseling that was being started. Scholarships were available for recovering alcoholics. He told me who to contact. For the first time, at age

[1] Muriel James and Dorothy Jongeward, Addison Wesley, 1971.

forty-three, I began to make tentative plans for what I would be when I grew up. My old interests in psychology and theater became integrated with my new interest in groups and psychodrama. I stopped drinking in November, and by the following September I was enrolled in school.

The process escalated. I was turned on by any kind of learning. My mind had been idle too long. In the program I was in, my classmates were mostly former junkies; young people who had been through a Synanon-type program and were also seeking new ways of life. These young people gave me fresh input. They were sixties kids, and as I learned to respect their views I was forced to reexamine many of my old values. The courses I took were designed for people who had dropped out of life, people who did not need another failure. I remember an English course that I took. The man who taught it was a magician and very knowledgeable about altered states of consciousness. In the course, our final project was to create something. I created a kite, grounded loosely but able to fly high. The crossbows were the tension between what is and what ought to be. The kite now hangs in my living room in Phoenix.

When I first started going to school, the simple mechanics of getting there were difficult for me. I had to drive an hour and a half each way, and the courses were at night. I was working on not making excuses. One night, the roads were flooded and the rain was coming down in buckets. I arrived in class drenched, almost an hour late. Everyone wanted to know where I had been, and I refused to tell them. I did not want to make an excuse. The teacher smiled rather ruefully and said, "Couldn't you just give us a reason?"

Many of my first classes were run as groups. I also started going to weekend groups around the state—touchy/feely groups, T groups, value-clarification workshops. And always I would return to Lee and process what I had done in light of my future goals and the baby steps I needed to take to accomplish them.

My plan for school was to proceed slowly, with possible ending places at each level. I completed the counseling course and got an Associate of Arts degree. I immediately entered regular college, transferring my credits. In a year and a half I had a B.A. in psychology. After that, I went to graduate school and started working toward a master's degree in social work. As I entered the School of Social Work, I also enrolled as a regular student at the Moreno Institute and began to spend my holidays studying psychodrama. By now I no longer believed, even secretly, that the world or my husband or my mother owed me a living. I took responsibility for financing my own college education. I went through the process of hooking myself up with the Department of Vocational Rehabilitation, which paid some part of both my undergraduate and graduate work. I applied for a grant, which I got. I took out college loans, which I am still paying back. I learned to deal with the bureaucratic red tape of grant application and loan application without impatience, seeing that as a part of the total picture. Whenever I was stuck, Lee came up with a practical solution.

There was excitement and a great deal of joy in this period of getting sober and finding myself. There was also sadness. My marriage did not survive my new sense of identity and autonomy. Jack and I worked at it. We went to marital therapy. He joined a group. But it was just too late. I needed to be free, and his sense of confusion about what was happening to me created a barrier that we were unable to break down. The two things that we had done best in our marriage, drink together and travel together, were no longer viable options. We seemed to be on separate paths.

Two years after I stopped drinking I left my old farmhouse in the suburbs, the house that I had worked on and painted, hammered and nailed, and loved, and moved to a small apartment in the inner city, near the hospital where I was then working as an alcoholism counselor and near my newfound friends. I can remember sitting alone on the floor of my new apartment, waiting for my friends to come with the truck bringing the few possessions I had chosen to take from my former home. Fear and excitement were churning within me. The sense of responsibility, the realization that I had really done it this time and I was going to have to take care of myself, was overwhelming. I felt very lonely.

Then the people began to arrive, bringing food and hammers and handmade macramé. My AA buddies, my group members, people from the hospital, and again I knew what I had learned so well in the past two years— I was not alone. For a few months I often used the telephone before seven or after eleven, calling Lee or another person and just talking. Slowly I began for the first time to create an environment that was really mine.

As my horizons expanded, my children also learned that there are many alternatives in life. My son became interested in alternative life styles and involved himself in metaphysics and food co-ops. My daughter became a carpenter. At my graduation from graduate school, the important people for me were present. My son, my daughter, my former woman therapist, now friend and surrogate mother, and Lee, my friend and surrogate father.

The last two years have been more of the same. I take risks. I make choices. I know that I am in charge of my life. After I received my M.S.W. I spent a summer in Beacon learning more about psychodrama. I then came to Phoenix to study with a psychodramatist here. I now have a job as clinical coordinator of an outpatient clinic for alcoholics and drug abusers. I supervise four staff members and two students, I design programs, I direct three psychodrama sessions a week. I have a small private practice and I continue to study psychodrama.

I have also assumed responsibility for my eighty-five-year-old mother. This is a constant struggle. She is an invalid. I have tried various unsuccessful ways of caring for her, and I recently made the painful decision to put her in a nursing home. It was difficult. It was the best decision I knew how to make.

Lee and I talk with each other on the phone. He sends me material for my program. He comes to see me and does some reality therapy counseling with my son, who is staying with me. Miles do not interfere with my continued sense of support. I know I am not alone. I have hundreds of projects waiting to be done. Gradually I have developed a small network of friends. I'm never bored. I'm not sure about Phoenix yet. It's good for my arthritis, but it doesn't feel quite like home. Who knows, I may try a new place next year. The important thing again is that I know that whatever I do it will be my choice.

11

Teenage Loneliness

A Suicidal Teenager Learns to Make Friends and Feel Worthwhile

Robert E. Wubbolding

Phil, a seventeen-year-old high school student, was referred to me by a high school counselor who described him as "suicidal and depressed." He was lonely, had no friends, and had considered killing himself. The counselor told me that Phil wanted to speak to someone outside the school, but that he did not want his parents to know he was seeking psychological help. I felt that I could help Phil, even though I knew that I was leaving the country in six months for a period of one year, in order to teach in Japan. Of course, the threat of suicide is always serious, but sometimes it is possible in a relatively short period of time to help a teenager learn better ways to live. I knew that if we could do this, Phil's suicide threats would cease.

Phil and I had several telephone conversations, and he described his behavior. He was spending most of his weekends alone in his room, listening to music. On the few occasions that he ventured out, he went to movies or museums alone. He also played baseball one night a week but rarely engaged in conversations with the other players. Communication with his parents was limited to topics relating to household maintenance such as meals and housecleaning. There was virtually no discussion about schoolwork, personal problems, or future plans.

During these telephone conversations, I tried to listen as a friend and instill the feeling of hope—that it was possible for him to feel better and to overcome his feelings of misery and loneliness if he was willing to work at it. I emphasized that there was evidence of his power to achieve happiness and success. After all, he had already experienced some degrees of success—he had always been a good student, he had interests and hobbies (music), and he played baseball. After talking to me for the first time, he had stated that he felt better, at least temporarily. These factors were proof that he had some degree of strength—strength, as I pointed out, that was achieved only through hard work—and so, in the future, if he achieved more success he could gain strength and feel better. Because of this existing strength, and even more because of his solid value judgment to improve his life, I believed that suicide was not imminent.

The next major task was to see him face to face. Since he was a minor, I would see him on a continuing basis only if he had his parents' permission. I had an important therapeutic reason for this communication between him and his parents, and that was to help him feel success in his relationship with them. If he could take this single step toward success and strength, I could reinforce it in the future and use it as an illustration that he was capable of reaching out to the people around him.

There was little risk involved in this plan, since the school counselor, who knew the parents, had assured me that it was very likely that they would be cooperative. Additionally, as stated above, my feeling was that though he was considering suicide, there was no clear or imminent danger that he would attempt it. Had such danger been present, I would have intervened directly. I also stressed to Phil that he needed to follow through on telling his parents fairly soon, as I would be available to see him for only six months. After that I would be taking my leave of absence.

The transcript below illustrates only some of the interaction that took place. Although not a complete record of all of the counseling sessions, it is an accurate account of the therapeutic relationship.

FOURTH PHONE CONVERSATION

PHIL: Am I bothering you?
REW: No, not at all.
PHIL: I still haven't told my parents, and I'd like to end it all. I don't want to bother people with my problems.
REW: Sometimes it's good for you to "bother" people with your problems. So when will you tell your parents?
PHIL: I don't know if I will.

REW: It would be good for you if you get over this hurdle of telling them. How about telling them this weekend?

PHIL: I could try, but then I've tried before.

REW: Well, at least you've tried. Trying is a success for you.

PHIL: I've read a book by Victor Frankl.

REW: What book? *Man's Search for Meaning?*

PHIL: Yes. Have you read it?

REW: Yes, it's one of my favorite books. How about telling your parents about seeing me and then call me and we'll talk about the book?

PHIL: I'll try.

REW: How about telling them and calling me on Monday at one P.M.?

PHIL: Okay. I'll try.

REW: Call me Monday at one in my office.

PHIL: Okay. I'll call you.

He wanted to know if I was truly interested in him. I tried to give him assurance that I cared and that I would be persistent in my encouragement to tell his parents that he wanted to see me.

I also felt it was crucial to help him identify even a small success, so I pointed out that he did "try" and had therefore achieved some degree of success. Thus, he need not view a decision on his part not to follow through as total failure. An increase in feelings of failure and inadequacy would not have been helpful to him.

The maximum plan for the future I was able to elicit was that he call me back in four days. It would have been better to have gotten a commitment to tell his parents at a definite time and place, but his decision, or value judgment, to tell them seemed to be too weak to press for a definite commitment.

PHONE CONVERSATION FIVE DAYS LATER

REW: What happened over the weekend?

PHIL: I didn't do it. I don't trust them and I got busy on Friday . . .

REW: [Interrupting him] How about this week? What's going on this week? Will you do it?

PHIL: We have exams on Wednesday, Thursday, and Friday. I'll have time to tell her on Wednesday.

REW: What time would be the best time?

PHIL: I'll be home at noon and the other kids won't be there, but I don't trust her.

REW: Will you do it even though you don't trust her?

PHIL: I'll try. But I've failed in the past.

REW: You haven't told her, but at least you've thought about it. That's something to your credit. How about telling her on Wednesday at noon and calling me at three?

PHIL: Okay. I'll do it.

REW: Fine, I'll be in my office at one o'clock Wednesday and I'll expect to hear from you.

This excerpt is an example of excuse making on the part of the client and of my attempt to break through the excuse gently by emphasizing reformulation of the same plan of action—telling his parents that he wanted to see me face to face.

Finally, Phil followed through on his plan to tell his parents that he wanted to undergo counseling. Without hesitation, they agreed to allow him to talk to me on a regular basis.

For several sessions we talked about many different plans, especially one involving an effort to speak to a girl in his math class and ask her for a date. One entire session was spent rehearsing his entrance into the classroom, placing his books on the desk, saying, "Hello, Ellen." We explored the consequences of this simple plan—for example, what she might say to him when he talked to her. He concluded that nothing disastrous would happen to him as a result of this interchange. However, while his value judgment to seek relationships was clear, his strength to follow through on plans was, at this point, insufficient, for he failed to speak to the girl, saying that he "chickened out at the last minute."

I decided that before he could follow through on his plans, he and I needed to be better friends. Though he had learned he could formulate plans (which gave him hope for a more pleasurable future), it appeared that we needed time to discuss his already existing strength and success. We spent approximately 50 percent of each of several sessions talking about books and movies. For example, he told me that he had seen *Jaws* three times and that it was an excellent commentary on human nature and how people react in times of crisis. We also talked about his baseball, and the fact that he had achieved some degree of success in that he at least participated in the game. He added that he had recently been able to talk to several of his teammates after the game.

It is crucial to note that this discussion was more than "small talk." I was able to reinforce his successes: he liked to read, he criticized books and movies in an incisive way, he was more than a passive observer of the media, and he could relate to others, as he had done at his baseball games. But what was more important, he was being given the opportunity to recognize that there were many aspects of his life that were not problem areas but that, in fact, gave him pleasure, strength, and a feeling of success. The resulting self-confidence, though still slight, and the deepened relationship with me would serve as a foundation for positive plans of action.

EXCERPT FROM THE FIFTH SESSION

REW: How have you been spending your weekends?
PHIL: I listen to music.
REW: Where?
PHIL: In my room, at home.

REW: Do you ever ask anyone to listen with you, a friend or your brothers and sisters?
PHIL: Never. I listen in my room at home, alone.
REW: Are you happy with that situation?
PHIL: No, it's very lonely to spend the whole weekend alone.
REW: How about asking someone to listen with you?
PHIL: My brothers and sisters are pests.
REW: Someone else?
PHIL: *No* thanks!
REW: Phil, describe your room. What's it like?
PHIL: There's a bed, a desk, pictures, chest of drawers, record player. I just close the blinds on the weekends and listen to the stereo.
REW: You close the blinds, even in the daylight?
PHIL: Yes.
REW: Sounds dreary!
PHIL: It is.
REW: Phil, if you want to work hard, I know you can feel better. I'm going to ask you to do something—just for one weekend. Are you willing to try?

PHIL: What is it?

REW: Would you keep your blinds open this weekend when you listen to music in your room?

PHIL: Wow, I don't know!

REW: It wouldn't be easy. But I think it would help you feel better—unless you enjoy your current misery.

PHIL: All right, all right. I see what you're saying.

REW: How about it?

PHIL: I could do it for one day, maybe.

REW: That's good enough. Will you really do it?

PHIL: I will. One day is not too much.

REW: Shake on that?

PHIL: Shake. [Shaking hands]

REW: Okay. Let's talk next week on how it went.

Phil was able to follow through on his plan and accomplished even more. He kept his blinds open for the entire weekend. This plan was minimal, but since "a journey of a thousand miles is begun with one step," it was an important initial move toward love and self-worth. The goal of this plan, formulated by me, was to encourage him to begin to reach out to others, even if in a symbolic way at first—opening his room to the light of the world around him. Subsequently he would open himself to friendships. It also enabled him to alter in a small way his present behavior, which had been bringing him pain. He realized that the plan involved little personal threat and that it would be a step in the direction of love and worth.

Sixth Through Tenth Sessions

Phil stated that, though he felt somewhat better, he would face a "do or die" decision in several months at the end of summer. We had spoken very little about suicide, even though it had been the original reason for the referral. It seemed to me that he would bring up the topic eventually, and that an effective way of dealing with him in the beginning was to help him replace his feelings of depression and loneliness by making plans to take him along the pathways of love and self-worth. Now, too, he felt enough trust in me to talk about suicide openly, knowing that I wouldn't be horrified and that I wouldn't put him down. I suggested that in order to make a good decision, he should think about the "do" choice at least as much and as long as he had been thinking about the "die" side of it. I asked him if he felt any glimmer of hope or had any positive feelings about how things were going for him. He said that at times he did enjoy life and feel hopeful. I suggested that it was through his own efforts he was able to achieve this and asked him what he thought could result from similar efforts in the future. He responded, "The 'do' could reduce the 'die' to nonexistence." I added that we could see each other for about three more months before I left the country and that I had hope and confidence that he would feel better by that time. He concluded that he wanted to "put that decision behind me."

Eleventh Through Fifteenth Sessions

The plan to keep his blinds open and the discussion about his value judgment on suicide seemed to have been a turning point in the counseling. He reported that he was growing in hope and self-confidence. He stated that "the first step is the hardest," and then that he realized in a concrete way he could change his behavior and feel better. Though I had previously recognized some existing strengths and had often pointed them out, this small personal success made a deeper impression on him and helped him both literally and figuratively to "see the light" and to "put that decision behind me."

He then progressed to formulating many positive plans, which he mapped out in detail, such as talking to his high school counselor to ask him about getting into college, filling out the proper forms, and having them notarized. All this, I suggested, should be discussed on an almost daily basis with his parents. Such discussion would not only keep them abreast of his efforts to go to college, but would provide a basis for deepening his relationship with them, a crucial element in his improvement. He also began to call his high school classmates and ask them to come to his house to listen to music, play the board game Risk (the only game he played) or study, and he tried talking to the girls who came to watch his baseball games.

Sixteenth Through Nineteenth Sessions

Phil described at length his success at a baseball game. He had approached several girls and been able to carry on a conversation with them. He noted how they had seemed genuinely interested in him and been enthusiastic about his decision to go out of town to college. This interaction illustrates that he had built considerable strength in his interpersonal relations, that he was now seeing himself as likable. He realized that there was a viable alternative to the grinding depression and loneliness he had felt previously. His behavior was considerably different from that of several months earlier, when he had been unable to say hello to the girl in his math class, and he was enjoying the change.

Gaining strength steadily, he was now able to make more plans to alleviate his loneliness. He went to a church picnic and later to a pizza parlor, at which he talked and joked with many of his peers; he went canoeing and was voted captain of his canoe, and played Risk with several friends.

REW: Phil, let's go back to Saturday night. Tell me exactly how it was organized.

PHIL: We were at the pizza parlor and Bob L. wanted to organize a game. He had three people. I said, "You need four. I'll play."

REW: In other words, you came forward and included yourself in the game. That's great. It must have been very satisfying to do that.

PHIL: Yes, it sure was.

REW: Now what does this tell you about getting involved with people?

PHIL: To get involved with people, I've just got to make the first move.

REW: Right. But what do you do—specifically?

PHIL: I've got to speak up and volunteer to do things.

REW: You're right on target. You know, you're a long way from when you stayed in your room on the weekends.

PHIL: Yeah!

REW: What are you going to do this weekend?

PHIL: Go to a party.

REW: How did that come about?

PHIL: At the pizza parlor, some girl told Steve she was having a party next weekend. Steve asked her if Phil was invited. She said I could come.

REW: In other words, Steve wanted you to come.

PHIL: Yeah!

REW: He must like you. So you *do* have friends, people that think you are fun to be with. You're starting to feel a lot of strength inside.

PHIL: [Smiling] I do!

REW: Phil, before we end I want to ask you about the future. Try to answer in terms of what you do now that you did not do in the past and what you are going to do in the future.

PHIL: Six months ago I walked around like a corpse, bleeding inside and hurting. Now I'm reaching out to people.

REW: What are you doing now that you did not do when you walked around like a bleeding corpse?

PHIL: I'm calling up people and volunteering.

REW: And you found out they like you.

PHIL: Yeah!

REW: How about when you go to college?

PHIL: I'll have to look for others, maybe science fiction clubs, maybe Star Trek fan club members.

REW: Right. Also, you can ask your roommates, classmates where they're from, what they're interested in, what they've done in the past, et cetera. The more you get involved with them, the better you'll feel.

This final session ended with our joint summary about recent successes and general plans for the future.

He had developed friends, could communicate better with his parents, and was ready for college. Significantly, he said suicide was out of the question. He recognized that there would be difficult days ahead, but that he had the tools to deal with them and could seek additional help on campus if necessary in the future. He stated that he would look at the good days, determine what made them good, and do similar things on bad days. I concluded that it would be well if we could talk again in the future, at the end of his first year in college, and that I hoped he would write to me after a few weeks away at college.

When I think back on it, I believe that in the beginning I stayed on the plan about the girl in his math class too long, since it hadn't worked. When I switched to other plans, and deepened the counseling relationship, he made progress quickly. On the other hand, I don't feel that staying with the former plan was totally wasteful. He learned that I wouldn't give up, that I wouldn't reject him when he didn't follow through, and that I genuinely cared about him. And this laid the groundwork for subsequent success.

12

A Middle-Aged Daughter's Dilemma

The Problems of Caring for an Elderly Parent

Pat Baldauf

When Marge phoned, she said she had read a local news article about me and reality therapy. She said she had a problem concerning her aged father and wondered if I could help her with what seemed to her was an impossible dilemma. We made an appointment.

The following day Marge arrived, obviously distressed and upset. I suggested we have a cup of coffee while she told me a little about herself and her family. It was apparent that she was an intelligent and energetic woman. Though college educated, her family responsibilities and related activities as a homemaker had kept her quite involved, leaving little time for an outside career. She had three children, one in high school and two in college, all still living at home. I shared with her the fact that we had some family situations in common—I, too, had high school and college students at home. We spoke of the challenges this presents, families living with emerging adults.

She spoke of her hobby, ceramics, and how she had enjoyed selling her work to gift shops and making gifts for her friends and family. I showed her some gifts my daughter had made for us when she had taken a ceramics class in an adult education course. She showed special interest in one of the pieces my daughter had made and commented about her work. She said none of her own children were interested in ceramics but were quite involved in sports and gymnastics.

Her husband was an account executive in an advertising agency. His work schedule kept both of them busy. He traveled, and sometimes he wanted her to entertain prospective clients in their home or join him out for dinner with them in the evening.

This was becoming difficult because of her increasing involvement with her aging father. She tried to visit her father daily. Lately she had had little or no time for her hobby, to which she had previously devoted a few hours a day, and she was spending less and less time with her family. In fact, she said, over the past six weeks she had begun to suffer frequent headaches and what her physician called nervous tension and insomnia. Her physician had prescribed Valium.

I said I was particularly interested in hearing about her aging father because I had an aging mother, who lived with our family. Though Marge had been appearing somewhat more relaxed than when she arrived, when she began to talk about her father, she cried. She related that her eighty-year-old father (her mother was dead) had become ill some months ago and had been hospitalized, and when he was discharged he had been unable to take care of himself at home. She said hospital authorities had advised her to investigate nursing homes, but she preferred that her father live in his own home. She had been driving several miles daily to attend to his needs, even though she had hired a home health aide who came in a few hours a day and a male college student who spent each night with him.

Making these arrangements had been a great deal of strain. She was constantly juggling schedules as problems cropped up with the home health aide and college student. The college student was nontalk-ative and unfriendly, or so claimed her father. The home health aide did not always arrive at the appointed time and sometimes re-quested days off, which meant that Marge had to find other help, sometimes at a moment's notice, and most of the time she elected to do the job herself.

I asked if she thought this arrangement could work out eventually. She began to cry again and said it might if her family would be more helpful. She felt they were selfish for not coming to her rescue by becoming more involved, helping with the housework, spending more time with her father, and running errands. She expressed fur-ther frustration that she had not been able to pursue her hobby, which had given her some enjoyment and relief from the daily routine of her life.

I asked her if she thought she could continue on her current sched-ule of taking care of her father's needs under the present setup and work out the needs of her family, her husband, and herself. She admitted it wasn't working and that her feelings of guilt and frustration, as well as fatigue from the daily traveling and aggravation with her father, were making her very tense and irritable and not a pleasant person to live with, and her family was letting her know this in ways that were not so nice.

I asked her if there were any way she could change the situation and still meet her father's needs and her own. She said she was really reluctant about making a decision because she felt guilty about talking about the possibility of a nursing home for her father. She felt no nursing home could possibly come up to the standards of care she had been giving him and wanted to continue to give. He had always been a very good father, had been there for her in times of need both while she was growing up and as a young adult, and because of this she felt she could not "desert" him. At the same time, she could see the nursing home as an alternative because she knew it would be impossible for him to live with her. She seemed reluctant to talk about the reasons she did not feel such a live-in arrangement would be possible, so I did not pursue it at that time. But I felt that Marge's feelings of guilt were intensified since she had been an only child and there were no other siblings to share the responsibility.

I asked her if she knew anything about nursing homes close to her home. She said she had some information about nursing homes in general and had had some comments and suggestions from friends about some things to look for if she decided to investigate homes for her father. I said I had done volunteer work and visited some of the local homes, and I shared my observations about the atmosphere and treatment of the elderly patients. I suggested we look in the yellow pages of the phone book to get some more names and numbers; she could then call and get the information she needed to make the best decision for her father. She said she had been told it would also be a good idea to call the social services and senior citizens' organization in the town to get more information about the nursing homes and how they are rated.

As Marge talked, I realized she knew she had to make a change. I could see that she really was more capable and knowledgeable about how to go about getting the information than I would have thought when, so obviously upset, she first began to explain the problem. She was basically a strong, responsible, and intelligent woman.

Before she left, we agreed that she would do some investigating of possible homes for her father and explain to him that the change would have to come. She seemed relieved to know what she had to do next but apprehensive about approaching her father. However, she said she would try. I asked her to call me within the next three days to tell me how she was making out. She said she would and thanked me for listening to her.

A few days later she did call, but was feeling quite discouraged about the information she was getting and the conditions and services in some of the homes she had visited. She was back to feeling guilty and wondering if indeed she was making the right decision. We reviewed once more the possibility of other alternatives, especially bringing her father to live with her, and again she said it would be impossible. I asked if it would be possible to narrow her list of homes down to two or three that might meet her pocketbook and her father's needs and then take her father to visit and let him help make the final decision. This seemed like a feasible strategy and one that Marge could handle, and she agreed to try it. We thought it would probably take a week or so to accomplish this, as she had to set up appointments. We arranged to meet two weeks later with the reassurance that she could call me at any time, particularly if she were feeling discouraged and upset.

She called only once during that two-week span, to ask some questions about one of the nursing homes in which I had done volunteer work—and I suspect to get reassurance that she was making the right decision about her father.

After about two weeks, Marge came to talk about what had happened during that time. She had investigated several homes and had narrowed the choice down to one she liked and felt would be suitable for her father. She explained to him that she would be able to visit him daily and that he would receive better care, meet other people, and probably have more fun. She took him for a visit to the nursing home, and when the routine of activities—cards, bingo, church, a cocktail hour, the chance to talk with friendly people, physiotherapy to make him stronger—were explained to him, he had seemed most receptive to the idea of this becoming his new home.

However, even as she spoke with me about her father's acceptance of the idea of going into the nursing home, she seemed uneasy and nervous. She talked about what his new life would be like, but also mentioned the possibility of inefficient help and care in this home, which she had chosen and which he liked. She kept repeating how guilty she felt about not having him come to live with her. When I asked if there had been any change in her family's attitude about his coming to live with them over the past few weeks, she said her father was difficult to get along with because of his demanding personality, and this had become worse with advancing age. While she understood her father and might be able to cope with that part of the problem, her husband simply would not consider having him in the home because he felt it would put too great a burden on Marge and be too inconvenient to work around, with his busy schedule, traveling, and unexpected dinner guests. We even discussed what might happen if her father did come to live with them on a temporary basis to see if there was any possibility of that working out before she made a final decision and arrangements for the nursing home.

As she considered it, doing her thinking out loud, she concluded that she would not be able to handle her father, husband, and children on a day-to-day basis. She said she had always shouldered much of the responsibility of keeping the home running. Her husband was busy earning a living, and her children had all they could manage with schoolwork and part-time jobs. She seemed to acknowledge for the first time that they were being responsible about their lives and naturally assumed that her father was her responsibility and that she could work it out. In fact, they had even expressed the opinion that he would get better care in a good nursing home. Marge could see that since she would not have much physical or moral support from her family, it would be very difficult for her to manage. So once again she seemed able to accept the idea that the nursing home would be the best alternative for her, for her father, and for her family.

I told her that I knew this was not an easy decision to make because my eighty-year-old mother had been living with our family for over twenty years, and if such a time came I would find it difficult to imagine having her in a nursing home under the care of "strangers." Since I had always been the only person who had taken care of her, I would have proceeded just as Marge had, and if my mother seemed to like the setting and people in the nursing home, chosen with her help, I would have to feel that that was the best I could do under the circumstances. The most important thing would be the proximity of the home, so that I could visit frequently. I asked Marge if her schedule at home would allow her to do this. Visiting would not be the same burden as caring for him day and night in her home. After thinking it over, she decided she could probably work it out on a schedule of every other day, and perhaps in time have the teenagers fix dinner once a week so she could spend a dinner hour with him— or perhaps have lunch with him once in a while.

As she left, she seemed a bit more at ease with the idea that, for the time being, this was the best way to relieve her guilt and not disrupt her family's life style.

I asked her if she would like to come and talk again after her father was admitted to the nursing home. There was to be a month's waiting period before he could be admitted. She agreed to give me a call from time to time while she was waiting. Her father would still be on the home visitation schedule and she would be getting him ready to move. She did call over the next several weeks just to talk about how things were going, and even though she was tired, she sounded a little more calm because she said at least she was not in a perpetual state of indecision.

Almost two months elapsed before I saw Marge again. Her father had been admitted to the nearby nursing home, and she said her frequent visits kept her abreast of any situation that arose. She could assure herself that her father was receiving excellent care, and she felt, in fact, that more attention was paid to her father by staff attendants because of her frequent visits.

I asked if the family was helping her work out the new arrangement, and she said it wasn't easy, but she was working on getting them to do more for themselves and for each other so she could have more time to spend with her father without being so exhausted. I pointed out that her schedule still sounded hectic and didn't seem to allow for any free time for her. She admitted that because of her continuing guilt feelings, she would stay longer and longer with her father each day. When I asked what she was doing in her leisure time when her husband was away, she said she didn't have any. I asked what she would do if she could make some free time in her schedule, and she talked of several ceramic projects she wanted to do. We worked out a daily schedule in which she would be able to work at her hobby for an hour a day and have a finished product for a gift shop to sell or as a gift for a specific friend. She said she realized that prolonging her visits with her father wasn't really helping him, since he would often doze off while she was visiting and she would continue to sit there, feeling guilty about leaving him but at the same time feeling guilty about not being home with her family. We agreed it might be good simply to explain upon arrival when she would have to leave, but that she would be back the next day or day after that. We also spoke of the possibility of her working out a rotating visiting system with the other members of the family so that "Gramps" would have something and someone different to look forward to for the coming days.

I asked her to call me about once a month and keep me in touch about how things were going. She did call monthly for a while, and she comes in periodically and we work on her schedule so that she can continue to have some "me" time and still be there for her father and her family.

Her headaches did go away, and so did her nervous tension. She has occasional insomnia, but is aware that she is still not totally comfortable with the thought of her father living in a nursing home. She also realizes, however, that this is an ongoing situation, and she is trying to face it realistically. She has developed the courage and strength to live with her decision. It was the least offensive option available. She seemed to know this even when she came for therapy but needed to review the situation with someone to find relief from her guilt.

Investigating the accommodations available for her father was extremely helpful to Marge in finding relief from that guilt. Sharing her findings with me was an important part of her therapy. It helped her to realize her own competence as a worthwhile person. It's important, too, to her feeling of self-worth to share some of what she learned about this problem, and for that purpose Marge wrote the following about her experience.

INVESTIGATING NURSING HOMES

The problems of aging and disabled parents in today's society are manifold, compounded by lack of knowledge on the part of the children of the parents about nursing homes, home, Medicare, etc. It takes a vast amount of time to investigate all avenues, let alone an abundance of energy when one is already under emotional strain of having to face the problem.

The most important consideration, I believe, is to investigate as many nursing homes as possible armed with as many questions as you feel are necessary. Keep your eyes open and talk to patients and settle on a nursing home only when you feel your parents would be comfortable there. *Then* take him or her there and introduce him to the person in charge, a few patients, and anyone else you think might be helpful.

The home I chose was recommended highly, and although it was much less lavish than some, I felt it was a more friendly kind of home. And there was a tremendous staff (nurses and attendants) on the premises.

I was taken through every inch of the clean, comfortable nursing home and was told that if my father preferred to eat alone in his room, it could be arranged. But they assured me he would soon want to take his meals in the pleasant dining room.

The home is all on one level and my father really seems happy there. His room is spacious and cheerful. Physiotherapy has made him stronger, and he seems to be enjoying life with persons his own age around him.

A book that was helpful and gave me insights and comforting feelings was *You and Your Aging Parent* by Barbara Silverstone and Helen Kandel Hyman.[1]

[1] New York: Pantheon, 1976.

13

A Commitment to Staying Married

Marriage Counseling with a Young Couple

Judith Jones Nugaris

Marty and Tammi Moore had been married six years when I met them. They had no children.

She had a wholesome "girl-next-door" kind of prettiness. Tall and slender, she dressed in cotton slacks and tops, always with a matching silk scarf to tie back her hair. Articulate on a number of subjects, especially nutrition and ecology, she read several books a week, sometimes on those subjects, but she also enjoyed romantic and epic novels and classical literature. She enjoyed gardening as well.

A stranger engaged in social conversation with this intelligent, well-read young woman who radiated health and beauty would have had difficulty recognizing the other side of her, which was her image of herself—an inadequate housewife clinging desperately to a marriage that promised little and to which she gave little.

A striking contrast to Tammi, Marty was dark and aesthetic looking, with a neatly trimmed black beard. He dressed casually in jeans, faded cotton shirts, and heavy boots. His job with a small company that manufactured electrical appliances was an entry-level white-collar position. It embarrassed him that almost four years after leaving graduate school, he still had no definite career plans. Although critical of his company's lack of sensitivity to employee needs and of its dedication to capitalistic values, he was conscientious and hard working and had earned two promotions. He claimed to feel intellectually and morally superior to nearly everyone at work, but regarded his work relations as amicable both with subordinates and superiors.

Tammi and Marty had met at a small midwestern college. She left college after they became engaged, ostensibly to work and save money for their wedding and marriage, but she confessed that, unhappy and unsuccessful as a student, she had found an acceptable alternative in marriage. When Marty graduated, he was accepted into a graduate program in psychology at a large western university. He had no clear goals, but, encouraged by supportive professors, he decided to pursue a master's degree in psychology.

Tammi, who saw the move West as temporary, found a job as a clerk in a department store and accepted the role of principal wage earner for the marriage. They rented a house with another couple, both students. They became vegetarians, gave and attended pot parties, experimented with drugs, and on weekends drank heavily.

Halfway through Marty's first term, he had an affair. He confessed to Tammi, asked for and received her forgiveness and understanding, and ended it. But the following semester he became involved with another young woman, this time a member of their circle of friends. He told Tammi that although he was unsure about his affections for the other woman, if Tammi didn't object he would like to continue both relationships.

This time Tammi was devastated but asserted herself effectively. She insisted that Marty make a choice, threatening separation if he did not give up the other relationship. He responded by professing a commitment to Tammi and their marriage and terminating the other relationship. (When we discussed this later, Marty admitted that he had been relieved by Tammi's assertiveness and that he would not have respected any other decision on her part.)

Tammi initially perceived her staying with Marty after his second affair as evidence of her commitment to the marriage. However, later she confessed that though her commitment was real, she also felt trapped and helpless. Overwhelmed by feelings of rejection, humiliation, and anger, she had clung to him in desperation, while hating herself for lacking the strength to leave. She reacted in the only way she knew—becoming more dependent on Marty and withdrawing from the rest of the world. One day following their agreement to stay together, she announced she had quit her job. To herself she vowed, "I'm not going to do anything any more." This began a phase of isolation, inactivity, and increased phobic behavior for Tammi.

Marty consulted me first. (Tammi was at that time seeing another therapist.) He was sophisticated about different approaches to therapy and had written to Dr. Glasser, asking for names of local reality therapists. During our first interview, I asked Marty why he had chosen reality therapy. He wanted a therapist who would relate to him, have some interest in him, he said. He and Tammi had been seeing a marriage counselor who had asked him questions but did not interact with him. I responded that I also thought the relationship between us was very important—that, in fact, I would like to spend the first three meetings getting to know each other and then decide if we could work well together.

Marty was overwhelmed by his wife's dependency and what he felt was his total responsibility for their relationship. It seemed to him that she did not function adequately in any area of her life. She did not drive, so he did all the shopping and household errands or provided transportation for her. In fact, she went nowhere without him. Whatever housework was done, he did—usually when he could no longer tolerate the clutter. He resented this not so much because he objected to housework, but because Tammi did not do her share. He also had the full financial responsibility for both of them. "I just can't handle the full burden any more. I feel like I'm living for two people," he said, sounding more discouraged and helpless than resentful or angry.

Marty spoke of unhappiness with other areas of his life. He found his job unstimulating and ungratifying, but he had no idea what he would enjoy more or find more meaning in. He had enjoyed writing in college and had thought he would like to be a writer, but he didn't really know what he·would write about.

It seemed to him that the most meaningful period of his life had been when he was an antiwar activist and draft counselor. But he had even come to think of that work as useless because he felt that every time he had helped one young man avoid going to war, another one had to take his place.

His social activities and relationships also seemed inadequate to him. He took evening courses at the local community college and enjoyed reading. He occasionally played golf with some of the men he worked with, but did not consider these men his friends. He found playing the guitar relaxing but did it rarely.

Marty seemed very likable to me, and he possessed the qualities often associated with happiness and success—intelligence, education, youth, and good health—but he viewed himself as a failure. His life was unsatisfying—it had no purpose or direction. When we talked about how to improve his life, Marty said his marriage was his first priority. It was the area causing the most pain. It would end in divorce if it was not changed soon. I suggested that if he could improve his marriage, he would feel better about himself and more confident to improve other areas of his life.

We both felt it was important that Tammi be involved in this process. But her present therapist refused to collaborate or join in any type of conjoint marital counseling. Tammi was becoming dissatisfied with her therapist, and at Marty's urging she made an appointment to see me. We got along well, and she decided to terminate her present therapy and join Marty in marriage counseling.

At our first meeting I was impressed with Tammi's youthfulness and intense unhappiness. Everything she said confirmed Marty's description of her life style. She did very little of value with her time, sleeping until noon or later and then watching television. She liked to read in the late afternoon, but she did take time off to prepare dinner. Then she read late into the night, often not going to bed until two or three in the morning. She explained that she was afraid to go to sleep, afraid that she would die in her sleep, and when she did sleep she was disturbed by bad dreams.

It was true that she did very little without Marty. The couples they visited or entertained occasionally on weekends they had met through Marty, and she was friendly with the women but had no contact with them outside of the get-togethers with the husbands. In fact, the only individual contact she had with anyone was with her husband and her therapist.

As a child Tammi had been a good student, although she began to be an underachiever in high school. She had a fine voice and had been encouraged by her parents and teachers to pursue an education and career in music, but she no longer sang even for her own pleasure.

During the first years of their marriage, she had had several jobs. She neither felt successful doing them or liked any of them.

They had gone for counseling to a local mental health clinic after Marty's affairs, and although the matter was no longer discussed, Tammi was adamant that it was an unresolved issue for her. She felt she carried the entire emotional burden for their relationship. Marty made little attempt to meet her emotional needs and was not affectionate or loving. She felt she would be willing to carry out the household tasks more adequately if he were more attentive. But, she admitted, Marty provided for her in one way—materially.

The second time Tammi and I met we talked more about her goals for therapy. I expressed my opinion that we needed to work on helping her to develop better self-esteem. She needed to learn to take better care of herself. I suggested that she couldn't really be an equal partner in her marriage until she felt more positively about herself. She agreed that she would like to make these changes but was dubious. "I understand that you think I would be happier if I were more self-sufficient, but—" she paused—"doesn't that let Marty off the hook? If I wanted to be so independent I could get a divorce."

I thought that she could be even closer to Marty if she were less dependent on him, that if she felt better about herself, Marty would see her more positively. Perhaps she felt that I was expecting a lot of her, but she would make the changes at her own pace with my help. Marty's help would be needed, too, I added.

She looked somewhat reassured. Not having felt really good about herself for a long time, and bothered by Marty's lack of regard for her, she hadn't known where to begin or what to do. She added that she did trust me, felt that I understood her, and that she wanted me to help them. We decided that our next step was to arrange a meeting with Marty and make further plans for working together.

The following week I met with Marty and Tammi together. After some reiterating of their complaints about each other, they discussed their respective views that each was carrying the responsibility of the marriage alone. Marty pointed out that he not only worked and carried the financial burden, but he also took care of household duties. Tammi countered that she did more housework than he recognized, and that any communication between them was due only to her persistent efforts. I asked them what was positive in their relationship, what kept them from giving up hope. Both said, as though it were perfectly obvious, that they loved each other. They had spoken of divorce as an alternative, and each often threatened to leave, but neither wanted to consider it as a real choice.

They agreed that the first two years of their marriage had been happy. Even at the worst times they maintained an active and mutually satisfying sexual relationship. Both said that they communicated their sexual needs to the other and that the other was responsive and loving. Fights, which usually ended in exhaustion, still were often followed by lovemaking.

Marty still respected Tammi. Initially attracted not only by her physical beauty but by her musical and artistic talent and intelligence, he was frustrated and disappointed now because she allowed all this to be underdeveloped and unused.

Tammi also expressed her admiration and respect for Marty. When she had met him she had liked his good looks and his daring antiwar stand. Having no motivation toward social or political activism, she shared Marty's views on most issues, but when they disagreed they had lively discussions.

They described close, warm times, now becoming rare, sitting in front of their fireplace with a bottle of wine, discussing books they were reading and philosophical issues.

Though it was not well articulated by either, it was my observation that they also shared a strong belief in the institution of marriage and monogamy. These values, combined with high dependency needs, provided a basis for their strong investment in preserving their marriage, but although I knew my clinical assessment of them was important, my personal response toward them counted, too—I liked them. I felt their pain and I wanted to help them. I told them at the joint meeting that completed the evaluation that I believed that they could, by working together with much effort and some pain, achieve a gratifying and successful relationship. I explained that since improving a relationship is a process that requires and utilizes the involvement of both individuals, I would like to meet regularly with them together. The objectives of these joint sessions would be for them to improve their communication and to understand better each other's needs and expectations and then learn to meet them. We would be discussing the changes they wanted to make and some specific things they could do to make these changes. Each of them also expressed a need for individual support—each had individual problems that needed therapeutic intervention. We compromised by dividing a two-hour weekly period into three parts. Each had a slightly abbreviated individual session, after which we all three met for about forty minutes.

Since each needed individual therapy and the marital situation was complex, I considered the advantage of a collaborator or co-thera- pist. But I am in private practice, and a second therapist would have added appreciably to the cost. More importantly, their trust in the profession had been seriously damaged by her recent therapist. Their trust in me, at this stage, was based on Dr. Glasser's recommendation and the degree of their pain. They were, understandably, unwilling to risk sharing their lives with yet another stranger.

They took turns being first to see me alone. Then the three of us met. They arranged themselves at a safe distance from each other in my office and I sat where I could face both of them.

Though they were critical of each other, they never demonstrated the noisy, emotional fights they said occurred at home. Each practiced restraint in expressing negative feelings toward the other.

Tammi nearly always opened the talk with an issue she wanted to discuss with Marty or an incident that had occurred during the week. Often she asked Marty if there was anything he wanted to discuss. He always deferred to her, though frequently I encouraged him to be more assertive in introducing his concerns, as expressed in individual sessions, into our joint sessions. He made excuses for his passivity—his particular problem could wait, he shared Tammi's concerns, or he wasn't ready to discuss an issue with Tammi.

Tammi accepted and carried the responsibility for communication and for dealing with problems, thus appearing to have the problems. Marty played the supporting role by conceding to her needs.

At one early session Tammi wanted to discuss two important plans— having a baby and moving to the country. Early in their marriage they had shared a dream to own acreage in a rural area. Now plans for having a family and moving sounded like only Tammi's dream. Marty said that he felt he was not ready to accept the responsibility of fatherhood and questioned, subtly, Tammi's ability to be an adequate mother, pointing to her problems doing housework and caring for pets. He was firm that he was not ready to consider yet whether he ever wanted children, so we postponed the subject, which distressed Tammi.

The issue of a country home, while embodying the same conflicts, seemed slightly less emotional. Tammi was certain they shared the goal of a home in the country where they could engage in light farming and escape from urban pressures. It was her childhood dream, and—along with having children—the fulfillment of her identity. But as the years slipped by they were making no plans, and she was feeling frustrated and discouraged. Marty, though he admitted he had once shared this goal, now put up barriers. Yes, he wanted to move out of the city, but he didn't want to be a "farmer." He doubted that Tammi would take responsibility for animals, and, besides, they couldn't afford to buy land, and if they moved he would have to find another job. The more Tammi pressed, the more elusive he became.

Tammi accused Marty of being dishonest with her. She criticized his indecisiveness as refusal or inability to plan for their future. How could she have faith in their marriage when he seemed unwilling to cooperate with her?

I pointed out that they were acting out their roles. Tammi was being the demanding wife who relied on Marty to do something to make the marriage better and who nagged to get her way. Marty was condescendingly patient in pointing out how unrealistic she was. But Tammi was taking responsibility for what was discussed in therapy and for dealing with their problems. By his "I'm handling everything, don't rock the boat" stance Marty created an illusion of self-confidence and strength, but in fact he was only depriving himself of the opportunity to share his fears and frustrations with his wife. Though they understood and agreed with my analysis, each had difficulty seeing how he or she contributed to the other's behavior or how to choose more successful behaviors. Tammi thought that once she gave up pushing and demanding for Marty to talk to her, they would never talk at all. And Marty was overwhelmed by her demands on him and rationalized that his stoic, unemotional, kindly tolerance was what was holding their marriage together.

I asked them to pursue the conversation, focusing on what each wanted in a country home. To Tammi it meant a small farm where they would be economically self-sufficient by raising a garden and animals. Marty envisioned a quiet, genteel life free of pressures, one that did not include caring for animals or doing farm work.

The animals were important to Tammi. "I'll take care of the animals. I can milk a goat," she said.

Marty countered, "You don't take care of our two dogs now. I have to feed them and clean up the yard. You never do."

"I do, too. You just don't notice." (She confessed, however, that cleaning chicken coops wasn't part of her dream.) She imagined purchasing a bargain—a rambling old farmhouse—and living in it after making a few repairs.

Marty objected, saying, "I'm not a handy man. I'm not fixing up an old house."

I encouraged them to spend more time, at home, sharing their ideas and dreams in order to find out what each wanted and to search for mutual ground. As they talked more over a period of time, their ideas became less romanticized, and they began to explore the actual problems and to make realistic plans.

I asked them to schedule some time each week for uninterrupted conversation with each other. It was in part an effort to neutralize the pressure from Tammi on Marty to pay more attention to her and his resistance to her. As I might have expected, Tammi was delighted with my plan and Marty dubious. His objection was that such talks would be contrived and artificial. I pointed out that since they acknowledged that they engaged in almost no constructive communication outside of my office, contrived conversation would be a good way to begin. They would undoubtedly feel awkward at first, but it would become more natural with practice. With reservations, he agreed to cooperate. Because of their tendency to misunderstand each other and to forget what plan they had agreed to try, we worked out the plan in detail in my office. They agreed to spend one half-hour each Thursday, beginning at 9:00 P.M., discussing a noncontroversial topic.

For several weeks they had difficulty carrying this out, each making excuses and blaming the other. I persisted, suggesting that they redesignate responsibility. By this time they were involved in the process and agreed to take turns for making arrangements and reminding the other of the time. I recognized each attempt as progress and suggested that they continue to avoid highly controversial subjects. Though this may have added to the artificiality, it enabled them to have an extended conversation that didn't end in a bitter fight. Eventually they used these times to discuss areas of disagreement and learned to argue successfully.

By now, in Marty's individual sessions we were focusing on what he could do to improve his life in addition to improving his marriage. He mentioned many things he wanted to do, like take courses in astrology or play his guitar more. He followed through on some plans and experienced some success, but was still apathetic and mildly depressed. His individual session often seemed too brief for him to deal with his concerns adequately.

One evening I asked him, somewhat routinely, how he could better get his emotional needs met in his marriage. He confessed that he was discouraged again about the marriage and proceeded to pour out the story of the previous weekend's events in a way uncharacteristic for him. He had spent most of the previous Saturday morning cleaning house while Tammi slept. When she arose, well after noon, she wanted him to go shopping with her. However, Marty wanted to visit a friend who had invited him to watch a football game. She complained that he avoided her and didn't want to spend time together. He resented her criticism, pointing out (to me) that if she had gotten up she could have spent all morning with him. They had spent the afternoon together—Tammi crying and Marty defending himself and trying to control her emotional outbursts. He described his frustration and confusion to me. He was again feeling that he had to do it all—the housework, then supporting and comforting Tammi. The worst frustration was that no matter what he did it didn't work.

I suggested that perhaps he would like Tammi to get up earlier on Saturdays and show more interest in spending the day with him. Denying this, he returned to his complaint about dirty dishes. Marty was lonely and depressed, didn't know how to get his wife to pay attention to him—yet he persisted in talking about dirty dishes. I chose to ignore his denial and pursue my perceptions. I told him that I thought he needed to learn to take better care of himself emotionally—to let Tammi know more clearly what, other than a clean house, he needed in their relationship. I said that he couldn't expect her to be responsive if he acted like an emotional Rock of Gibraltar. He had tears in his eyes as he answered that I was right, but he didn't understand what he should do. I said that I could not tell him, but I was sure he could learn. It was my impression that he was more open with me than with Tammi. He confirmed this, explaining that her pressure to know his thoughts made him uneasy and increased his feeling of inadequacy. I pointed out that she was also more important to him, thus it was safer to be more emotional and show his inadequacy to me. However, since she was the person who could meet his needs, it was essential that he learn to express himself to her.

I told him it would help if when we met with Tammi he would bring up some of the concerns he expressed to me privately. We would be in a better position to try to work out their difficulties so that both his and Tammi's needs could be met. He didn't have much confidence in the plan, but agreed to try it.

We noted that we had used more than our allotted time. I wondered if one of his present needs was for a regular fifty-minute individual therapy hour. He said that he thought it would help—he missed the full hour he had had before Tammi had begun to see me—but he also considered it important for her to see me and for them to meet with me together. Since they couldn't afford three hours a week, he saw no way to meet his need. As this was the most assertive I had known Marty to be in regard to his own needs, it was important to respond to him. I asked him to discuss it with Tammi and to attempt to work out a way to have a full session.

Tammi joined us and Marty explained, rather apologetically, that he couldn't seem to make adequate use of the shortened time. She was understanding and affirmed her own investment in their therapy being mutually productive. The outcome was that Marty and Tammi each had a fifty-minute session each week, with the exception of one week a month when we all met together. This format continued until a later phase of treatment.

Tammi's involvement in her therapy also deepened with longer individual sessions. Earlier in her therapy I had been concerned about her isolation and limited activity. She now expressed dissatisfaction with her life, especially the extent of her dependence on Marty.

We made plans, based on modest objectives, for her to do things on her own. She said that she would like to attend a church, as a way of expressing and confirming her personal religious beliefs. She also thought she might like to sing in a choir. Although he didn't want to go himself, Marty agreed that on the following Sunday he would take her to a church of her denomination that was near home. I supported this, feeling it would enhance her self-esteem. Her faith was important to her, and besides I saw a potential source of congenial friends and support.

The following week she reported she hadn't gone. "I feel guilty because I really wanted to go," she said. "I never feel guilty when I don't do things that I don't like, like the dishes. Also I thought that you would be disappointed in me, and I don't like that."

I assured her that I was sorry that she hadn't accomplished what she wanted, but that I didn't think any less of her because she hadn't attended church.

"I know that, of course. It just seems like an expectation, and I don't like to think that I'm doing something because someone expects it of me." She went on to explain, "It's like when my parents expected me to get good grades. I resented their expectations even though I wanted good grades."

I responded to this by pointing out that her perceptions of others' expectations and criticisms were interfering with her use of therapy to achieve her goals. I suggested that we attempt to sort out her goals from what she thought Marty or I or her parents wanted of her. As we talked more about how she perceived herself and how she wanted to change, I talked about "growing up" and learning to be "responsible" for herself. My use of the words "grow up" and "responsibility" bothered her. "I don't want to grow up," she said. "I don't want to lose something—I don't know how to explain it— but I think it's a kind of innocence. Do you understand?"

I confessed that I didn't understand but wanted to. As we talked more, I learned her fear of growing up was related to her fear of death and losing her parents. "I'm sure that it's related to the summer that I visited my grandmother, when I was eleven," she explained. She believed that was when her phobias began. "I was supposed to stay two weeks, but something happened that my parents couldn't come to get me. The first two weeks I had fun because my grandmother lived on a farm and there were woods to play in. But when Mommy and Daddy didn't come, I was really upset. They called and explained, but that didn't help. I couldn't sleep, and I was afraid that either I or my whole family would die before I ever saw them again. I couldn't eat much and I lost a little weight. But no one seemed to notice anything, or to pay any attention. Finally, my parents came. I think I was there about six weeks. When I got home I tried to explain to my mother how I felt, but she kind of brushed it off. I became more withdrawn after that. I was still frightened of dying, or of Mommy or Daddy dying."

"That must have been very frightening," I empathized. "Any young girl would be upset and might feel that she was being abandoned."

"I've thought a lot about it," she continued, "and other things that happened in my childhood. I think that my fear of death now must be related to something that happened that summer or maybe something else, too. If I can just understand what, I think I can find the key. Isn't that what you do in therapy? Find the cause of the problem in order to understand it?"

"You've already gone over it a great deal, I imagine." Tammi acknowledged that she had. I tried to be noncritical in disagreeing with her treatment plan. "I don't know whether we could ever pinpoint the exact beginning of your phobia," I said, "and even if we did you can't change those childhood events now. But you aren't a child now, and you can learn to handle your fears differently than you did as a child."

Tammi was doubtful. "I really trust your judgment and your knowledge, but I feel like if I could just understand what caused my fears, it would help." I said that her insight was already quite good, and this had not helped her.

"Then what do I do?" she wondered.

Since in reality therapy we have learned that although phobias may have started in the past, when they continue they are tied to the present, I suggested that we work on overcoming her fearfulness now by helping her deal with day-to-day obstacles. I recognized that my expectation that she do things away from home was unrealistic at this point and suggested that we talk about times when her fearfulness interfered with something she wanted to do and how to cope better with that fear.

Going to sleep at night was a fearful experience, and she decided to go to bed when Marty did, a behavior change for which she was rewarded with an improved sexual relationship. She still thought of death before falling asleep, but she discovered that if she refrained from reading all night, she could fall asleep in spite of feeling frightened.

However, this did not end Tammi's resistance to change, nor did she cease her examination of the past. Reluctant to assume more responsibility, she seemed to be saying, "I'm just a frightened little girl. Please don't expect any more of me."

During this time her relationship with Marty was improving. Fights were now controlled and no longer led to threats of divorce or desertion. Marty still didn't talk to her as much as she would have liked, but she agreed not to question him about his moods. If a bad mood was related to work, Marty told her that, and if something involving her was affecting his behavior, he told her that, too. He recognized that better communication would benefit his relationship with his wife and appreciated her efforts to allow the time he needed to approach her at his pace. He did begin to share more of his thoughts on some low-risk but important topics. Tammi was gratified to learn that Marty would talk to her without pressure.

That summer they looked at houses for sale. They had not decided to buy a house, but they agreed, at my suggestion, to obtain some factual information about real estate as a step toward dealing with their disagreement over a place in the country. This led to a confrontation over conflicts about commitment. Marty admitted that owning property represented a commitment to a "settled life" and giving up the freedom to go any place any time. Tammi recognized that she would be making a commitment to "settling in" to a life that up until now she had considered only temporary. She would be giving up her dream of moving to the country.

In spite of these reservations, they seemed more comfortable with the new phase of their marriage. Tammi felt confident enough to renew her pressure to have a child, and Marty, although still resistant, agreed to discuss it. He finally decided he would eventually like a child but reserved time to "work out conflicts about fatherhood and some of the problems in the marriage." Tammi admitted that she would like to feel more secure about the marriage and more self-confident before having a baby. But with Marty's new positive attitude, she was able to invest new energy into treatment with the goal of preparing for motherhood.

At a midsummer meeting they informed me that Tammi was pregnant. Both were simultaneously frightened and delighted.

I shared their feelings. Tammi's self-esteem and confidence had grown noticeably. But could she respond to the ever-present needs of an infant? And if she became more dependent on Marty, how would he react?

We shared our realistic concerns both in individual and joint sessions. Looking back, the pregnancy seemed to mark a turning point in therapy. Not only did Tammi and Marty renew their commitment to each other and to continued growth, but the new responsibility and stress brought their gains into sharper perspective.

Marty expressed it best. "We're going in the right direction. Not long ago I would come home from work some evenings and just sit in the car for half an hour because I didn't want to go in the house. It was like I would recharge myself to prepare for the battle that I knew was going to take place. It was pretty terrible, but now I think we've reached the point that we're dealing with the problems. And our views and expectations of each other are more realistic."

As Tammi's pregnancy progressed into the third month, she experienced all of the classic symptoms, especially fatigue. As a result she was discouraged, self-deprecating, and more demanding of Marty.

Marty, though understanding, was caught between his sense of responsibility to Tammi and his needs. He responded to Tammi's physical needs, helping with the housework, taking her for doctor's appointments, but began to withdraw emotionally and to experience periods of depression.

Our primary focus in both individual and joint therapy now was to deal with new pressures created by the pregnancy and preparation for parenthood. We returned to our previous arrangement of half an hour with each individually and a weekly joint meeting.

Marty and Tammi demonstrated their renewed commitment to growing in tangible ways. They began house hunting in earnest, and in the middle of the winter, only two months before Tammi was to deliver, they moved into a pleasant suburban home.

Tammi had decided on natural childbirth and found an obstetrician who would support her in this and allow Marty in the delivery room. They took classes in the Lamaze method and were pleased with their success in learning a method that requires mutual cooperation and trust. This helped to further develop their communication skills.

In the second trimester of her pregnancy Tammi was bothered by a return of her death phobia. Previous to this she had been free of disabling fears for several months. Now she reported that as she was falling asleep at night, she became short of breath and thought she was having a heart attack. She was determined to overcome her fear and learned that she could control her nighttime panic by not giving in to it and by asking Marty for reassurance. She said that though being pregnant seemed to take a lot of energy, when she was not feeling frightened she felt very alive.

Tammi also discussed other fears commonly experienced by expectant mothers. She worried that she would not be able to endure the pain of childbirth and was concerned about her limited energy and how she would manage housework and child care. As we talked, her self-assurance increased. Her doctor had assured her that she was in good general health and would regain her strength in time. We talked about how she had accomplished more only recently and how she could again use what she had already learned.

More importantly, and related to her inactivity and fearfulness, she realized the danger of overdependence on one's child and her vulnerability to this. She resolved not to be a clinging mother, but to develop interests of her own so that later, when her child needed to separate from her, she would be able to accept it. I encouraged her to find other expectant mothers with whom she could share concerns and experiences. She found the Lamaze class more comfortable than she had expected and introduced herself to some of the women. This was the first time that Tammi admitted she needed friendships or support from other than her family.

Marty also had doubts and fears. His greatest fear was that he would not love his child sufficiently, that he would not know how to meet the needs of or relate emotionally to a baby. The Lamaze class helped him, as the importance of his role was defined and supported. His sense of involvement and significance grew, and he began to anticipate the birth.

As the time for the arrival of the baby neared, Tammi and Marty decided to take a vacation from therapy. We terminated one month before the expected delivery and decided they would resume therapy after they had had a few weeks to adjust and could either bring the baby or feel comfortable about getting a sitter.

Marty called two weeks later. "We had a baby girl this morning." Her name was Jennifer, and she was healthy and doing well. Helping to deliver her had been the most profound experience of his life. He was very happy and already very emotionally involved with his daughter.

When I talked to Tammi, she was still tired but elated with her success. Yes, childbirth hurt, but she had coped with the pain and felt stronger than ever.

Three months later Tammi and Marty resumed therapy. They brought Jennifer, a beautiful and thriving baby. Her parents still showed the warm glow of success and pride despite the midnight feedings and hectic schedule. Both enjoyed their parental roles and shared the responsibilities and pleasure. Nevertheless, some of the pre-pregnancy problems had surfaced.

For Tammi, housework, which had always been difficult, had now become impossible. Marty had ceased sharing ideas and feelings and wanted only to talk about Jennifer. Marty admitted to falling back on his pattern of emotional withdrawal, but said it was because Tammi was always tired, made extra demands on him, and was not available to listen. Their sexual relationship, always a source of pleasure, had waned. Tammi felt fat and physically unattractive and attributed lessened interest to breastfeeding and fatigue. Marty felt rejected by her lack of interest, which had begun during pregnancy. She felt that he sublimated his sexual energy. Although each expressed a lack of trust in the other, a sense of loss, and a desire to recapture this part of their relationship, both resisted plans that would focus on this problem.

Despite this, we found in the next few weeks that both had made noticeable growth during the pregnancy in their commitment to each other. Each verbalized without ambivalence their investment in strengthening their relationship. The focus of our joint session again was communication and dealing with specific issues in their relationship.

They agreed they rarely spent time together any more sharing thoughts and experiences and planned to reinstate the structured conversations. After about three months they reacquired the pattern and no longer needed to schedule talk times. Tammi had less need to make what seemed to Marty unreasonable demands, and he shared himself more openly.

Now they agreed to work toward a home in a rural area and a target date two years hence.

Marty wanted to commit himself to using his individual therapy sessions to working on his conflicts about a career change. The major barrier was Marty's difficulty in making any decisions and his lack of self-confidence. He and Tammi discussed what careers would fit into their life style. When Marty considered computer programming, Tammi worried that he might be placing financial security ahead of altruism and assured him that she would sacrifice some security for his job gratification. He insisted he would not sacrifice altruism for materialism—ethical values were important to both. He also wanted to leave time to share in the care and rearing of Jennifer.

Marty made another step in his effort to be more open and told Tammi that her approval and support were important to him. She gladly assured him that she would support him in whatever career he chose.

He still dreamed of being a free-lance writer, but realized that, given average success, it would take years before he could earn a living that way. My suggestion that he consider jobs that provided experience in writing and use of his present skills was incomprehensible to him. He admitted that he hadn't sufficient confidence in his writing to offer it as a skill to a prospective employer.

He was stymied by the idea of an actual change. I recommended reading on career planning and changes. He did this, but slowly, taking several weeks to buy the book and a month to read it. He enrolled in a creative writing course, but missed a lot of classes and finally dropped out—but this had a positive side, as he found "I resent time I spend away from home now. I want to see Jennifer before she goes to bed."

He still said he wanted to write, so I suggested he keep a journal. Again his poor self-image became the issue. He doubted the value of his ideas and personal day-to-day experiences—his personal thoughts and mundane experiences required self-exposure and might not stand up under self-criticism. We continued to talk about what he might write, and several weeks later he did begin a journal.

It was my hope that by recording his ideas Marty would see them as having value and enhance his self-worth. Perhaps he would also develop the habit of writing. In the ensuing months he spoke of his journal periodically and became increasingly involved with writing in it. I never asked to see it, he never offered to show it to me or discussed what he wrote, but my impression was that this activity had therapeutic value. My evidence was his involvement with it and his increasing sense of self-worth.

His relationship with Tammi was now a source of satisfaction and support. He had improved his ability to express needs and emotions and was optimistic about further efforts to discuss concerns and take more responsibility for his needs. But the relationship was not free from tension and mistrust.

An opportunity for him to deal with this occurred that summer. We were meeting on a day when there was a minor accident at a nearby nuclear power plant. Each had heard the news report, Marty at work and Tammi just before he arrived home. They discussed the event briefly before leaving for our appointment. Each discussed with me individually their upset over the other's reaction. Tammi felt Marty had reacted casually to what she considered a major threat to their safety, deprecating her understanding of the danger and scoffing at her concern. Hearing the news broadcast, he had been alarmed and had considered calling Tammi, but had decided that would only frighten her. When he arrived home, she immediately suggested that perhaps they should leave the area. To calm her, he played down the danger. She still wanted to leave.

After some defensiveness about her irrationality and his own upset, he admitted that, "I'm afraid she'll take the baby and leave me. I have this picture of coming home from work and she's gone, with Jennifer, and I'm alone." He said he hadn't told Tammi about this fear, only how crazy she was to want to run away in panic.

The ensuing joint discussion was clarifying to both. Tammi had no realization of Marty's fear of being left and quickly reassured him that she had no such intention. She was offended that he still regarded her as that impulsive and irresponsible. She had only wanted to impress him with the extent of her concern because he seemed too casual. He confessed that when he heard the news report he had thought of evacuating immediately, but had decided that was an over-reaction.

I intervened to reinforce Marty's need of reassurance. Tammi still had difficulty perceiving Marty as needing anyone. What she heard was his lack of confidence in her stability. Marty, with my assistance, was able to explain that his criticism of her had been his way of expressing his fear. She finally understood. Each made some progress in understanding the needs of the other, as well as in developing communication skills.

The next month Tammi received word that her mother, who lived in another state, had suffered a serious fracture, which required hospitalization for a week or two and then relative immobility for several weeks after her return home. After lengthy discussion, Marty and Tammi decided that Tammi would go to help care for her mother. This meant taking Jennifer and staying for an indefinite length of time.

All of them handled the separation quite well. Marty was acutely aware that this separation was much different for him than when Tammi had previously visited her parents. Before he had welcomed the time alone. Now he was lonely, called Tammi often, and anticipated their reunion. He was aware of how important they were to him, and this was a good feeling for him.

He spoke more easily of missing Jennifer than of missing Tammi and could not explain this. It would be several months before he could speak comfortably about his emotional needs in his relationship with Tammi, either to her or me.

Tammi, though harried and physically run down, showed new strength after Jennifer's birth. She now recognized the importance of having sources of satisfaction in her life besides the baby and wanted friends, other women with similar experiences and needs. I suggested that perhaps what she needed was a mothers' group, a group of women who met regularly to share the concerns, problems, and satisfactions of being a young mother.

Together we explored possible resources, including the local YWCA and some suggestions found in a women's magazine. Tammi made several phone calls and discovered that there was no group that met her criteria in her community. However, several people were supportive of her idea and helped her to make contacts with other women who might share the same interest. She decided to organize her own group. She enlisted the assistance of her Lamaze instructor, with whom she had developed a friendship, and began making phone calls to young mothers. With organizational and leadership skills that surprised both of us, Tammi succeeded in gathering together a group of young women, which became an ongoing support group. The group grew and even began to meet occasionally in the evenings in order to include husbands in special programs. For the first time in their marriage, Tammi introduced Marty to her friends. She was pleased with Marty's increased esteem and recognition of her contribution and success.

Tammi and Marty decided to have Jennifer baptized and began attending a church, where they were invited to join a couple's group. As they became a part of their community with new friends and acquaintances, they recognized the value of these resources to their marriage. Tammi was no longer dependent on Marty for total emotional support, could be more supportive of him, and make new contributions to their marriage.

We began to talk about when she would terminate therapy. Tammi asked to taper off gradually, unwilling to completely give up what was still, except for Marty, her major source of support. We agreed to meet biweekly for a while, and she would join Marty and me for monthly meetings. This happened naturally, as her visit to her parents occurred during this period. Later in the summer Tammi was again pregnant and terminated her individual therapy.

While I was still seeing Tammi weekly, there were changes in the joint meetings. They no longer saved issues to discuss with me, but continued discussions that had begun at home.

One evening they were having an animated conversation about their plans for moving to a country home, a plan now rather well along. They were not arguing, but exchanging ideas and inquiring about each other's opinions and preferences. Toward the end of the session I remarked on how well they were communicating. They acknowledged that they enjoyed the progress they had made in this. "You don't need me any more," I said. "I think you're ready to stop these meetings." I pointed out that not only did they converse quite comfortably about emotional and controversial issues, but had reported to me that they were able to handle problems at home without waiting for our session. They agreed with my evaluation but hastened to add that they didn't feel entirely confident.

When they returned the next week they said they had talked about my statement that we should think of terminating marriage counseling. There were still some unfinished issues, but both admitted making progress, and they *had* accomplished their goals.

I assured them that I thought they would continue to progress together and pointed out that neither could set the individual goals for the other.

Marty, who confessed that he was mildly disappointed that he had not been ready to terminate as soon as Tammi, wanted to feel free to move at his own pace. With new assertiveness he stated that he would continue until he accomplished what he wanted. He now felt pressure from within to deal with his career dilemma. He was writing more in his journal and writing letters. He made outlines for articles but balked at the idea of submitting anything to a magazine. He began exploring different career opportunities more seriously and subscribed to a newspaper from the area where they planned to move. On an impulse he sent a hurriedly prepared resumé in response to an ad for a job that was filled by the time his application was received. But this action seemed to give him confidence to continue. He carefully wrote a new resumé and sent it to several companies he thought might have suitable positions for him.

The kind of job he wanted was still a dilemma. He now began to see that his indecisiveness was a barrier to having the control he wanted over his life and a problem in his relationship with Tammi. Previously he had defended this characteristic as careful, methodical decision making.

He was also moderately anxious about having a second child, pointing out that he was an only child and had no experience with families larger than three. He still was having difficulty asserting himself with Tammi, particularly in letting her know of his own needs and wishes, but in this area he also made increased efforts to change.

One evening he began by saying there was something he wanted to tell me about immediately. Tammi, in her sixth month of pregnancy, had become more dependent on and demanding of him, reminding him of earlier, unhappy days. Though he understood that she was genuinely tired and not feeling well, he resented her demands and felt inadequate to meet them.

"The other evening I didn't do something she wanted me to . . . I don't remember what it was. She got angry and berated me like she used to, accusing me of not caring, not loving her. She called me names and cursed me. I knew that I was supposed to comfort her and calm her down, reassure her that I love her. I resented having to do it, but I did. She did calm down, and everything was okay. But I still felt kind of resentful. So I told her how much it hurts me when she calls me names and curses at me like that." And then he said, somewhat incredulously, "For the first time in our marriage she told me that she appreciated me. She said that she 'puts me through a lot' and she appreciates my putting up with her."

To Marty this was more than sufficient reward for his effort.

Marty is currently still in therapy but is making progress in his personal relationships with both Tammi and his daughter. This progress is carrying over to other relationships at work and with his parents. He is also making definite, realistic career plans. He speaks of his plans confidently, with expectation of success. We are beginning to talk about when he will be ready to terminate.

When I last saw Tammi she informed me that she was feeling good about herself and her life. "I think differently now, I don't feel helpless. I don't worry about those other women that Marty had affairs with any more, and I did for a long time. It's a relief to feel secure." Marty added that he was glad that she was no longer bothered by that. He had considered that phase over for him when the affairs had ended.

Tammi added, "I've decided something else recently. I'm going to sing again. I've started practicing. My range is higher than it used to be. I used to dream of making it big for Columbia Records, or something, but there are a lot of things that I can do, professional choirs and things like that." She sounded excited, self-assured.

We were in their comfortably furnished living room, where they were helping me plan the writing of this history. We spent almost two hours talking of our experiences together, of their impressions of the the process, and of how they perceive themselves and their marriage now. Tammi served tea, and they showed me the library where Marty had spent many hours building two walls of bookshelves.

(I had heard about all of the frustration these bookshelves had caused him.) He proudly showed the completed project and said it was worth all of his time and work.

Certainly, everything isn't perfect, they agreed. But they are no longer frightened or depressed. Now they can talk to each other. Tammi recalled that she used to think she couldn't survive if the marriage didn't. Now she knows that she would, and that she stays in the marriage by choice, rather than necessity. Marty added that he now regards Tammi and "his family" as a source of support and pleasure rather than a burden. He looks forward to coming home from work.

They both feel confident to cope with their difficulties and whatever they have to face in the future.

14

"What's Got Into Dad?"

A Middle-Aged Father Improves His Family's Life

Edward E. Ford

I have said that the clients who come to a counselor are a little like people who are brought to an emergency room. Some have chronic illnesses that have suddenly become acute, others are victims of accidents. Mike was an example of the first, a man with chronic problems that had seemed mild for years but had suddenly become acute.

Externally, Mike thought his life had been going along fairly well. He had been married to his wife, Julie, for twenty-five years. Two of their six children were happily married. Another two were around the house occasionally—they were not yet married—but basically well launched in life. He had a good income as an accountant, and his wife had an interesting job running her own old people's home just next door to their own home. True, Mike's son Chuck, a sophomore in high school, was failing several courses and doing poorly in the rest, and his daughter Christa, a freshman in high school, seemed increasingly moody and withdrawn. Still, Mike was deeply shocked when his wife told him that either he seek help and start putting his family's life in order or she was taking the kids and getting out. She was giving him only one last chance to change what she perceived as an unhappy, chaotic family life, and she meant what she said.

Julie, who had read my book *Why Marriage*[1] and attended one of my lectures, suggested that perhaps I could help him. He seemed

[1] *Why Marriage: A Reality Therapist Looks at Married Life* (Niles, Ill.: Argus Communications, 1974).

161

a gentle, sensitive man, willing to try something new because he was, above all, deeply confused by what seemed to be happening around him.

It seemed obvious as we spoke that while Julie's professed concern was about losing control of the kids, Mike's was about losing Julie. The thought that she would take their last two children with her when she left, if she did leave, upset him much less than the prospect of his being without her. Whatever the strains in their relationship, the depth of his need for her was apparent. I had not yet met her, but she had demonstrated her interest in him by taking the trouble to read my book and urging him to make an appointment with me. Eventually, I knew that we would talk about his relationship with his children, especially those who were at home, but I decided to begin, as I always do, with the area where I felt it would be easiest to build strength. That was his relationship to Julie. I was sure she would cooperate.

But at this point it was important to know more about Mike. I asked him what he did for fun, whether he got any exercise (or ever had enjoyed exercising), and what if anything he read. My clients are often a little surprised that I begin with what they might regard as one of their less serious problems. They are still more surprised when I begin with something they have not regarded as a problem at all. Mike had not come to me to discuss his reading habits or his physical condition. However, I saw him as a man no longer young, probably in substantially poorer physical condition than he needed to be and further in time from his last significant learning experience than he should have been. Julie wanted Mike to shape up their family life. A first step, I thought, was shaping up Mike. You know the Arabic proverb: If you have but two loaves of bread left, sell one and buy hyacinths to feed your soul. We would get to Mike's bread problems in due course. I wanted to begin with a few hyacinths for his soul.

When I asked Mike what he had been reading lately, he said that he had been reading very little. What did he do with his leisure time? Well, when he came home from work, he usually turned on the television. He had at one time read more. I asked him what the last book was that he could remember reading and enjoying. It turned out to be James Michener's *The Source*, which is about an archeological excavation, a romance and history of the Holy Land worked into a description of a dig. I asked Mike if he found archeology interesting. To my surprise, he said he had once been a member of an archeological book club. I asked about some of the books he had received through that club, and he was full of information, visibly brightening as he remembered this long-forgotten but interesting part of his history. I asked if he thought watching as much television as he was was helping him. He responded that it was "just something to do." I then asked him if he would consider watching television twenty minutes less every day and reading instead. He said he would, and I asked, "What are you going to read?" Whenever one of my clients is making a decision like this, I try to help that person to be as specific as possible, to actually visualize themselves doing whatever it is they decide to do.

He replied, "Oh, I don't know. I'll get something from a bookstore."

"What bookstore?" I asked. He named a bookstore.

"When are you going there?" He suggested he would stop on the way home from our session. "What will you do if they don't have anything you like?" He said he would try the library. By now I was convinced he meant it, and I asked no more questions.

When I showed concern for his physical condition, Mike indicated he had never been particularly athletic but was now unpleasantly aware of a slight but steady weight gain and recently a shortness of breath. I asked if he were willing to walk a mile every day. He was skeptical at first. "What good would that do?"

"Will it make things worse?" I asked.

"Oh, no," he said.

I asked if he had some other sport or physical activity he preferred. He didn't.

"Well, then, do you or don't you think you might feel better about yourself if you felt a little better about your body?" He promised to add a walk as well as a little reading to his daily routine.

The picture I had from Mike of how Julie thought their home life was going led me to think that Mike was exercising very little control over anything, including himself. Julie's complaint was that whenever she left the house everything fell apart, and Mike could not disagree. I wanted to help him realize that if he could take control of himself, he would be in a better position to take some control of his family life. As he took up these other activities, he found he had less time and significantly less interest in watching television, and this, as far as I was concerned, was helping.

When we began talking about his relationship with Julie, I reassured Mike, as I had when we first met, that I had seen many men as upset and baffled by what was happening in their lives, including their love lives, as he was. I couldn't make any ironclad guarantees, but there was every reason to think that, with attention and effort, things could become dramatically better. I say this because I mean it, and because I mean it, people believe it. I have indeed seen many cases of "middle-age slump." Husband and wife have separate lives but decreasing enthusiasm for each other and their children. They may sleep together, but lovemaking is rare or perfunctory. Whatever pride there once was in parenthood seems a fading memory. If there are children still at home, the basic needs—I mean physical needs— are attended to, but little more is done. The children are raising themselves. Sometimes this is a result of fatigue. Money worries may have forced the wife to take a job she didn't really want or the husband to work longer hours than he would have chosen. In short, their priorities become misplaced, and their past dreams of middle-age enjoyment together recede. They give in to the passive pleasures of television and movies, and the effortful activities that make life a pleasure begin to disappear. Life together becomes dull, routine. They need to reset their priorities and relearn how to live with one another. As they do so, their self-respect returns, their affection for each other with it, and their children's respect and affection for them follows suit. I was confident that a turnaround like this was possible for Mike, too.

I asked Mike about his sex life with Julie, and he admitted that it was practically nonexistent. I asked him if he had ever thought of getting a divorce. Often, raising that possibility early in any discussion of the health of a marriage delivers a valuable shock. Mike had never wanted to divorce Julie—he loved her. Well, then, did he think that marriage without any physical affection or intimacy was a good long-term idea? He admitted that it wasn't and that he wished things could be different.

I asked him to describe what if anything he and Julie did together. How did they spend time together? He answered that usually when he came home from work, she went next door to the old people's home. Sometimes she would come back and cook a meal for him and the children. More often, she would grab a bite with the old people and leave him and the children to fend for themselves, which they did, but usually not together. On the weekends he had his chores to attend to, and she had hers. They were both busy, but their activities rarely involved both of them.

I asked Mike if he thought his relationship with Julie could improve if he made an effort to spend a little more time with her. He felt it could, but seemed puzzled as to how to start. I suggested, for openers, that he just go next door for twenty minutes or so each evening. What would he do there? I didn't care. Maybe he could help. If he couldn't, he could still be there and share a little time with Julie. The total time investment I was calling for at this point—twenty minutes reading, twenty minutes walking, and twenty minutes with Julie—was less than half of what he admitted he spent watching television during the evening. I suggested also that he ask Julie if she would join him on his walks. He doubted that she would, but knowing she had read my book and sent him to me, I suspected strongly he was wrong.

He was—the walks became regular practice. As for the visits to the old people's home, Mike—who had been almost a total stranger to the people living under his wife's care—found himself caught up in conversation and passing whole evenings there. And, of course, that meant he was with Julie, too.

As she saw Mike making an effort, some of the warmth crept back into their relationship. At her suggestion, the two of them enrolled in a course I was giving on parenting. This provided an opportunity for them to work out together the problems Christa and Chuck were having, and provided them with further time alone, since they had to drive more than an hour to the place where the course was taught. Their first new parenting decision was to try to make the evening meal more of a family event than it had been.

Julie tried to get back from the old people's home each evening to cook, and Mike helped by cleaning up after dinner. However, at the start Christa and Chuck were having none of it. Or at any rate, they did not regard supper as in any way an obligatory appearance. I urged Mike not to force them to come directly but only to place certain conditions on their participation. I meant that if they were to eat what was prepared, then they would have to eat it *when* it was served, not later, and participate in the cleanup. There was always cold food around. If they wanted to eat that, they could. If they wanted the hot prepared meal, then they had to take it on the terms offered.

More was involved than food. I spent several sessions going over in detail the skills needed for enjoyable conversation, especially with children. I explained the use of questions that open up conversation, such as asking opinions, or having the children explain something. Such questions might include, "How do you compare this high school with the last one you went to? Show me how to adjust the carburetor! What do high school kids mean by _____ [then insert a word you've heard but don't understand]?" We engaged in role playing, in which I would be Mike and he would be Christa or Chuck. Then we would play a stressful encounter, and together we worked out better ways of handling his children. Mike began to develop painfully, slowly, steadily an ability to converse with his children.

Sometimes only one child would come to the meal. Sometimes both would come. Sometimes neither would come, and he would dine alone with Julie, which was always good, too. But the overall pattern was that "suppertime became a super time," as Christa eventually put it. Whichever child was sitting it out in the living room watching television began to feel left out of the fun. Before long, nearly every evening saw all four of them gathered at the table. In time, Mike, who had never shared any of the cooking responsibilities with Julie, made a plan to cook dinner. The children would occasionally be drawn into cooking, too. Julie loved leaving her chores at the old people's home to come back to her own home and sit down to an already prepared meal. Mike would never have guessed before he actually saw it how much this could please her, and he derived his gratification from her enjoyment.

As Mike began to care about seeing these meals go well, he became aware of how generally careless most of the other arrangements were in his home. He contrasted the way he felt about his work as an accountant, where he was very meticulous and proud of results, with the way he felt about his home, where little—except, now, the evening meal—seemed to happen according to any plan. He noticed, for example, that there had been no time set for the evening meal before he set one. In other areas, things seemed equally slipshod. Whenever he tried to introduce a little greater order, he ran into resistance— a passive resistance from Chuck, an active hostility from Christa.

Patterns that have been set for years cannot be displaced overnight. I urged Mike to think of himself as the principle of order in his family. He was the hub where the spokes came together. If his relationship with Julie could become so much better, then so could his relationship with Chuck and Christa. Eventually the family would start to agree on times and methods of how to run the house and live together more amicably.

Mike's overtures to Christa all seemed to be rebuffed, which was painful for him, but even the pain was a good sign. If you remember, when he first came in he had been concerned about his relationship with Julie but hardly seemed conscious of the fact that he also had a relationship to maintain with Christa and Chuck or that there was a problem there at all. While helping him to cope with his children's rejection of him, I urged him to think of himself as providing a model for the other family members of how a good family member conducts himself—how he keeps trying even when others offer no encouragement. For example, I urged him just to stick his head into Christa's room before he went to bed himself and say, "Good night, honey," Or, I suggested, he could give her an unexpected kiss once in a while. None of this brought any immediate change in her behavior toward him. However, her behavior toward her mother and her brother changed very noticeably. She started dropping in next door to help Julie, and her fighting with Chuck stopped almost entirely.

Much of Julie's initial distress when she gave Mike his ultimatum had been caused by the constant shrill and hate-filled fighting between Chuck and Christa. She saw Mike watching television passively while the children shrieked at each other. He did not intervene and did not even seem to notice, as if it did not concern him. She felt it ought to, so she was very pleased when Mike's brave efforts to reestablish loving contact with his daughter brought these visible results elsewhere in the girl's life.

Mike's relationship with his son Chuck seemed to have less to do with the emotional quality of their interactions than with some of the things that boys Chuck's age care about—the car, stereo equipment, liquor, and especially money. Mike thought Chuck was very wasteful with money, and he took the boy's spending particularly hard when he began failing his school courses. Further, as communications between Mike and Julie improved, they learned that both of their children, but especially Chuck, had frequently touched them twice for the same weekly allowance! The parents had been speaking so little that they only learned about this hoodwinking weeks after the fact.

In one of my classes that Mike and Julie had attended, I had discussed allowances. I had mentioned that I had found with my own children that they appreciate and handle money much more when they earn it themselves. Mike suggested that perhaps he ought to cut out allowances, which would make the children responsible to earn their own money. I told him it had worked in my home.

Chuck was upset by the sudden loss of income and expressed his displeasure. "It's not fair, Dad." Mike agreed with his son that it wasn't fair (a technique I taught him to cut out arguments), but that it was what he was going to do. Chuck sulked for a few days, then startled everyone by going out and getting a job. The new job did more for the boy than just restore his budget. It provided him with a sense of respect for himself, which was reflected in his efforts to improve his academic standing at school. It also provided an area where he and his father could talk and where Mike's years of work experience as an accountant could shine a bit. Mike was proud of what Chuck accomplished in his job—the boy saved money for a dream trip to California, where a friend's family had a house on the coast—and Chuck sensed his father's pride and responded.

Before Mike came to see me, Chuck had been relying for quasi-paternal advice on his older brother, Tony. Tony had had his own problems when he was living at home. Julie remembered that he had once responded to her request that he help in the old people's home by saying, "Dad doesn't give a damn, why should I?" But Tony had managed to leave home when the time came and set himself up with an apartment, a job, and law school at night. Once when things were particularly tense with Christa, Chuck had gone to live with Tony. The boys were close, and Chuck was impressed that Tony was impressed with the change in their father. Those family members who were at home had seen only a gradual change. Tony, living away from home, remembered the "before," and seeing the "after" he asked, "What's got into Dad? He's a changed man."

Mike is a changed man, but the things he has learned to do are things almost anyone can learn to do, and most of us half know already. In a kind of thank-you letter Mike wrote me, he said:

My goal is to help them [his children] get along by doing what you did for me, that is, getting them to look at what they are doing, make a judgment, and figure a better way. My job is to teach my children what I have learned."

15

"I Don't Live There Any More"

Giving Up a Failure Identity

Ronald C. Harshman

Jeanette was having severe difficulties in getting along with her mother and other members of her family and had been lonely and depressed. She had been seeing another counselor for over a year, but she was still having suicidal thoughts, and her general life situation did not seem to be improving. Jeanette realized that she was not getting better. In addition, it was apparently the practice of the other counselor to involve some of his patients in working for him, and Jeanette was doing secretarial work on that basis. She was trying to back away from the therapeutic involvement but didn't feel secure enough to make the total break. She was at a loss to know where to turn when she heard me talking about reality therapy on the radio.

She phoned my office to ask me some more specific questions about reality therapy. She told me a little about herself and asked if I thought she could "do something," as she put it, to function better. I talked with her long enough to determine that she had already made the decision to terminate her therapeutic relationship with the other counselor, and then I told her that it would probably be a good idea for us to meet at least once.

Jeanette was thirty-three years old at the time of her first visit and had been married to her husband, Bill, for about ten years. They had three children, who were then nine, seven, and two years old. Superficially, at least, it seemed as though Jeanette's life might have been very satisfying. She was an attractive woman, a concerned mother, and a caring wife. In addition to the work she had been doing for her other counselor, she was bowling in a league, involved in a community babysitting service, and active in her community league organization (a group of community people who had volunteered to organize community-based recreational activities).

Jeanette blamed many of her problems on the fact that she was left home with the children for long periods of time. Her husband was a supervisor for a company that had plants in many areas of western Canada, and he had to travel to these places. Jeanette found Bill's absences very difficult to handle, and each time her husband left town Jeanette felt lonely, then depressed, and when he returned she greeted him with a great deal of anger.

What was especially frightening for her was that, while Bill was gone, her negative feelings had begun to be directed toward her children. Recently she had been having fantasies about her youngest child, Christopher. She imagined herself hitting him in the head with a hammer, and although she had never physically abused any of her children, just having such destructive thoughts was very disturbing to her. She was concerned for her children's safety, and her fantasies had convinced her she was "crazy."

Typically, when Bill returned from a trip she would be cool toward him. It would take a fairly long time for them to attain any feeling of closeness, and by that time he was off again on another, necessary business trip. Their relationship seemed to be in a vicious behavioral circle, both self-destructive and self-perpetuating.

As Jeanette continued to tell me her concerns, she indicated that her relationship with her husband had deteriorated to the point where she felt very negative about their sexual relationship. This relationship had been a positive factor during the early stages of their involvement, and now that it was deteriorating Jeanette was becoming progressively more concerned. She complained that they did not talk to each other, and even when they did become involved in activities together, there was never any carryover. They would do something, but when that was done, each returned to his own world and continued the cooler relationship.

I tried to assess with her some of the positive elements in Jeanette's life. For example, she had once taken some modeling courses and was very attractive. She was obviously respected and cared about by friends. She was receiving positive feedback regarding her involvement in the babysitting service. However, Jeanette chose to repudiate these experiences and felt that she could not begin to feel better about herself or her situation.

We talked about the differences between reality therapy and the approach to counseling with which she was more familiar. We agreed that, as she had already lost confidence in her previous counselor, it would be appropriate for her to look for part-time work elsewhere. I made it very clear that I did not want to get into a "witch hunt" with her and try to find all the reasons for her negative feelings. I wanted us to begin looking honestly at what she could do to make things better in her life. Jeanette seemed willing to try to do this, but she doubted that it would really help her.

We began therapy on a weekly basis and immediately started to look at the things Jeanette could do to alter her situation. She resigned from her position with her former counselor and was offered a supervisory job with the babysitting service. This confused Jeanette—she couldn't understand why these people would want her to take on more responsibility. Why didn't they see how "sick" she really was? Again the dichotomy—she saw herself one way and others perceived her quite differently.

After a lot of discussion, Jeanette was able to recognize how she had been putting herself down, and she could also accept the fact that she needed to stop doing it. It was clear that her former counselor had spent a great deal of time trying to find all the reasons in Jeanette's past that were making her feel lonely and depressed in the present. We were able to talk about the destructiveness of this process, and although Jeanette, on a "head level," could appreciate the need for change, she found it to be an extremely difficult habit to break.

Bill was planning to be out of town during the following week, and Jeanette and I spent a great deal of time talking about what she could do to keep herself productively busy during his absence. She mentioned that she had long wanted to fix up an office for Bill in the basement of their home, and although she had been thinking about doing this for quite some time, she had never actually done anything about it. We talked about her need to really accomplish something, and she was able to accept the challenge of putting her intentions into practice.

It is interesting to note that the issue of Jeanette's building resentment toward her husband's traveling had been discussed with her previous counselor. His way of dealing with the problem had been to advise Jeanette that it was most important for her to "share" these feelings with Bill. Unfortunately, this "sharing" became more of a "dumping" experience. Jeanette chose to inform her husband of her feelings as he was preparing to leave on his business trips. Of course, at those times Jeanette was feeling very depressed and angry, and Bill really couldn't do anything about her feelings. Quite predictably, he would get on the plane feeling helpless and Jeanette would go home to brood in anger.

We agreed that it would be a good idea for Jeanette to try approaching this upcoming trip from a somewhat different angle. As a result, Jeanette decided that she would simply tell Bill that she knew she would miss him, but that she was going to make a commitment to him that she would try to keep herself productively busy during his absence.

Although I found Jeanette to be a very sensitive and feeling young woman, it became quite clear that she had really built a very high wall around her own "inner core." By this I mean that she had really learned to anesthetize herself emotionally. She was denying her needs and feelings and didn't know who she was or where she was going. I felt that it would be crucial for us to be able to come to grips with the "real" Jeanette. In order to do this, we would have to become involved in a relationship that would be so meaningful to her that she would accept the possibility of giving up the failure identity into which she had so destructively locked herself. I knew that Jeanette would need time to allow for this to occur, and I was convinced that the trust and involvement in our relationship would have to be earned rather than asked for. And I realized that although Jeanette wanted to be able to trust, her previous experiences had been very negative. It was important for me to allow her to move at a pace with which she could feel comfortable.

During the following week, Jeanette was able to follow through and get a good start on her redesigning project. She was able to clear the area she was going to use for Bill's new office, and she was also able to complete the portion of redecoration that she had set herself to accomplish while Bill was gone. When Bill returned home, he expressed very genuine relief and happiness. This was the first time that Jeanette had really followed through and done something constructive during his absence. Jeanette's pride in her own efforts, coupled with Bill's positive response, did a lot to help the couple as they began to alter their destructive behavioral cycle.

During the next three to four months, I continued seeing Jeanette on a weekly basis. We were able to look realistically at what she was doing, and we were also able to find better ways for her to spend her time and deal with her feelings. I felt it was necessary that Jeanette be able to discuss her involvement in therapy with both her husband and her children. Jeanette agreed that it would be important for her to be honest with her children and to tell them that although she was having some difficulties, she was now doing something constructive about them. We discussed various ways to approach each of the children, and Jeanette decided that it would be best to speak to them individually.

Jeanette was able to recognize that her negative feelings about Christopher were making her suffer severe guilt feelings anytime she planned to do anything without him. When she went bowling, she took him to the alley where they had a babysitting service. Anytime she was invited out for lunch, she refused on the grounds that she did not want to leave Christopher with a babysitter. As we discussed the situation, Jeanette began to realize how she resented her lack of freedom, and how this resentment was undermining any positive feelings that might have come out of the time she spent with Christopher. It became clear that it would be healthier for Jeanette to have some specific times to be able to do what she wanted. She agreed that it would help her feel better about doing this if she first spent specific time with Christopher, doing something "special," and then left to do "her own thing." Jeanette learned to plan her time with her children more effectively and still allocate time for herself. As she did this, she began to feel better about what she was doing in both areas.

Although Jeanette found talking about therapy with Bill and the children difficult, she felt very proud once she had been able to be honest with them. What made her feel particularly good was the direct and meaningful support her family gave her. I had met with Bill on one or two occasions and found that although he was supportive of Jeanette's involvement in therapy, he found it difficult to understand why she was so unhappy within herself. He acknowledged, however, that he had seen some very significant and positive changes in Jeanette since she had started therapy with me, and he wanted to be involved in as supportive a way as possible. Bill agreed to offer his assistance in both planning and carrying out some more positive interactions between the two of them. They were able to start spending more time together, and after an enjoyable outing such as playing in a community volleyball game, they continued the involvement by going out for coffee and talking afterwards.

Jeanette and I continued to establish an increasingly meaningful relationship, and as she continued to gain trust in our involvement, it became more possible for us to look at the prospect of her starting to build a more healthy and positive identity. Although we could talk about almost all of Jeanette's concerns, the one area that remained outside our discussions was the one of sexuality. In spite of the fact that Jeanette had initially mentioned her concerns regarding her sexual relationship with Bill, she avoided any attempt to look at the problem. A major stumbling block was the way she perceived her own sexuality. In spite of my intuitions, I felt convinced that it would not be advantageous to push Jeanette too much beyond her own comfort level, so I simply continued to remind her that this was an area we would have to talk about at some point.

It was during our sixteenth session that there finally appeared to be sufficient trust on Jeanette's part to allow me access into that part of herself which she had so skillfully, but destructively, locked away. We were able to talk about many of the fears and negative feelings she had about her sexuality. It became clear that she had been punishing herself relentlessly for incidents that had happened many years ago. Prior to her relationship with Bill, she had had intercourse with two different men. After the second encounter she had contracted gonorrhoea, and as a result she had been seeing herself as both a "total slut" and a "horrible person." Jeanette needed to look at the entire episode to see that although she resented and regretted that one sexual encounter, it was now she herself who was maintaining the liaison with the relationship, which had long since ended.

After a very long discussion, Jeanette was able to realize that she still saw herself as a "microscopic slide of gonorrhoea cells." I could now use the strength and closeness in our relationship to confront Jeanette with the need to choose between maintaining the failure identity into which she had locked herself or strengthening the new success identity she had begun to establish through our involvement. This proved to be an extremely difficult ordeal for Jeanette, but it became quite obvious that she really wanted to move in the direction of health, and that she was going to use the vehicle she now had—our relationship—to try, desperately, to abandon her self-concept of failure.

Jeanette was now able to realize the connection between her present difficulties and that "ancient" experience, which she had not allowed herself to reconcile. We discussed the fact that Jeanette was, in effect, telling herself that she did not really deserve to have a good husband, a good marriage, a nice family, or a good reputation in the community because such things are not obtained by "sluts" or "horrible people." Our ability to discuss and evaluate the situation indicated the degree to which Jeanette was really prepared to allow me into the previously forbidden "inner core." For the first time in many years, Jeanette openly recognized and evaluated her self-perceptions. She was able to be honest with herself about her emotional needs and feelings.

It is necessary to understand that the relationship that had developed between Jeanette and me was now at the point where she could cling to the strength of my caring and begin to let go of the "failure" identity that had been such a great part of her life. It is important to recognize that this type of connection does not enter a therapeutic relationship without some degree of risk. The therapist must be sensitive to the potential dependency that is involved in this kind of situation, and he or she must be able to handle that dependency in a responsible and health-provoking way. I do not personally believe that a patient's dependency on his or her therapist is a negative thing. We must accept the fact that in many instances the therapeutic relationship is the first one in which the patient is really able to trust, care about, be cared about by, and be dependent upon a responsible, mature, "important" (in the life of the patient) person. I believe that the effective handling of our relationship really became a decisive factor determining the direction in which we were able to move.

Quite predictably, Jeanette came to our next session with very ambivalent feelings. She expressed the fact that she felt a great weight had been lifted off her shoulders, and she was most enthusiastic about the challenges that lay before her in terms of finding out who she really was. Once she had been able to allow me into the "inner core," and as a result of the trust that she now had in me (and us), Jeanette was also able to join me in getting over the prohibitive wall she had built around her own "real self." She obviously felt quite positive about this aspect of the process.

On the other hand, Jeanette was now experiencing some very definite confusion and fear. She had known me for such a short period of time, and yet I was the first man who had ever been able to accomplish the feat of getting over the "wall." As a result, Jeanette came to the session feeling that the only logical explanation for her feelings must be that she was falling in love with me.

The openness and trust that was inherent in our relationship allowed us to discuss these ambivalent feelings fully. I felt that it was extremely important for me to be able to help Jeanette in clearly and honestly defining what she was experiencing. With some assistance, Jeanette was able to see that it was certainly inappropriate for her to compare the relationship she had with Bill to the relationship she had with me. I was able to help Jeanette recognize that the feelings she had for me were quite valid and meaningful, but they did not mean that she was falling in love with me. Realistically, there was an extreme closeness between us. Jeanette had been able to allow herself to become involved in a situation in which she could both give and receive honest caring. The fact that I had been able to gain entry into the "inner core" was primarily a result of my being a skilled therapist.

As a result of our discussions, Jeanette was able to see that she had much more invested in the relationship with Bill than she did in the relationship with me. As she was able to differentiate the feelings she was experiencing, she was also able to recognize that once she felt more comfortable within her own "inner core," she would be able to allow Bill to enter, and at that point it would become clear that the relationship with Bill was the real "love" relationship. Jeanette and I were sharing a very meaningful, real, caring relationship, and she was able to accept the value and uniqueness of this involvement. As we talked openly about what was really going on, Jeanette became increasingly more comfortable with her feelings, and more importantly, with their validity and meaningfulness.

Once we were able to work through these feelings, Jeanette really began to move quickly in therapy. Whenever she began to slip, I would teasingly refer to her perception of herself as "a dishful of gonorrhoea." At first Jeanette would get quite angry with me for confronting her with this vivid image of how she saw herself. But then, because I felt our relationship was strong enough to allow her to believe in the fact that I cared a great deal about her, she began to perceive the teasing as my way of letting her know that I knew when she was putting herself down. I felt that her anger was a manifestation of her frustration with herself for getting back into old habits, and she really understood that she was not getting angry with me.

With some encouragement, Jeanette was able to muster up the confidence to go back to the modeling studio where she had previously taken courses. To her surprise and great pleasure, she was welcomed with open arms. The modeling agency was looking for women in Jeanette's age range, and she not only began to get some assignments, but she was able to start teaching part time at the studio. At this point, Jeanette began to feel increasingly more comfortable with the thought of abandoning her "failure" identity. Now she really had an investment not only in developing but in maintaining her new and healthier identity.

Jeanette and I began spacing our sessions, and I saw her less and less frequently. She did have some setbacks, but she became more and more able to deal with these in healthy and productive ways. Her relationship with Bill improved significantly, and her relationships with the children became more meaningful and positive for all concerned. Jeanette was much more able to enjoy her involvement with her children, and she was also able to see them as healthy extensions of a healthier self. As Jeanette's own self-concept improved, so did her ability to accept the good things she had going on in her life, as being both appropriate and real.

Although Bill continued to travel, Jeanette was now able to handle her feelings more effectively and responsibly. She was planning her time more efficiently, and the time spent with her children began to be more meaningful and enjoyable for the children as well as for Jeanette. She was also able to start dealing more honestly with her mother and other members of her family. Jeanette was no longer looking into her past in order to find scapegoats for her present depressions and loneliness but was able to see that, in spite of the focus of her previous counseling program, her mother was really not to blame for Jeanette's poor self-image.

It has now been over two years since I first saw Jeanette, and I still hear from her occasionally. She is doing much better and is feeling positive about the degree of control she has over her own life. The negative and destructive thoughts have not returned, and the relationship with Bill is continuing to grow in a healthier and mutually rewarding manner.

16

New Perceptions Needed

A Middle-Aged Woman Stops Blaming Others for Her Problems

Richard Hawes

Carol was forty-seven when she came to see me and had been chronically distressed with regurgitation, severe depression, psychosomatic tendencies, and alcoholism most of her life. Two years later, when I told her I was considering writing her case history, I asked her if she would like to write it herself. She said she would. She had a long history of varied therapeutic experiences, and she chose to relate them as well as her personal history to show how different reality therapy was from any previous experience in her erratic and unsatisfying life.

From our first meeting on I tried to create a warm, trusting relationship based on open and interesting conversation as free of value judgment from me as possible. As trust developed between the two of us, we began to focus on and analyze specific situations in Carol's life, considering her attitudes and behaviors, the consequences of her actions within the given situations, and optional ways she could approach the persons and/or the situation in a more effective manner. Initially the emphasis in therapy was on problem solving, and in the following history Carol presents typical examples taken from different areas of her life. During the first three or four months of our weekly meetings, hardly a session went by where we did not discuss at least one of these situations.

Gradually the emphasis in therapy changed. Our conversations began to emphasize ways Carol could use her time and energies toward more enjoyable experiences rather than continuing problem solving or making plans to diminish or eliminate negative behavioral patterns. While the first phase of the treatment procedure was helpful and indeed necessary, this shift to the positive, self-creative use of time and energy seems to have marked a significant change in her day-to-day experiences and her mental and emotional orientation toward life in general. Here is her story, in her own words, regarding these phases of her therapeutic experiences and the insights she has gained.

PERSONAL HISTORY

The undertaking of this writing fell on April 13, 1978, which marked the eighth anniversary of my father's death. It would also have been my brother Dave's sixty-fourth birthday—had he survived the brain cancer that killed him four years ago. Just a few weeks previous to this writing my employer died of a heart attack in his sleep, and I began this task without anything but a great deal of dark gloom, wondering how I could put down anything that indicated any kind of achievement. As I wrote, I began to feel better, mainly because I discovered that my pathways were not as dark as I thought, and that my course was a better lighted way than I had ever previously known.

I was the youngest of five children, born when my mother was thirty-seven years old, which she felt was too old to bear a child. She told me later that she hid me behind doors so that people would not know she had had another baby. I was told that jokingly I was referred to as "excess baggage," but I don't remember being lonely or unloved. I remember that this was a busy and active family. I adored my three brothers, who always seemed to be around to hug and tease me.

My grandmother took care of me until I was nine. When she died, the unit of family life disappeared because it was about that time that all of my brothers went into the service. My mother managed my father's bakery shop, working as many as twelve hours a day. I rarely saw her except on weekends when she was mostly in bed with her feet propped up on pillows. She cooked for us but, as I remember, served only my father. My sister and I helped ourselves.

I was a fat child in a neighborhood that had few fat children. I had an excellent appetite, which I did not find difficult to elevate to gluttony. My mother being an excellent cook, and my father a superb baker, I was surrounded by enough good things to keep me busy until I realized that I didn't look at all like my contemporaries. By this time I had developed a malocclusion of my teeth, had undergone surgery for strabismus, and was prone to chin abscesses. I was not the cute, plump child of my infancy and felt that I was being rejected by my classmates because of this. In my eleventh year, I thought that if I looked like all the rest, they would accept me. With a determination I have not equaled since (where did all that strength come from?) I dieted like a Hollywood starlet—only to be foiled by my mother, who was certain that bread was the staff of life. She tempted me, and a year later I recapitulated. However, as a means of fighting her and fighting fat, I learned to regurgitate, and I started using it for many reasons—when I was bored, when I was angry, when I simply needed to stuff food and didn't want to keep it all down. I don't think that at the time I realized I was setting up a behavior pattern—that I would continue to use regurgitation indefinitely as a means of reacting to situations I couldn't handle, but that was what happened, even though I regarded it with disgust and loathing. Although I knew it wasn't routine or accepted behavior, I could not bring myself to talk about it for years. I didn't regard it as an effect, but thought of it as my entire problem.

I was about thirteen when my oldest brother, who was just starting out in psychiatric practice, suggested to my mother that I might benefit from therapy. If he had taken me to see someone at that time, I think I might have accepted the idea. But I was in defiance of my mother and would have done nothing she suggested.

I was a poor and inattentive student, and the only jobs open to me when I graduated from high school were clerical. Although not really advancing or learning in any specific area, I read a great deal, had no friends, continued to throw up, and that became my life.

In 1969 my mother died and I returned home to live with my father. I had not known my father well. He was a quiet, shy man who never had a great deal to say to me. My mother talked for both of them. He was a baker and had strong hands. When my mother felt I needed to be punished, my father was asked to administer the slap. Although this did not happen often, I learned later that he greatly disliked being put in this role. Once, our dog had urinated on some new chairs and my father, as usual, was called to deliver justice. He came to me with tears in his eyes, begging me to tell my mother that he had acted accordingly, but he could not bring himself to do it.

I had some idea at that time that if I returned to my father's house, we could mutually benefit. He was eighty-five, very spry and independent— he shopped and cooked for himself and gardened. He loved taking long, solitary walks and could still do this when I moved back. Perhaps a severe hearing loss from which he suffered most of his life had helped him become self-sufficient. He found it easy to be alone and quiet and had learned to amuse himself. His mind was alert, and he enjoyed reading in both English and Yiddish.

He loved going to the movies, and the biggest treat I could give him would be to take him on a Saturday afternoon. Although he had enjoyed his solitude, once I moved in he seemed to enjoy my companionship. He enjoyed having someone who would walk with him, talk with him, and take him to the movies. But he also wanted to make the decisions, and this created conflict. I wanted to be a model housekeeper. I had my own ideas of how to fill his needs and a notion that enjoying oneself was frivolous. So we went our separate ways—often in anger and chagrin.

He was continuing his walks, but soon needed the assistance of first a cane and later a walker. He started to fall, coming home bruised and cut, and eventually he broke his glasses and dentures. He then became depressed and slept most of the day, missing meals, complaining a great deal of gastric distress, and finally I felt that the greatest service I could do for him would be to move him to a senior citizens' residence where he could get more attention. He went under protest, declaring that he would be better off dead, and two days later he died.

I did not feel guilt about his death immediately—that came later. What I felt was relief—there had been so many arguments. His deterioration and depression had been difficult for me, and I learned that an occasional nip from the brandy bottle helped to relieve the tension. This became habit with me, and weekends were designed to drink myself numb.

Seven months later my oldest brother died, and that did result in depression. For six months I was unable to do anything but go to work, work as I could, and feel that I had failed in every respect, my job included. I had about three months psychiatric treatment at this time, but as soon as I started to feel better, I ended treatment, dug deeper into my work situation for some kind of safe retreat, and thought I could short-circuit all feelings, good and bad, by drinking at home at night. This was my way of life, and I assumed it was the best I could do.

Experiences in Psychotherapy

The first was a psychiatrist who wrote on blue paper and wore a monocle. I saw him five times. Then there was a man ready to put me in a hospital on our first encounter. (I didn't say a word for the entire hour—could that have been the reason?) I saw him only once. The next man seemed to know less than I (was that possible?) and I saw him twice. Then the man in whom I felt my first real confidence. He said, "I know how you feel." I saw him every two weeks for two years until I felt less depressed. I don't know that I came away with anything positive, but at least he was someone I could trust, someone I could talk to—I could not talk to my mother or my sister about my ideas, feelings, and situations.

After the initial two years, I saw him only occasionally for "mop-up" sessions during the next five years. He did try to interest me in going back to school, and in fact, I did get some college credits through his direct influence that I enjoyed tremendously. His office as well as his conversation was a treasure of literature, art, and music, and somehow I did fancy myself to lean in this direction, but did nothing to prove it.

It would be nice to say that at this point I had been restored, but all the while I continued to throw up, continued to have difficulties relating to my mother, and seemed to have less and less energy. My obsession with dieting continued, and I found it was easier not to eat than eat and then regurgitate. My energy sources were so low that it was physically painful for me to move. It was difficult for me to concentrate or perform, and just being at my desk at work sapped what little energy I had. I started to feel guilty for not being able to do my job, felt that I lacked honor in this regard, and once again crawled into my depression as an escape. I found no interest or meaning in anything I did and questioned the necessity for being alive.

The lack of self-esteem was so strong that I did want to end life. I didn't have the necessary medication around to take that step, but I tried by using multiple Miltown and Coriciden. Not being knowledgeable about the effectiveness of these, all I achieved was a twenty-four-hour stupor and enough concern on my mother's and family physician's part to get me admitted to a hospital's psychiatric unit for three months. My therapist was called but did not immediately respond, and my internist reached another man. My hospitalization took me out of two unsatisfying situations—my home and my job. As for the stay itself, I can only remember I was frightened and horrified that I might be permanently stamped by my association with the unit and my breakdown.

My shrink came to visit every morning at eight o'clock and pulled me into a little examination room off the ward while I was still in pajamas and groggy with the previous night's medication. I think I really hated him because he was in complete control of my situation—I had to rely on him for my release. Later I came to regard him as quite a nice human being. Through his support, I managed to find another job after the hospitalization. I had thought I would never be able to work again because of the stigma.

For four years I saw him weekly. I managed to expound on how much I hated my mother and I continued to vomit. I went back to school and dropped out of enough classes that I thought my return to City College was an impossibility.

Now things become rather indistinguishable. There were a number of jobs, none exciting, all marked with the feeling that I was not doing well. There were a number of therapies and therapists, but nothing that worked for me.

Although my mother in the last ten years of her life suffered severe emotional disturbances, being committed to sanitariums at least three times and having electroshock therapy on several occasions, I continued to move back and forth between her home and other locations. I returned to her home when I was too weak and sick to be on my own, thinking I could draw on her "strength." Nevertheless, when she died I thought all of my problems would end. I liked to think she had created them, not I—that all my habits, subterfuges, and self-deceits would disappear into her grave. Nothing could have been further from the truth.

During the next seven years I saw two other therapists for short durations. There was no effect, nothing I can remark on, nothing I took with me from either.

Reality Therapy

I decided to try another therapist because of a persistent gastrointestinal distress with no pathology indicated on the x-ray. The only explanation on which my internist and I could agree was marked mental and emotional constipation. I had proved that the passage of time does not necessarily make one wiser; that is, I still threw up, still had no friends, still felt unworthy in my job situation, and by this time I was securely addicted to alcohol. A positive perception of life around me was not possible because of the limitations and restrictions I had placed on myself. There did not seem anything beyond work and drink, and I pitied myself endlessly because I could not turn to my family.

In previous situations it had been my assumption that all I had to do was sit in the therapists' offices and some miraculous transformation would take place. Now for the first time I am beginning to understand that change does not occur in the therapist's office and by talking about change. I had to *do* something—behave differently in my everyday contacts and thereby develop more helpful perceptions of myself and others.

Changing habits and attitudes is not easy. First I had to recognize my contributions to disturbing personal relationships and realize that my best chance to feel better was to look for ways to change my thoughts, my actions, and my feelings. This takes a certain amount of self-effacement. Then it takes persistence in applying these new and different ways in a variety of situations. Following are four examples to give you an idea of some of the changes I'm making.

My relationship with my sister has not been a satisfactory one for me or her. She has for years assumed the role of an authority figure with me. She has treated me as a child, and as you will see from this example, my actions usually did nothing to dispel her notions of me.

Of course, our experiences in growing up were not always strained, and occasionally we had fun together. Part of that fun was to bestow on each other what I call "terms of endearment" in the form of nicknames. My favorites for her were "Crawley Van Grope" from the L'il Abner cartoons and "Crummy." Recently, during one of our telephone conversations, I addressed her as "Crummy." Her sharp reply was, "Don't use that name with me; I find it very demeaning." Feeling that she had completely misunderstood my affection for her and that she had broken our childhood bonds, I became furious, hung up the phone, and then, I am somewhat embarrassed to admit, tried to pull the telephone jack from the wall. Still infuriated, I called the telephone people to have the phone disconnected. Once my rage subsided, it seemed too much of an inconvenience to be without a phone, so I canceled the order for the disconnection.

Still simmering, I decided to call her only when necessary and respond with a cool politeness when she called me—that would teach her!

In the old days, I would have carried on this ridiculous performance for days and sometimes weeks. This time my thoughts were gradually changed, spurred on by three very significant questions, which persistently come up in therapy. "How are my actions helping me?" "What do I want?" and "What can I do to make the situation better?"

Jostled by these queries, it gradually occurred to me that she was justified in stating her preferences. She was asking me to be considerate of her feelings, which are just as important to her as mine are to me. Realizing this is the first step. The next step was to apologize to her for my behavior, which is not the easiest thing to do when one is conditioned to believe that the other person is the one at fault. With these sorts of changes on my part, perhaps in time we may be more than just sisters—I hope we will be friends. I was able eventually to show her that my attitudes toward her were changing by showing more understanding of her needs. Later I was able to tell her I was sorry I had called her "Crummy."

In another situation, with a friend of eleven years, the same sort of changes on my part were helpful in bolstering my self-respect. A few years ago, my friend married and moved out of the city. Her marriage was a difficult one. One evening she called me out of misery, expecting a reassuring discussion or at least some sympathetic understanding from me. Rather than this, I cut her short, using sarcasm and criticism as my cutting edges. Severely damaged by her crumbling marriage and my approach to her, she hung up. My response (typical for me at the time) was to tear up her telephone number and address.

A year passed before we met again. She called me at work, but my feeling was not to offer any invitation to meet with her until she offered first. Perhaps we were both frightened of the other's rejection, but the conversation ended without any further attempt to pick up the friendship—something that I truly desired but would not act upon.

From time to time I would think about our deteriorated relationship and frequently wondered what would happen if I called her. Through our discussions in therapy, I was encouraged to do this. It helped during the sessions to talk over the different responses she might give and what I would say. Finally, I got enough courage to call. Her response was very receptive, and we began to make plans to renew our friendship. My persistent self-pitying philosophy characterized by the phrase, "What's the use?" was dealt a serious blow by this experience, and our continued contact has made my life much better.

At work, I'm learning not to let other people's manipulative behaviors overwhelm me and chip away at my own sense of well-being. One of my co-workers often arrives late and is fully aware that our employer disapproves of this. One morning recently a particularly troublesome piece of correspondence was not sent on time. Our boss called the office to talk with her only to find that she was late. He called her at home to let her know of his upset over her performance. That afternoon, she burst into the office demanding to know why we didn't cover for her. She followed that up by not talking to me and slapping papers on my desk as though I were responsible for what had occurred. This intimidating approach had worked well for her in the past, because I had no idea how to respond other than to be a "shrinking violet." This time, because in our sessions we had discussed different responses that could be given in such a situation, it was different. When she had settled down somewhat later in the day, I asked to talk to her privately. I told her in a very calm and direct way that I wanted to remain friendly with her and that I would appreciate her handling future situations differently. I could hardly believe it was I talking. I was not falling into my usual performance, full of tears or feelings of guilt, neither of which were relevant, justifiable, or helpful to her or me. Stating this, I took my exit quickly and carried on with the afternoon's duties. She was quite visibly affected by our talk, and although she didn't apologize, her behavior for the next few days was quite subdued. During that time I found things to talk to her about in a friendly and considerate way, and I also expressed my appreciation for her treating me better. This approach has remarkedly improved my self-respect and our relationship.

This last example involves my following through more directly with working situations. I'm responsible for the Medicare/Medi-Cal billing in our office. A little while ago, one of the billing notices, which should have been processed sometime earlier, was found among a batch of old papers. My first impulse was to become emotionally upset, attempt to cover up the find, put it aside, and perhaps lose it again. I was sure that when the doctors or other office workers found the oversight, they would somehow castigate me or treat me in a miserable way. Once again during the therapy session, we role-played some of the approaches I could make to my employer. The plan I followed was to take a straightforward approach by calling the Medi-Cal office to see what could be done. I found that probably up to 80 percent would be paid and that an appeal could be made for the Medi-Cal portion of the bill. I then went to the physician personally and told him what had happened and how I had worked it out with the Medi-Cal office. Much to my pleasant surprise, he warmly complimented me on the job I had done. My worries about being badly treated were all for naught.

One of these experiences by itself may seem small, but the cumulative effect of all of them has given me a sense of confidence I had not before realized was there. An additional major difference in this therapy is that sessions are not the painful ordeals for me they once were, and I wonder why the concept of self-improvement should ever have to be served up in the form of a bitter tonic. My previous experiences in therapy have been rather remote and formal, except for my first therapist, who was closest to the father I would have chosen, had I been able to make that choice. However, he was a sad and melancholy man and I was a sad and melancholy patient. The healing process here is cheer, accompanied by positive yet realistic ways to handle everyday situations. It is not easy to practice self-annihilation under these circumstances.

Because of the ease and informality of our conversations in the session, I find I am in turn easier in my conversation with others. Because I feel a freedom of expression, I am more free to relate in a more congenial manner with others. As a result, my thoughts about people are better and I spend much less time in the dark atmosphere of blaming and complaining. I've become much more cognizant and therefore much more able to devote my time and energy to more personally pleasurable pursuits. Recently a lady gave me two of her garden-variety camellias. My old response would have been to throw them away, because I would have felt too pressured from daily events to take time out to find a vase for them. But I brought them back to the office, found a vase for them, found the time to look at them and admire their form and color, and even enjoyed the few garden bugs that were still clinging to them. I'm beginning to see that closing my eyes through alcohol to events around me is not going to improve my circumstances. When I drink, I cannot enjoy the sun as it is now shining through the window, or the color of my cat's eyes, and enjoying these simple pleasures to me is as major an achievement as winning a gold trophy might be to someone else.

The cumulative effect of experiencing the good feelings associated with successfully completing these various plans at work and in my personal life have helped increase my emotional strength. My gastrointestinal distress has shown marked improvement, and I've been without alcohol since November 1976 (thirty-three months as of this writing). My overeating and regurgitation have decreased significantly. I'm relating much better on a daily basis with my companions at work, my sister, and my friends. What's becoming very pleasing is that I'm finding more motivation to structure my time in more enjoyable and interesting ways.

What lies ahead for me? My private devils are still lack of motivation, an inability to see things through to their conclusion, to finish what I have started. Application to time, order, and self-discipline are goals not yet fully achieved, but I'm working on them.

What I'm learning to do in my life is to continue to strengthen my self-respect and self-confidence. I'm even beginning to think that I could promote my intellectual capacities to a greater fulfillment. These are all aims in writing and not completely accomplished in fact. The major accomplishment is that I could not have told you I wanted any of this one year ago.

Carol has gained mental strength and wisdom by providing herself with new experiences—meticulously practicing these new ways in various areas of her life, reflecting upon and evaluating their consequences, continually clarifying her values and purposes in life, setting up further objectives and plans to reinforce those self-prescribed experiences, and practicing more and more until her new attitudes toward herself and others are well inscribed in her mind.

Three years ago she was beset by the distressing notions that regurgitation, alcohol, and depression were the best she could do. She felt that enjoyment was a "frivolous occupation." She bolstered these ideas by assuming that this was her only way of life, and incredible as it seems, she supported that notion by believing that "there was nothing remedial to be done." Even after her previous experiences in therapy, she had the rather dubious idea that personal transformation would somehow miraculously happen by just "sitting in the therapist's office" or waiting until her mother died.

As Carol gradually began to take increasing responsibility for her thoughts and actions, she began to experience an emotional well-being, fleeting at first, but gaining stability with time and effort, that she had not had before. She continues to learn that she is able to choose different and more personally rewarding uses of her time and energy. Her perceptions of life are more clear, more realistic, and more positive. She is taking herself and her previously distressing personal situations less seriously—in fact, she is finding less and less time to be bothered with them.

It's interesting to note here that as Carol wrote this chapter she used the experience as a way to reflect on her present life and was able to catapult to a few more moves. One of these was to provide herself with more experiences in groups. A second was to sign up for a course, preferably in religion or philosophy; to that end she recently completed a course in Judaism at Yeshiva University of Los Angeles. And a third came directly from this experience in writing. She had for some time thought that she would like to write, and the positive responses she received from people who read her manuscript during its formation encouraged her to sign up for a writing class in children's literature. These commitments have provided alternative group experiences comparable to those of a professional nature.

Carol and I have talked about her signing up for Alcoholics Anonymous. She had gone for four months prior to seeing me, and we frequently talked about the value of the experience. She went to an occasional meeting after we started therapy but could not seem to sustain the effort to continue and make the total commitment the group requires. Her past experiences in group therapy had done nothing to encourage her to renew that kind of experience.

Perhaps the highlight of her recent activity has been her volunteer work at the Children's Museum, where she assists and escorts children through the museum's various adventures. Her latest assignments are helping the children use crayons to trace from newsprint, working in "Grandma's Attic," where the children learn to make butter using antique kitchen equipment, and leading groups of children under the city streets to learn how our city transports gas, electricity, and water. She helps the kids into slicker rain coats, boots, and hats and has, as she notes, "a ball doing it." She's quick to add that this is the kind of therapy she has been seeking. Carol still maintains contact with me as she continues to make changes in her life.

Recently, Carol phoned to tell me that she has made application to volunteer at Children's Hospital. During the conversation, she remarked, in what would seem to be an understatement, "You know, my extracurricular activities seem to be taking precedence over my work."

Good going, Carol.

17

The Road Back

A Delinquent and Depressed Sixteen-Year-Old Boy Is Rehabilitated

Melvin L. Goard

Before a young man chooses Speck Homes, he is told that his only other choice of the moment is to be locked up. At the judge's option he will go either to Oklahoma State Training School for Boys or to the adult penitentiary. He has been on probation, in a psychiatric ward in jail, or in trouble long enough for all other programs to have failed to rehabilitate him. When a judge thinks our program at Speck Homes can help, he asks us to come to jail or another court-related facility to explain the Speck Homes alternative. If one of our ten places is open, I do a series of psychological tests and then meet with the young man, his parents if possible, and the judge.

Because of our location we consider it necessary to make two concessions in screening the boys who enter. We have three buildings—our offices, our public school, and a home. We have no fences and are part of a historical section in the oldest part of Oklahoma City. Originally we took only boys convicted of multiburglary charges. That was because we wanted to exist harmoniously in the community, where many of the people don't even know what we do. After we had proved that we were creating no problems, we extended this to include young men who have been convicted of multiple charges of armed robbery and assault with intent to kill. The only concession we make to the community now is that we don't take anyone convicted for murder or rape. That is a philosophy we would like to change someday, but we have developed this program slowly, with careful consideration of public relations and community reaction and support, and so far it has worked, and we are accepted. We have never once created a community problem, never had a fight occur in the community or inside our facility. Our boys have never used unacceptable language to a staff member or done anything to offend anyone in the neighborhood. Eventually we will try to include in our admission policy any young man who needs us.

One other policy has already been changed. Originally we accepted the young man only if he had parents who would make a commitment to become involved in the therapeutic process at Speck Homes while their son was there. That rigid policy prevented us from admitting some boys we felt were salvageable. We now have developed a half-way house for boys whose parents are not involved.

When I went to detention to meet Vincent and his mother, it was for a briefing on all aspects of Speck Homes. Vincent was a sixteen-year-old Mexican-Indian who during the interview was polite and quiet and answered only when we spoke to him. He had been on probation for two years and had recently been arrested for assault and battery with intent to kill. Juvenile court had decided that to protect himself as well as others, he had to be removed from society. He had two options—to be incarcerated at the State Training School for Boys, a correctional facility, or come to Speck Homes.

It was important for Vincent and his mother to understand that if he chose Speck Homes, he would stay with us until we decided he was rehabilitated. If he went to the training school, the state would determine the length of the stay. If he were willing to serve time and get it over with, he might be free sooner. At Speck Homes the staff would determine when he was responsible enough to return to society, and our determining factors are tough. Because of our high rehabilitation rate, the court has never questioned our decision when we have sent a boy home or to our halfway house. Our successful program covers so many aspects of the boys' lives that we have earned a reputation with the district attorney's office which enables our young men to leave Speck Homes and return to society with a clean record. Vincent would have to stay long enough to show us he could be responsible for every phase of his life. He would eventually have to prove that he was capable of going to school full time (8:20 A.M. to 11:30 A.M.) and working full time (2:00 P.M. to 11:30 P.M.) simultaneously. He would be attending group therapy programs, both with the boys and with the parents, and be counseled individually by our staff. Somehow, at the same time, he would have to find time to help in the maintenance of our buildings and the daily housekeeping.

For Vincent, there was another important consideration. He was a chronic runaway, not only from home but from any agency to which he had been assigned. If he would not stay with us, we could not help him. We asked him to make the commitment to stay. We explained a little about our philosophy of therapy and living, which is completely based on the principles of reality therapy, and which we explain in greater detail after a boy enters.

At this time we were aware, as we always are, that we were talking to a young man who was very sophisticated when it came to conning a representative of the law. Young men like Vincent have had a lot of experience getting and staying out of jail. They see us, and truthfully so, as an alternative to detention, and they'll say almost anything they think we want to hear.

Vincent's mother was eager for him to choose Speck Homes and agreed to enter the parents' therapeutic program. Vincent considered the possibilities and chose as most young men do. He entered Speck Homes in February 1977.

He had been living with his mother and her three younger children. His parents were divorced, and his oldest brother, who had also been involved in antisocial behavior, lived with his father. Vincent spoke bitterly of his father and had little or no rapport with him. His mother, in her turn, had little control over Vincent. In fact, Vincent liked to boast that he never allowed his mother to hassle him, which meant, "I do whatever I want." And what he wanted was a life free of the responsibilities society expected him to assume. Weekends were spent getting high and partying, using marijuana, alcohol, STP, acid, or whatever drug was available to him. Although he was enrolled in ninth grade, he had been in and out of school for the last year. He made low grades, talked all the time in the classroom, and did none of the work. He claimed he had done well in elementary school and had not started doing poorly until he entered high school. He blamed his father for this, saying it was because his father had had him transferred to a new school.

Vincent is small framed, dark skinned, and has scars on his hands and face that he claims were made by friends with a lighter while fighting when he was drunk. He had a neighborhood reputation for getting into fights frequently. His records showed him to be highly emotional, impulsive, and hot tempered. He seemed to lack the ability to think through a situation and showed immature reasoning and judgment.

On his first day with us he went through a briefing program. Each of our boys is given a small white handbook to familiarize him with all aspects of our programs. They personalize it with their names, and as they live with us add any comments about their goals, special activities, or anything they wish to make it theirs. We review it carefully with each boy to be sure he understands all the rules, which have been set by present and prior residents and may be reevaluated if necessary. They cover every aspect of behavior pertinent to people living in our setting, such as standards of cleanliness and smoking and visitation regulations, and are very specific. Breaking the rules can result in removal from Speck Homes and returning to court. The handbook, which the boys have dubbed the "bible," also tells the incoming resident what to expect regarding his education, recreation, counseling sessions, and every other facet of life within Speck Homes.

It is not unusual for any institution to do this with new residents, but what makes our manual unique is what appears on the first page, titled "Orientation."

There's got to be a lot going through your mind right now. You've been to court and have been sent to Speck Homes. You may have been thinking you were going to "get off" and go home. That really doesn't matter now. What does matter is that you broke the law and you are here. If you're willing to accept it, you're being offered a chance to change some areas in your life so that you won't ever have to get busted and sent to court again.

At Speck Homes, you'll be dealing with personal responsibilities. All boiled down to that it simply means that there is a pay-off for everything that you do; and you've got to accept that pay-off. Here, you'll be expected to "pull your weight." You will have chores to do and rules to follow. We will allow you to be accountable for your behavior without excuses. You are also going to have the chance to find out a lot about yourself and your parents.

At Speck Homes, you will be dealing with care. The staff here will probably be different than what you expected. They really do care about you, and because they do, they will give you no slack. They will be doing their best to get involved with you and to get to know you as a person. How you respond is up to you. The staff is here for one reason, because you are worthwhile. You will be treated by staff in the same way staff would want to be treated if they were residents here. They not only want to see you stay out of trouble, but they would also like to see you be happy and proud and feeling good about *YOU*.

At Speck Homes, you will be dealing with your life, and the chances to make it different. You've got the chance and what you do is up to you.

From the first day, Vincent was told his rehabilitation was his responsibility, that we were all here to help him in any way we could. Each member of our counseling staff posts his schedule, and Vincent could sign up for individual counseling when he chose to discuss any problem he wished or any area on which he wanted to work or that pleased him. Later in the handbook he is told that "honesty is the key." Honesty is sometimes rough, but it is the only way to get help. He was urged to get involved.

This advice seemed to have little impact on Vincent. From the moment he entered Speck Homes, Vincent was extremely withdrawn. When forced to communicate, he did so belligerently. He had a briefing on what his duties would be and was told what his first job would be—picking up the yard. He chose not to talk to anyone the entire first day. When he was checked five minutes after going to bed, he was fully dressed. Told by the night counselor that he needed to undress, he replied, "I will when I'm ready to go to sleep." Our counselors know that not fully undressing is behavior commonly seen in insecure residents, but we have our rules. Vincent was asked to step into the hallway, where he was told, kindly, that it was appropriate to undress before getting into bed. After waiting a few minutes, he quickly took his clothes off, ran and jumped into bed, pulling the covers over his head.

This behavior was typical of the first fourteen days. He ate little and preferred to be filthy, and while he participated only sparingly and spasmodically in the program, he did stay in sufficient control to remain at Speck Homes. He did his work, committed no crimes, was not involved in disruptive physical behavior, and made no attempt to run away, but he showed very little improvement. These were tense times for him and the staff. We approached him repeatedly to be more cooperative, but he resisted.

Everyone on the staff is completely trained in using the techniques of reality therapy. They take the 120-hour training program that I give, and some have taken additional workshops elsewhere. None of the background information on any boy is shared with the staff. I am the only one who knows the nature of his offense. It's necessary to tell the staff what type of drugs or reaction from specific drugs they must look for. Other than that, as far as the staff is concerned each young man is the same as any other when he enters, and he receives the same treatment.

However, once the young man becomes a part of our program,

his records are available to everyone, including him—everything ever written up about any resident while he is at Speck Homes is available for him to read. Every week the staff meets separately with each resident to discuss his previous week and plan the next. Nothing is ever discussed without the resident being there to hear what is being said about him. There are no hidden agendas or hidden consequences. The resident has access to the files, the log entries, and at the weekly staff meetings he hears each staff member report what has been put in the logs. He may read it if he wishes. And any staff member has the same access to everything that is going on with any young man. The staff knew with Vincent they had to be firm, consistent, avoid getting emotional, and try to be kind and warm, not easy when you face repeated rejection. None of this helped. We tried whatever we could think of to show him we cared about him, that we wanted to be involved in helping him try to find new and constructive patterns for his life, but we faced constant frustration for our efforts. Attempts at conversation were rejected. Offers to play ball were spurned. We tried to spend time with him, but he withdrew completely. He would talk to no one. He seemed intent on hurting himself, and it even seemed that he almost enjoyed the pain. Even at Speck Homes we rarely see a young man this destructive.

We continued to treat him with the same consistency, and it was in this vein that Mr. Jones, a counselor, had to both discipline him and ask him to come up with a better plan one night in mid-March. The boys were preparing dinner and Vincent refused to help, explaining tersely, "I told you I wasn't going to eat." Mr. Jones sent him outside to think about what he had said and suggested he return with a different approach.

Vincent sat down on the back steps of his cottage, and it was there I had my first one-to-one encounter with him. He was sobbing and crying loudly. Instead of becoming involved with whatever had caused him to be in such a state, I surprised him by my first question. "Do you remember the last time you attended an Indian festival, Vincent?"

His reply was defensive. "What do you know about Indians?"

I responded with a simple truth, "Not much." But the one festival I had attended had at least given me the knowledge that trying to talk about it with Vincent could be the breakthrough we were looking for.

He raised his head and looked at me—the first time in thirty days he had looked a staff member in the eye.

The next morning I found a note on my desk:

Since you know nothing about Indians I am going to make you something to show what Indian life was about.

I was elated. This was Vincent's first positive response after thirty days in the program. True, it was written rather than oral, but it was better than the arrogance and withdrawal to which we had become accustomed.

Vincent's gift to me was an example of Indian culture made from scraps he'd found around the cottage. It was a replica approximately six inches high of a cradle board used by Indian women to carry children on their backs. It had intricate bead work, and made use of leather and rabbitskin, with snake rattlers hanging down from the bottom and Indian feathers on both sides. It showed great artistic skill as well as Vincent's understanding of his native art, and because of its small size it must have taken tremendous patience. For us, this cradle board signified a tremendous breakthrough. It told us never to lose hope with any boy and never to stop trying, and it gave us the courage to look for more positive responses from him. We had become accustomed to receiving positive responses from boys fairly soon after they came to live with us, but with Vincent we had waited what seemed to be a long time. We all needed something to carry us through another thirty days. It is difficult not to give up when you have no response at all—we are, after all, only human, too.

Our goals for Vincent still had to be small in scope to be attainable. One of the areas on which we concentrated for the next thirty days was simply encouraging him to wash his hands before pitching in with the kitchen chores. Our concern about his reluctance to wash before fixing meals was twofold. Not only were we enforcing our own rules, but health regulations dictated clean hands. Every time the housemother asked Vincent to wash, however, he would become angry and arrogant. This seemed to us to be Vincent's most significant "small" problem, and one that caused us the most concern during his second month at Speck Homes. Throughout the ensuing weeks the housemother's log noted repeatedly, "Vincent and I are still fighting the cleanliness battle each morning." Asked to wash his hands, Vincent would pout and sulk for the rest of the day and refuse to speak to any of the staff members or other residents—but his intransigence was still met with continued patience and persistence tempered with love and kindness. Perhaps because she never became angry or upset with him when she asked him to wash his hands, the housemother's patience led Vincent to his first positive response to another staff member other than myself, to her. One morning after breakfast, Vincent made his first open comment, and he did it in the presence of the other residents. He told the housemother that her breakfast had been okay.

That same day another staff member managed to break through Vincent's sulking, withdrawing behavior. Vincent was helping to prepare dinner by making chocolate pudding, when he apparently spilled it all over the floor and made a tremendous mess. A staff member walked in just after the spill. Vincent was probably expecting a scolding, but instead the staff person simply commented, "I'm glad to see you're involved in preparing the meal." It was a subtle point, but one that apparently impressed Vincent. All his life he had waited for the rebuke, waited for the put-down, had had little positive reaction to anything he had done. So he stopped to wait and find out what was coming next. Still no criticism. After a short time he realized there would be no other reaction—and he turned around and went about his other responsibilities. For the first time in sixty days, the log entries by the night counselor, Mr. Koch, noted that Vincent's attitude had improved even if only slightly, and that Vincent was in a better mood that day.

The next morning Vincent awoke at four-thirty, three hours before the normal wake-up time. A staff member told him there was really no need to get up so early, that it would probably make his day too long. Vincent did not respond in his usual negative way. Indeed, his attitude toward returning to sleep was pleasant. It may not seem like much, but for him this was a big step. And we were continuing to see the light.

On April 12 the housemother noted in the log: "No problems whatsoever with Vincent. He actually volunteered to wash his hands, adding a little wryly, 'even though it does hurt me to do it.' " In the log after that, she added: "The battle of the hands was a long hard one. I won, or maybe we both won."

What she did not record was that she was exuberantly happy with this small success, the battle of the hands. Nevertheless, we were still a little skeptical, and wondered if Vincent had only relented in one area to become more adamant in another. This did not turn out to be true; the positive change he had made stayed. He continued to wash his hands, and occasionally he even looked at staff members during conversations. For the rest of it, he got up and went to bed on time, made his bed, and fulfilled other minor responsibilities, doing just enough to stay in the program. The staff considered it a tremendously positive month, considering the long period of initial frustration. We felt Vincent had found something at Speck he had never experienced. He was staying, and that seemed a miracle. We knew that we could not use the same yardstick for each boy, but with Vincent we were learning how the smallest change in his behavior meant we were starting to succeed.

Most of Vincent's communication with us until now had been written, not verbal. His notes to staff members appeared often, and they were angry—with us, with his family—and they showed his extreme hostility about being at Speck Homes. It was almost as though the notes were a challenge to us to give up on him. One note even asked why we kept him, why we did not send him away, as obviously we were not helping him.

Gradually his notes grew less bitter, and he began to communicate in his group therapy sessions. All our boys are required to attend— just attend—a minimum of ten hours a week of group therapy. Boys start participating when they wish to, but from the first every boy must attend. Vincent attended for a long time before he seemed to be listening and before he talked. As his verbal communication increased—he started talking quite a bit to the other residents in group—the note writing decreased a little.

In one session, three of the boys were discussing what they had been doing—what changes they had been working on in their lives. Vincent suddenly started to cry. His tears were unexpected—we had been working at that moment with one of the other boys. Nothing had been said to him, but he apparently related to that young man's recollection of things that had happened to him as a child.

In private counseling Vincent was still trying to spend a substantial amount of time dealing with the past. We will deal with the past as long as the boy feels it is necessary, but we do not encourage it. In Vincent's case, we had now spent several months going over the past. Indeed, we had gone over every bit of it in great detail. I could not see what could be resolved, spending time in this unconstructive way. I felt we had to move forward, and that continually rehashing

the past gave Vincent an excuse not to. I told him that if we did
not move forward, I would no longer talk to him. He said nothing,
but I felt my response was appropriate for the time and that we
were ready for a new beginning.

I think it's important to note, however, that I did not do this until
I felt Vincent and I were involved enough with each other that he
trusted our friendship. I had spent even more than my usual time
showing him I cared about his future. I would sit beside him at meal-
time, visit him in the classroom, offer to play pool, try to share in
interests and at all times to develop conversations about anything
at all which would interest him.

Vincent took my ultimatum well, but continued to fluctuate in
moods so that we never knew what to expect. One day he would
talk, would seem to want to get involved in our program, and the
next day he withdrew and remained silent again. We were still getting
letters from him, and most of them centered around one point—
care. He seemed not to know what the word meant. He asked us
what the other boys meant when they talked about "caring." We
had learned in working with the boys not to talk about giving and
receiving love. "Love" often has a sexual connotation for this age.
Instead we use the words "warmth" and "caring," words that are
more comfortable and less threatening. But for Vincent even the
word "care" was uncomfortable. He had had so little care in his life,
he had no concept of the meaning of the word. Sadly, he could not
recall even having heard hearing the words "care" and "love" used
by his father or mother when he was a child—his parents were uncar-
ing and unloving, unable or unwilling to give either. So, since Vincent
had never experienced care or love, his letters now expressed an
interest in learning to know more about them.

Gradually he started to reach out to find out more about Speck
Homes, to learn more about himself and his school. At this point
we began to talk more about his artwork, using as a starting point
the Indian piece he had designed for me. We knew he had outstanding
artistic ability. We suggested he might consider painting a mural
on the basement walls. We hoped this would give staff members
the opportunity to become more involved with him, and that it would
also allow him to express himself in a way that would be more meaningful to him. Vincent took on the project, and during the next three
or four weeks he was allowed to paint whenever he wished, after
fulfilling his basic chores and responsibilities. As he worked, he encour-

aged some of the other fellows to come over and sit down. He was eager to show them what he was doing, which is probably unusual for an artist. This was the first time he let anyone other than our staff into his life.

Vincent's depressions began to decrease, and his withdrawal declined in direct proportion to his increasing expression through his art. He had not done a 180-degree turn, but there were more happy moods, or at least more neutral ones, and the negative behavior was diminishing. Vincent was learning for the first time how to share.

The impact of Vincent's changing attitude illustrated to us again how important it was to be friend as well as mentor to the boys. Not until this happens are we able to help the boys in our program change their attitudes and behavior, learn to make the responsible decisions for their own lives that they must to succeed in society. In the beginning it is very difficult for me or my staff to understand from moment to moment all that troubles the youngsters, but we can always be their friends. And as we get to know them we learn more.

Vincent tried again in a group session to discuss his past, his background. We got nowhere, and Vincent told me he didn't think I knew how to help him. I was desperately trying to figure out how to help him take a step into reality when I found this note in my car:

After family group, when I was looking out of my window thinking, I came up with things that are important to me. Using the tree is the only way that I can explain. I want to reach out and break off a limb and see what the grain looks like. There was something in the way—the rules of Speck Homes and the window. I feel myself reaching out to you to find out what your grain is like. I think that something is in my way—the selfishness in me.

Vincent had helped give us better insight into his feelings by expressing himself in writing. It was a tremendous aid at that point in his stay at Speck Homes for him to be articulate at least on paper. For the first time he was saying that he really wanted to know what other people were like.

Shortly after this, Vincent began to establish meaningful relationships with other staff as well as other residents, although it was difficult to determine how effective these new relationships were. His moods and depressions still seemed to change from day to day. During one counseling session Vincent told a staff member he felt depressed and did not know which way to turn. The staff member encouraged him to clarify what he was saying. Vincent said he did not know whether he should "care" about others in the home. He still did not understand the difference between caring and noncaring.

On May 1, 1977, Vincent and I spent almost two hours in a counseling session. We began by talking about the Indian cradle board, and he explained each of the board's intricate designs and what each part meant in the Indian culture. He was giving me something I had never had before—knowledge about something he knew that I didn't. He told me that inside of that papoose on the cradle board he had put the representation of an arrow and a key. He said, "This key is the key in regards to my heart." I realized that we were beginning to make some impact about caring, and that the only way he knew to relate the word love was through that design. When he put the key inside of the papoose, he was giving us a chance to unlock his heart. What he was saying was, "That represents the key to my heart."

We talked about that, and our discussion evolved into a lengthy dialogue about trust, care, and love. Vincent said he would like to trust someone. He said that care to him was simply allowing someone to take care of your personal items. I learned now that, while Vincent was still confused about what "caring" really meant, he wanted to learn the real meaning—he had many times heard the other boys talking about the pathways of giving and receiving care and warmth.

As part of our reality therapy program, the boys are taught the steps of reality therapy. They discuss failure identity and success identity. Each boy has a chart, which he often carries with him, and in thinking about how to learn to be responsible, he places himself on the chart—where he is now, where he would like to be, how he can move himself along into better pathways. The boys talk about all the steps to becoming a fulfilled person, which includes giving and receiving love, which, as I've said, we refer to as "warmth" and "care." The problem with Vincent was how to figure out a way to teach him to give and receive warmth and care when he did not understand what they were.

Vincent had showed that he had feelings about animals. We got a dog for Speck Homes and asked Vincent to look after him. We talked with him about the dog's needs and feelings—for example, hunger, pain, whether or not the dog wanted to play—and what

Vincent could do to meet the dog's needs. He could not meet needs until he learned to recognize what they were. While learning, he was becoming more involved with the dog—Vincent played with him, disciplined him, and even spent time talking with him.

We were now able to draw analogies. Vincent learned to care for the dog. That was not difficult—puppies are irresistible to anyone who likes animals. What we were doing now was to help Vincent understand that people have needs and feelings, too. We were able to help him begin to respond to other people in a healthy, positive manner. We stressed how Vincent could, through his interaction with his fellow residents, come to understand others and "know" their feelings.

First, we talked about not doing to the dog what he would not want our counselors to do to him, like ignore the dog or be unkind to him. Then we talked about his not treating the other boys as he would not want to be treated. It was, simply, the Golden Rule— treat the other boys as you would want to be treated.

Vincent was now beginning to see himself as others saw him— the withdrawal, the refusal to talk. He responded by trying to seek more information about himself and other people. For the first time he was initiating questions, trying to learn about people, how other people showed warmth toward each other. He asked me one day exactly when I had first found out what love meant. It was difficult to answer, since I had never thought about that before, about people teaching love. It was something most of us just feel, and here was a boy who had to learn it. Again, a reminder of how far we still had to go.

One of the many ways we practice involvement at Speck Homes does not involve the staff. It is a contract plan for the boys—they agree to spend about twenty to thirty minutes at a time rapping with each other. They meet in sessions that are for them like counseling sessions. The staff does not participate, and often does not know what is being discussed, but the boys learn a lot about each other, talk about what is going on in their lives. An older resident might take the responsibility for counseling a younger one and telling him what positive changes he himself has made. Although this is not mandatory, we encourage the practice.

Initially, when Vincent made his contract to have a counseling session, he never said a word. Now he was reaching out for conversation, and after his experience with the dog he felt he could make a contract with a peer and possibly help that person. His first contract was a simple one—it had to be to succeed. He would become involved with another resident, a boy named Steve, by teaching him Indian beadwork. We talked first about how he made allowances for the dog. It was only a puppy and made mistakes. People made mistakes, too, and Vincent had to try to understand this in working with his peers.

All this time his mood was steadily improving. However, while he was interacting more with other residents, he was still spending too much time by himself. He still told one of the other boys in a rap session that he hated people. "I have found that people I have tried to trust and become friends with ended up screwing me around one way or another." He indicated he did not hate people for what he had done or not done, but for what other people had done, or at least what he "believed" other people had done to him.

He was able to teach Steve the beadwork, and his success led him to volunteer to give a class on Indian beadwork to several boys. This was the first time he had chosen to become involved with a group. He planned the lessons, did it well, and gave of himself in a way he never had before. He had finally learned it was not necessary to write letters. It was all right to speak if he wanted to communicate. At a family group meeting he had spoken about the earlier note he had written us about trying to understand people, using as an example the wood grain of a tree. After this meeting he wrote us again— the last of forty notes we received during his stay. The ending shows us how far he had progressed in accepting responsibility.

I feel that I have been selfish in trying to get the things that I like from you and I see that I was wrong in telling you that I felt that I was doing my part and you wasn't. You have done an awful lot for me. You have made me feel wanted, worth being around and most of all you helped me see myself as a person. Last night during family group therapy what I was talking about was when I was looking out the window, thinking I came up with some things that I think I feel are important to me, using the tree as an example. I wanted to reach out and break a limb off and see what the grain looked like. There was something in the way, the rules of Speck Homes and the window. I want to get to know people as people. I feel myself reaching out to you to find out what is growing inside of you, to see what your grain looks like. Something is in the way; I see it as the selfishness in me. The plan that I have come up with to don't ask for so much from you, be happy with what I get and let time take its place and better understanding of one another. Time will be the judge and we will have better understanding. I see the selfishness hurting me. You might not see it, but I do. I feel that I should do something about it to keep from hurting myself. I don't want anything that I don't earn in the way of a friendship, a relationship with people. I want to be able to say to myself, I really have done my part and look where it has gotten me. This is my last note. I am writing this last time. From now on I have found that I can talk and I don't have to write letters.

He was right—he had learned to talk with all of us. He wanted to discuss a large range of subjects—living at home, animals, dealing with other residents—and his conversation was relaxed. A sense of humor began to show. He smiled during group counseling, and although he still had moods of depression, they no longer occurred daily, but only about once or twice a month, and he knew how to handle them. He would become involved in activities or relate to the other residents, and the moods would pass. Vincent was also doing well in our school, and was rewarded for his continued progress with the privilege of working outside.

Getting a job while continuing to live at Speck Homes is one of the mandatory aspects of our program. In Vincent's case, doing well in our school was part of his rehabilitation, because he had not yet graduated from high school. He also had to continue in all the involvement programs—group counseling, the contracts, and the family therapy sessions, which his mother was attending with him. But leaving the grounds to work was a major step forward in assuming responsibility—gaining worth and recognition away from Speck Homes.

We have an arrangement with a nearby hospital, whereby we agree to provide the hospital with working personnel but the boys get their own jobs. We give classes on applying for jobs, but only provide the opportunity for the jobs, not the jobs themselves. We have also arranged with the hospital that the boys start at the bottom. The boys call it either "the Pit"—washing dishes—or "the P & D"—a combination of laundry and dishes. Some of our boys are obviously capable of starting at a much higher level, but we ask the hospital to start the boys at the bottom to give them the opportunity to show they can move up. We have had some phenomenal success stories at that hospital. One of our young men is an orderly in the intensive care unit, one works in engineering, and one has gone on to work in inventory. But they all started at the bottom.

Vincent worked his way "up" to helping clean the food-processing department, getting very good grades on the job. We decided he was ready to return home to live with his mother. Before we made this decision, however, Vincent had to save up a minimum of $500 from his paycheck.

Before he can leave us, each of our boys has to set an amount that he will save and then save it. An older boy not returning to live with his parents might have to save $1,000 before he leaves our halfway house, as he might well need it. This is a further step along the path to success.

At this stage, if a young man does not have parents to whom he can return, or if he prefers not to return to live with his parents, he goes to our halfway house. But whether he goes home or to the halfway house, he is going to be with people who understand and practice the training in reality therapy our boys get while at Speck Homes, for many of the parents take our reality therapy training course.

Vincent's mother was one of those parents. She had become very involved in our family training program, and from the start she realized we were trying hard to communicate with her son and trying to help her to learn to do the same. As she saw his progress, she became more and more enthusiastic. She was able not only to show she cared for her own son but, later, to reach out and help others benefit from our program. Shortly before Vincent left Speck Homes, she organized a one-day workshop in reality therapy for other parents in the community with problem children. She arranged for a staff person at the home to give the course for a slight fee, and she solicited parents to take it. It was a big success.

She found further benefit from the changes she was able to make in herself. By increasing her communication skills and ability to become involved with the people around her, she made excellent advances at work and was better able to support her family. Vincent went home to a mother who was feeling a great sense of achievement in her own life and was very pleased that her son had learned to become responsible. She was eager to have him home and start anew with him.

In October 1977 Vincent left our school and returned to the one in his own neighborhood. He was unable to continue working at the hospital, as the hours conflicted with school, but he did get a job at a pizza parlor. His employer was impressed with his helpfulness, his industriousness, and his good attitude.

May 1978 was another exciting time for Vincent and for us. He entered the cradle board in a young people's art show in Oklahoma City—and he won first prize.

Vincent is now in the United States Army, training guard dogs in Korea. He is writing letters again, but these are very different:

Mr. Goard:

Hello, how you doing? Well, I finally made it to Korea. It's okay, but it's a dirty place. I'll be here a year or I should say 12 months. I should be coming back to the States around 11 Jan 80. Would you send me some pictures. I'm already lonely for familiar faces.

I'll write when I can. Right now all I'm doing is pulling guard duty cause we're having field practice or something like that. I wanted to come see you over Christmas but, I didn't cause I was so busy. There really isn't an excuse I don't know why I keep trying to make one. I really want to see you and Matt, and Mrs. Goard. I feel guilty now, cause I know I could have made time. I'll make up for it somehow. I hope you write back.

I never realized how much I really miss seeing the people I love until I put so much distance between us that I can't visit until 12 months pass. But, when it does I'll be back. You can bet on that. I've only been here about a week or two. I'm starting to get lonely—Sure, there are a lot of people to talk to and I do talk to them and have fun. But I'm lonely inside. You know that empty feeling. Oh it's just a period of my life when I have to adjust to being on my own. It relieves me though to let someone know. Anyway, I'm enjoying being over here, or should I say I like the different atmosphere. The people over here are friendly.

[Then follows a description of his work and a couple of pages showing how a friend who knows Korean writes in Korean and translates into English. The closing of the letter is:]

Take care and write soon.

Love,
Vincent

Working with Vincent gave us at Speck Homes a new awareness of what involvement is. He taught us that signs of progress are not always easy to see—that we must keep searching. But he also taught us that there is always hope of success, and that we should never accept failure in ourselves or in the young men who come to us.

18

Never Give Up

Assets and Alternatives with the Severely Handicapped

Bart P. Billings

Severely depressed, Florence Johnson took an overdose of sleeping pills and crawled into bed to die. Life seemed to hold no other option for her. Her husband, with whom she had never had a good relationship, was in prison for attempted robbery. He had a long record of drug abuse and incarcerations and would not be released for at least several years. Before his imprisonment he and Florence had been involved almost exclusively with people who lived in a drug culture—they all used drugs or sold them, or both. Her mother and sister had long ago disowned her, and because they considered Florence to be detrimental to her only child, a son, who had been two years old at the time, had undertaken his upbringing. He was still living with them, and Florence did not relate to him in a loving maternal relationship. She felt rejected by the people significant to her and had never experienced success through achievement in employment, school, or other interests such as hobbies.

Waiting to die, Florence lit a cigarette. As she slipped into unconsciousness, the bed caught fire. Neighbors saw the flames and called the fire department, and Florence was saved from death—but now she had new problems. She had been burned on many parts of her body, including her neck and arms, but it was her legs that were the most severely burned. Despite expert medical attention, neither could be saved. Both legs were amputated.

This was the patient I was summoned to see for a psychological evaluation. It was apparent that because of my job as a clinical psychologist in the Physical Medicine and Rehabilitation Center, this patient would eventually be transferred from the burn unit to the physical medicine ward, and I would be one of the people responsible for her rehabilitation.

A review of her chart indicated she had been in our hospital many times. She had a long history of emotional problems and had been diagnosed by psychiatrists as a paranoid schizophrenic who was dependent on drugs and had an unstable personality. She had been seen by our psychiatrists, but no results were recorded in the hospital records. Her history also indicated she had made many trips to our emergency room complaining of dizziness and headaches, many stab wounds (one of which left her right arm numb and painful), lacerations on her face, abnormal vaginal discharges, lower rib and abdominal pain, vomiting and weakness for two days (which may have been the result of drug abuse), hives (which resulted in severe itching), overdose on Librium, intramenstrual bleeding, and pain in her left leg. These problems had all occurred in the last year.

Having reviewed all the available material on the patient, I proceeded to visit her in the burn ward. Upon entering, I put on the hospital gown that is mandatory for infection control. Florence's room was halfway down the ward, and in passing I could look into other rooms where patients were being treated for burns in oversized tubs. Florence's room was occupied by four patients. She was in the far corner, next to another patient who had suffered very severe burns. In fact, all of the patients were in great pain, and due to their medication not really attentive to what was going on around them. A cloud of depression seemed to hang over the room, and I felt very unwelcome. All four acted as though they didn't want to see anyone, Florence even more than the others. She turned away from me in a way that indicated she would rather be left alone.

My first look at Florence revealed her to be an attractive black woman in her late twenties. It was difficult to get her attention. Besides being drowsy with medication, she was severely depressed, disinterested, and not able to make contact, eye or otherwise. She tried to withdraw from the interview by pulling the sheets up as far as she could without actually covering the burns on her neck and arms. As she did this, she seemed to blend into her surroundings—the white walls, uniforms, and floor—and gave the impression of crawling into nothingness.

The purpose of this visit was to make Florence aware of what services I would be providing her, what to expect in the future. My services were only one part of a total rehabilitation program. Eventually she would have physical therapy to help strengthen her muscles and teach her how to use prosthetic devices, occupational therapy to help her develop the skills necessary for daily living. She would be learning to use her new prosthetic limbs in a way that would enable her to engage in everyday activities. She would be working with physiatrists—physical medicine and rehabilitation specialty physicians—who would be monitoring her progress physically and coordinating the efforts of the total rehabilitation team. Our psychological services would help her deal with many of the problems that had interfered with her emotional stability and help her deal in the present with the emotional and physical problems she would be experiencing in learning to adjust to her new physical limitations. Our vocational services would take a look at Florence's interests and abilities and develop a suitable vocational plan with her. Social workers would investigate such possibilities as welfare and social security, and make arrangements for the assistive devices she would need, such as a wheelchair and prosthetic limbs. And she would progress to our prosthetic-orthotic section, where she would adjust from temporary prosthetic devices to permanent prosthetic devices—artificial legs.

After explaining as much as I thought she would be able to hear in fifteen minutes, I decided she had had enough for our first encounter. The only response I received from her might have been expected—an expression of total despair. She told me eventually that at the beginning she had felt worthless, not even capable of committing suicide without messing it up, and her life was now worse than before.

During the following weeks, I visited Forence several times, and I was able to gain her interest long enough to give her some tests, to determine her intellectual capabilities, vocational interests, and personality development. The tests were useful, as they gave us the information that Florence, although unaware of it, had the capabilities and abilities to engage in various types of vocational training. Even though putting the information to use was a long way down the road, this was one of the things that enabled me eventually to help Florence look at herself in terms of assets—indeed, it was the beginning of the attempt to help Florence develop an asset value system and move away from the comparative value system that was contributing to her present emotional state.

From the start, I tried to make Florence realize that comparing her capabilities to those of others would not necessarily help her. She needed to know what she could do with what she had rather than think about what she could not do with what she had lost. Throughout most of Florence's life, her value system had caused her to disparage everything she tried to accomplish and never allowed her to see what her capabilities were. She was always surprised when made aware that she could do many constructive things and that she had many alternatives to turn toward in her life.

The initial psychological evaluation was completed and the process of continued psychotherapy started. The psychological evaluation contained information that could be used by other professionals working with Florence, as the summary shows.

The patient appears to be quite rigid, touchy, difficult, and oversensitive. She will be a difficult patient to rehabilitate psychologically, since she has lacked any kind of successful pattern throughout most of her life, resulting in low-level self-worth feelings. Complicating matters, this patient relates poorly and tends to escape from reality pressures, and her own unacceptable impulses become need-fulfillment fantasies. The suicide attempt that this patient recently made, placing her in her present physical condition, is an indication of her lack of self-worth and need to escape reality. In rehabilitating her, a program must be set up where the patient can visualize her assets and be totally aware that she can succeed at short-range goals. These goals can be as minor as showing up on time for physical therapy. It should be noted that the patient does have a normal activity level, which is a plus to rehabilitation, and has the capacity to maintain rewarding social relationships, which can be tied in with her rehabilitation program while in the hospital.

When Florence was moved to the physical medicine and rehabilitation ward (PM & R), she started her involvement with physical therapy, occupational therapy, psychology, social work, and vocational counseling. Team meetings were held, including all of the therapists working with Florence, and plans were developed. In one, Florence was to be rewarded for positive attitude, appearance, and general behavior, the rewards taking the form of compliments to her.

During the initial part of Florence's rehabilitation program, I saw her from two to four times a week, but not necessarily in my private office, doing psychotherapy. Many times I would visit her in the gymnasium, while she was working in physical therapy, or while she was working in other parts of our program. She went twice each day for both physical and occupational therapy. She was seen by the ortho-dist in the prosthetic and orthetic shop as often as necessary, from once to several times a week as she was adjusting to her temporary pylons—the interim prosthetic devices prior to final prosthetic limbs. The physiatrist would see her on rounds every morning and check on her overall health and on her stumps, to determine if they were developing decubiti ulcers (pressure sores), also noting her progress in all other therapies. I also saw her on rounds in the morning approximately two to three times a week with the other members of the rehabilitation team.

For the first three to four weeks of the rehabilitation program, Florence remained depressed and spoke sparingly. One of the techniques I used during psychotherapy to move her away from her depression was humor. For instance, while she was looking at the floor, I would ask her what she was looking at, and mention that I would bring some bug spray along if she found anything that moved. What worked best to establish eye contact with her was being direct as well as being humorous, and asking her to look up so I could see the color of her eyes but also to get the feeling we were in the same room together. There were times when she continued to look down, and I reversed roles with her and purposely looked at my feet while talking to her. After a while, it became obvious to her that this was not an appropriate way to relate to people, and she learned better ways to communicate nonverbally.

Initially our goals in therapy were directed toward helping her become involved with other people in her daily activities. When she was on time for physical therapy, we rewarded this behavior by mentioning how reliable she was. When she smiled at people and looked at them, we discussed how attractive she looked and how she could see what other people were feeling by looking at their faces and observing expressions. Florence was asked to bring back to our therapy sessions information on who was working with her, how well she liked them, what it was that they were doing that she liked, and how she could be more helpful to them in doing their jobs. By talking about these people, who were new in her life, she was learning to communicate more effectively with them, but there were still some people she had a difficult time dealing with. There were people who also lacked communication skills—and empathy.

Although her depression stayed with her much of the time she was in the hospital, she went from being completely depressed and uncommunicative, to showing interest in her surroundings by starting to ask questions. Later she began to initiate questions with the people trying to help her, many of them inquiries about the various things they were doing. Florence was trying to determine how everything was fitting together to help her in her rehabilitation. During the first few months this was the only noticeable gain in her relationships with the people helping her. But this was a big improvement—from not talking at all and looking at the floor to listening to people when they spoke to her and sometimes responding to them.

It was easiest for her to learn to relate to her physical therapist, since they were working together twice a day and there was physical contact between them. As is the case in many rehabilitation facilities, one of the first positive relationships that develops with the patient and anyone else takes place in physical therapy because of nonverbal communications like touching. Although very selective about whom she would talk to, she did develop friendships with one or two of the nurses on the PM & R service. The nurses she was involved with were people who were outgoing and caring and expressed a great deal of interest in her. She still spoke only to those she saw on a regular basis. Other nurses whom she saw in passing, or those whose personalities did not lend to their initiating conversations, she more or less ignored.

During several of the staff meetings with the nursing, physical therapy, occupational therapy, and orthotics staff, reports indicated that Florence was expressive only if she was reinforced on her progress and engaged in conversation only when it was initiated by the therapist. Since this is what worked, this became the focus of our therapy plan—whoever was doing therapy would emphasize to her how well she was doing. Some of the nurses and therapists commented that they felt she really had very little chance of moving into a meaningful life once she was discharged from the hospital. I had to have enough faith in Florence at this point to reinforce those staff members who feared her problems were insurmountable.

Faced both with her depression and now with some nonverbal staff discouragement, it became difficult not to give up hope. In addition, we felt genuine concern about her trying suicide again. In dealing with this, we continued to talk about how to make her more aware of the alternatives in her life—there were still many things she could do, activities in which she could still be involved, jobs for which she was employable. We were trying to make her aware of the potential she had that could be developed. By helping her see that there was more to life than she had experienced previously, we hoped that she would develop enough interest and motivation to give her the incentive to go on living.

During the last month of her hospitalization, Florence was placed in group therapy once a week. Here she was able to relate to others with problems similar to hers. But more importantly, she discovered to her surprise that the group included people who had "worse problems" than she. She became acquainted with people whose injuries had left them paraplegic or quadriplegic, and this helped her to understand what we were explaining to her about her assets. She was helped further in the group as staff from other agencies and departments came to explain their services and tell the patients how these could be utilized when they were discharged.

For the first time since she had been hospitalized, Florence showed an interest in getting more information about the job possibilities open to her when she left us. She had never really worked and had never known how to regiment herself in a continuing activity such as work. It was hard for her to visualize herself working at all, and even harder for her to imagine that she could work in a position where she had to present herself in an organized and mature manner.

In going over her earlier test results, we were able to narrow down her interests. The vocational areas that stood out significantly were clerical and receptionist. She had had very little exposure to these areas, but was at least aware of what receptionists did, since her initial contact had been with a receptionist in many of the agencies she had gone to. But at this time it was extremely difficult for her to accept the idea that she could overcome her handicaps sufficiently to work in an office where she had to be comfortable communicating with many different kinds of people. Yet, because she had shown interest, I talked with the rehabilitation counselor from the State Department of Rehabilitation, and we both sat down with Florence. The three of us reviewed her test results and then explored her potential for the vocation. She agreed that although this represented a life style completely contrary to the one she had been living, it was a life style to which she aspired, and that if she could eventually get this kind of job, she would be getting exposure to and contact with the kind of people she had liked and admired most of her life. It was an exciting new goal for her and, we felt, a realistic one. The rehabilitation counselor would help her enroll in courses to learn the skills she would need when she left the hospital.

All therapies had been progressing and were now to the point where we could see she would be leaving the hospital soon. We were still very concerned about her depression, even though her attitude was improving steadily through her involvements with all of us. However, it was the renewal of an involvement from another time in her life that proved to be a tremendous aid in planning with Florence what she would do when she left. It was an extremely fortunate coincidence that her sister had a job in our University Medical Center, in Food Services. When Florence was initially hospitalized, her sister had visited her on the ward. When they were younger, Florence had cared a great deal for her sister, who remembered times when Florence had spent what little money she had for shoes or clothing for her.

Even though she had disapproved of Florence's recent life style, her sister did not want Florence to die. The relationship they had had earlier in their lives was still alive, and after her sister started dropping in during the early stages of Florence's hospitalization, it was strengthened. As the sisters became friendly again, Florence's mother, too, became involved in wanting to help Florence, and this was a tremendous aid for us. Both mother and sister felt that if Florence could not be rehabilitated successfully, she might attempt suicide again, so the more they saw that Florence seemed genuinely to want to change her goals, the more interested they became in helping her, and they offered to take her into their home when she left the hospital. Her sister, who was especially supportive while Florence was in the hospital and remained a source of strength when Florence left to go home, was included in several of the therapy sessions in hopes of developing this relationship.

In therapy we were making specific plans for Florence to leave the hospital. Commitments were made, not only by Florence but by her sister and the rehabilitation counselor, on what each would do to help Florence adjust to life on her own. Her sister would help her with a serious problem—going out in public. Florence found it very difficult to be seen with artificial legs. Her sister attempted to ease her into this by offering to accompany her on shopping expeditions and trips to the movies. Initially these attempts failed—Florence would not leave her mother's home. Eventually, however, she learned to overcome her embarrassment and also to wear long skirts, which made her more comfortable. The rehabilitation counselor dropped by her home to visit and take her out as well. Together they viewed sheltered workshops and schools, and later they submitted applications for employment and training programs.

Our hospital had initiated another program that was very helpful to Florence both while she was there and when she returned home. I had arranged with three community colleges nearby to give college credit to students with disabilities for a training program we give on helping disabled persons. As part of the course, the students who come to us work with patients who have disabilities similar to theirs. They learn a great deal about our program, and our patients have an opportunity for a relationship similar to a big brother or sister with a peer who shares their disability. When we call the college requesting a peer counselor, we describe the patient, and they send us a student who matches our patient as much as possible.

Shortly after Florence's arrival, we phoned the colleges for a peer counselor for her—to involve her with still another person, and one who had overcome some of the difficulties she would be facing. The young woman who came was white, five years younger than Florence, and had lost one leg at the hip while quite young. We explained Florence's problems to her and introduced them. Florence was still very depressed, but after looking over her peer, she asked her first question. "How did you get here?"

The peer answered, "By car."

Florence continued, "Who drove you?"

When the peer counselor answered, "No one, I drive myself," Florence was visibly impressed. This was something she obviously had never even considered doing—and shortly it became an important goal for her.

Unfortunately, this first encounter did not have such a positive effect on the peer counselor. When she left the hospital, she went back to her car, where she found herself sobbing uncontrollably—and she cried for about forty-five minutes. During this time she realized that she was overcome with sympathy and grief for Florence, and that meeting Florence had brought back many of the feelings she herself had had when she lost her leg. She went home and phoned me, and we set up some appointments for the two of us to talk about these feelings. She really did want to help Florence, and she continued to see her both at the hospital and when Florence went home.

When Florence and I talked in therapy about alternative ways for her to meet people—responsible people—she mentioned that one way she could become involved with such people would be to attend church. She had been active in her church when she was younger, and had enjoyed it. Her peer counselor's father was a minister in a local church, so the peer counselor was able to be sincere when she encouraged Florence to attend a church of her choosing.

With encouragement from both of us, Florence started to attend services. She was greeted warmly and was accepted from the start. In fact, her disability seemed almost an advantage to getting involved, since people immediately put themselves out to help her, a person who had experienced such a traumatic injury. Many people volunteered to help with transportation, and this made her feel very welcome. She attended services several times a week, went to church picnics and other social activities, and attended Bible study groups. These groups met in people's homes, and she volunteered the use of her home, too.

While she still needed a lot of encouragement to continue with both her church activities and other socializing, she now found this quite readily available from different people within the church. She eventually made friends with some of them, and they visited her at home. She began to spend—and still spends—a lot of time in church-related activities.

This was a significant step for Florence—moving from having a few people in her life to having many on whom she could depend—and one that was important to her sense of worth and accomplishment.

All of this involvement was necessary at this point, or Florence might have slipped back into her depressed state—doing nothing but staying home and watching television. Even with all of our encouragement, at times she wanted to give up and do just that. At these times I always explained to her patiently that none of us intended giving up helping her make her life better than it had been in the past.

We were working with many agencies at that time, still trying to rehabilitate Florence so she could find a job and be able to feel truly independent. As often happens when dealing with government agencies and depending on many other people, I was not able to move as rapidly as I would have liked. As an example, her rehabilitation counselor was promoted to a position in another part of the state, and it took a long time before Florence was assigned to another—in all she had four different counselors in her first year. There were times I spent more time working with these agency people than with Florence. Nevertheless we accomplished a lot, if not our most prized goal.

The Department of Rehabilitation helped her with driver's training, helped her get into a clerical training program, assisted her with her transportation, and got her the necessary equipment to continue her training, such as books and supplies. The Welfare Department helped her buy a wheelchair and prosthetic limbs and provided assistance with food and housing costs.

Just as in the hospital Florence had slowly but surely become more and more involved with the staff and other patients, when she left we continued trying to involve her in more activities and with more people. Perhaps at this stage one of the most significant accomplishments was her learning how to drive a car with hand controls. Florence had not driven prior to the injury, had never had a driver's license. One of the goals we set up in therapy was to accomplish this—which would show Florence in a very direct way that she could still do positive things with her life, things she had never even tried before. Through occupational therapy, driving school, and with assistance from Vocational Rehabilitation, Florence got her driving permit and later her license. Here was visible proof that she could succeed in obtaining a goal she had had a hand in developing, and with this her confidence grew. We had been telling her she could succeed in obtaining her goals, and now she had done it—and the effect on her was excellent.

She was able to go out and complete applications for employment and training and get more actively involved in a vocational training program to become a clerk-typist and receptionist. She has continued up until now working toward these goals, and is finishing the training program, learning to type, answer phones, improve her grammatical skills and other communication skills, and establish a regimentation. Florence is optimistic about obtaining employment in the future and being able to move off welfare and provide a living for herself and her son.

Florence continues to see me, and her depression is still with her at times, as might be expected, but we continue to work on areas of her life where she can make improvement and feel better about herself. At one session she told me that since she was living in the same home as her son, she would like to work on becoming an effective mother. It has become important to her to help her son lead a more positive life than hers had been, and she would do anything possible to see that her son does not turn out like her husband. She had difficulty controlling her son—he did not follow her instructions when, for example, she told him when he should return from school, he spoke to her disrespectfully, and he spent time with friends whom she felt were inappropriate—so she brought him along for family therapy.

We talked about the importance of school and education—how one had to prepare for the outside world. Florence used herself as an example of how difficult life could be without an education or a goal, and without adhering to society's standards. Florence was able to talk about herself effectively because she had had to solve so many problems and had been able to overcome some of them through working on her education. She also talked about her recent involvement with people who were responsible and how that had helped her. She was an effective role model, and her son began to realize how hard she had worked to get to where she was now. As he developed more insight into understanding his mother, he was more able to see what areas he had to work on if he wanted to be in a better situation than his parents when he became their age.

By bringing her son to therapy, Florence was also able to benefit. She realized she was attaining another goal very important to her— she was becoming an effective and caring mother. In the past it had been easier to neglect him, to let him do as he pleased. Now, by following through on recommendations made in therapy, she was able to enhance her self-image as a better mother, and when her son started to change his behavior, treat her with more respect, and follow some of her rules, her good feelings were reinforced still further. She continues to be very attentive to his needs and is doing a good job as a mother. She is eager to help him get a proper education and the discipline necessary for his future development as a responsible member of society.

When this was written, Florence's husband was still in jail but she was talking to him on the phone periodically, giving him information about her physical progress as well as her progress as a human being. One day she told me she had told him, "You can come back and live with me as my husband if you get involved in a training program that will help you become employed or go back to school to better yourself. If you don't do this when you are released, I will not allow you into my home."

Florence is now waiting for employment, but she is not discouraged.

Her story does not end here—it is just beginning. We know the future will not be easy for her. She will be facing many more changes that may be difficult. But the difference is that she is now involved with people. When problems arise she can talk to them, and they will help her work out her difficulties.

When I asked her for permission to tell her story for others to read, I asked her what she thought the most important part of her therapy had been. She answered, "From the beginning, you *cared*, and you never really gave up hope of me becoming a better person."

19

Aunt Martha's

A Group of Boys Becomes Constructive and Caring Through a Community Center Program

Kathleen Kahn Miner and Phyllis Mitlin Warren

What we do, we just do things we like and as we do 'em just start to realize that you can do stuff that's fun without gettin' in trouble and get attention without breaking a window.

These were the words of one of a group of boys who had been referred to Aunt Martha's. Although Aunt Martha's Youth Service Center started in Park Forest, Illinois, in the early 1970s as the community's response to the need for help for runaway youth, by 1979 youth with almost any kind of problem could get help.

Gary Leofanti, the director, regularly gives training programs that teach the principles of reality therapy. Sometimes the young people take these courses, but all the personnel, including over two hundred volunteers, always do. One of these volunteers, Anna, a very patient and nonjudgmental woman who had been very successful with one-on-one counseling, was asked by Phyllis, the coordinator of the out-reach program, to take on a group of ten-year-olds that had been referred to us by the police and one of the local elementary school principals.

It was obvious from the start that this group was very cohesive and that it had enormous strength. Phyllis thought that if she could work with the boys within the group and utilize that strength by channeling it constructively, she could better help the boys.

They had been caught throwing tomatoes at a senior citizens' build-ing. In addition, they loved racing across the roofs of the shopping center and had involved themselves in stealing large-wheel bicycles, and a few had progressed into more serious illegal activity—like setting off explosives on the railroad tracks. Besides all this, the principal had told us, they had driven their classroom teacher to resignation.

Anna and Phyllis made a plan for working with the group that started with a weekly meeting of the group with Anna. Later they would utilize some of the many other resources available through Aunt Martha's.

The first meetings were pandemonium. Anna was discouraged, and no wonder. Their idea of communicating was to run around wildly, pushing and fighting with each other. Anna mistakenly thought that if they went out their behavior might improve. They went to a restaurant for Cokes, and when they finally stopped chasing each other around, they tried a seemingly harmless prank—how many straws could they attach end to end before the chain broke? (Enough to encircle several tables.) Then they "progressed" to a throwing fight using little coffee cream cartons for weapons. These break and splatter beautifully when hitting a solid object such as a wall or floor. It was at this point that Anna removed the boys from the restaurant, to avoid being thrown out.

During her regularly scheduled meeting with Phyllis, Anna said, "I'm not a counselor. I'm a glorified babysitter." Phyllis had to convince Anna that progress was being made. Some of the boys had attended the first meeting only because their parents had insisted. (One of the original boys told us later that his initial reaction had been, "I'm not going to no stupid ladies to talk about trouble.") But the boys were continuing to attend, and now it was voluntary. Ten- and eleven-year-old boys would not keep coming unless they were getting something out of the meetings that fulfilled their needs. Phyllis felt that by being there every week and volunteering to spend time with them, Anna was demonstrating her sincere friendship and the fact that she cared for the boys, and that they were responding by coming back every week. Phyllis convinced Anna there would be no quick results—they had to be prepared for a lengthy process.

Fearing she would be forever banned from all the local restaurants, Anna decided to meet with the boys in her home. She had four children and considered her house damageproof. The boys put a hole through one of her doors.

But during the third month the boys' behavior gradually began to improve. Some of the aimless running around and shoving subsided, and the energy was channeled into safer, more organized activity. There was more verbal communication with Anna, and she became part of the group. It was far from perfect, and there was a great deal of regressing, but the boys had evidently decided that Anna wouldn't give up on them no matter what they did. She was demonstrating her friendship and caring through her accepting, nonjudgmental attitude and by her dependability in "always being there." They liked her and enjoyed the meetings, as evidenced by the fact that they continued to come without coercion.

The meetings were very simple. In nice weather they went to the parks and played baseball or tennis, or else they played basketball in Anna's driveway, which had a hoop over the garage. In bad weather they listened to records, talked, or played games like Monopoly. They began to plan their activities ahead of time. Each week the boys decided what to do at their next meeting—the first step toward accepting responsibility for their own actions. The discussion necessary to plan the new outings led to cooperation and cut down on the fighting. The boys even learned how to quiet a member who attempted to dominate a conversation.

When their behavior had improved somewhat, Anna decided to risk the local restaurants again, and they started to go out for pizza once a month. Each person paid for his or her own pizza, and the outings went well. Later they even decided to abandon their blue jeans in favor of suits when they ate out.

With the advent of summer, they added trips to the Lake Michigan Dunes and local lakes. They also drove into Chicago and went to several baseball games.

At this time several of the boys were receiving more attention in the two hours a week with the group than they were receiving in the rest of the week at home. This is not to imply that the parents were deliberately neglecting their children, but rather that, overwhelmed with burdens and responsibilities, some of them did not know how to make more time for their children.

After the first year, the meetings were switched from Anna's house to the village recreation center, and a short time after that they moved to Aunt Martha's, where they continue to meet.

During the first two years, the major responsibility for keeping the group going was Anna's, with Phyllis, the coordinator, in the background supervising. Phyllis's role was to meet with Anna every other week and discuss what was happening in the group. She would then make suggestions for group activities or for helping individual boys with various problems. She was also available for Anna to call at any time for help with specific problems, consultation, or moral support.

Anna was helped from time to time by various teen volunteers who had also gone through Aunt Martha's training. There were several volunteers (one girl and two boys) who met with the group for a few months each. The group was friendly but distant to these helpers. It seemed necessary for this group to be involved over a long period of time in order to establish a relationship.

By the end of the second year, Anna was wearing out and wanted to be relieved of her responsibility. A new volunteer, Priscilla, had just completed training a month before and had done well in several individual cases. She was a solid, stable person with a good sense of humor who liked sports and outdoor activities and seemed ideal to replace Anna.

Phyllis asked Anna to stay on with Priscilla for a few months so there would not be an abrupt change. After one month, Anna found the job so much easier with a co-leader that she decided not to leave. This is exactly what Phyllis had hoped would happen—she did not want to lose Anna as a volunteer. Anna and Priscilla have now been working well together for almost a year.

The boys' initial reaction to Priscilla was mixed. They were polite but wary, and they tried a few pranks to shake her up. One boy hung out the window of her car while she was driving. Her automatic reaction was to holler at him to get back in, which he did, but not immediately.

Priscilla saw this as a portent of things to come, and since she didn't want to be cast in a policing role, she discussed the situation with Phyllis. Phyllis suggested that it be thrown back into the boys' laps. They were now too mature and had come too far in emotional growth to act like this, and Priscilla should insist that they deal with the issue as a group problem.

Priscilla decided to have a discussion with the group before the next outing. She started by telling them, "Guys, I want to talk to you about a problem I have."

BOYS: Okay.

PRISCILLA: I don't think it's fair that we can't all have a good time when we go on a trip.

ADAM: What do you mean?

PRISCILLA: Well, when I pick you up at your parents' homes, I feel responsible for you until I take you home. If you do stuff like hanging out my car window, I worry and start to yell at you. I can't have fun when I'm worrying and I don't like myself when I yell.

CARL: Wow, I never thought about it like that.

DAVID: Yeah, it's not fair if we're having a good time and spoiling yours. What do you want us to do?

PRISCILLA: What do you think you could do?

ADAM: Well, we could promise to behave, but we'd probably forget and do something anyway.

BENJAMIN: We could help each other to remember. Like, if one of us gets goofy, we could say, "Hey man, cool it."

PRISCILLA: Is that how you want to handle it?

BOYS: Yeah, we should try that.

PRISCILLA: Okay, sounds good to me.

She had asked them to be involved in determining how they would behave so everyone could enjoy the outings. This appeared to satisfy their need to be treated as equals and encouraged them to respond in a mature manner. They stopped testing Priscilla, and from then on they accepted her as one of the group.

The boys continued to discuss how they should act, particularly on outings, and began monitoring each other's behavior. Several boys took the lead and subsequently emerged as leaders and positive examples for the others.

During the first year of involvement, Phyllis suggested to Anna that the group would be good candidates for Aunt Martha's Structured Outdoor Activities Program. This program provides an incremental, close-to-home series of outdoor experiences culminating in a five-day survival experience. The preparation normally takes place in a small, supportive group meeting once a week over a four-month period, and referrals to the program had always been individual. We felt, however, that these boys, already a cohesive group, should participate as a unit. This was the youngest group ever accepted into the Outdoor Program, and the leader initially believed that certain portions of the program would have to be adjusted for them to succeed.

The objectives of the Outdoor Program are to reduce recidivism, improve communication skills, improve self-concept, increase group socialization skills, and increase the participation of youth in their community. This is accomplished by interaction and communication facilitated by leaders who are skilled at guiding and directing youth into planning and carrying out positive, challenging activities.

The Outdoor Program consists of three phases:

Phase I—Introduction to Outdoor Activities

The boys were interviewed individually by the leader of the program, Bernadette, to determine their interest in outdoor activities and their willingness to commit themselves to all three phases of the program.

Each of the boys agreed enthusiastically to the program and seemed excited at the prospect. Then began weekly group meetings that included a variety of activities. Initiative games were utilized for quick involvement and to assure fun and group success in a noncompetitive atmosphere. In a game like All Aboard, which has simple rules and instructions, each member of the group is challenged to climb a small area, such as a tree stump, with at least one foot on the stump and the other foot not touching the ground for a ten-second time period. This may seem like a simple task, but it does take interaction, trial and error, and cooperation.

Values clarification exercises are also presented, usually in the form of questions posed about issues relevant to the group, such as school rules, communicating with parents, or peer pressure. These questions stimulate discussion without imposing the values of the leaders, and serve as a way for people in the group to examine their own thinking and values in relation to others in the group.

Eventually this group planned activities such as hiking, caving, camping, and backpacking, and they raised a portion of the cost of their wilderness trip by obtaining pledges from friends and relatives for each mile of a twenty-five-mile hike.

But the first meeting proved difficult. The boys were, according to Bernadette, "uncooperative and unruly" and reluctant to participate in any of the activities she suggested. Asked what they would like to do, they suggested Crack the Whip and Bernadette concurred, anxious to utilize the enthusiasm generated by the fact that all the boys were in agreement. The game was conducted on a fairly steep hill and when it was Bernadette's turn to be on the end, they cooperated—to force Bernadette to fall to the bottom. Somewhat shaken up, she later described the game as "wild and woolly," and Crack the Whip was not added to her repertoire of initiative games.

But the boys had participated enthusiastically as a group, and after that first forty-five-minute meeting they were successful in gaining some degree of interaction and involvement. When Bernadette ended the meeting, the boys protested, but her intent was to end the meeting at the height of their enthusiasm and involvement.

It had become evident, both during individual interviews and at the first meeting, that the success of the group was to some degree dependent on the attitude and involvement of one boy, Adam. The other boys looked to him for leadership, but unfortunately, according to Bernadette, he was "one of the most negative kids I've ever met."

At the next meeting, also a planning session, the boys were again uncooperative. Bernadette responded by telling the group, "Okay, you guys, it doesn't look like you can handle this any more this week— I'll see you next week." The boys were surprised that they were being held accountable for their behavior, but her manner was matter-of-fact, not judgmental, and left the door open for a successful meeting next time, which is exactly what happened.

Given the next opportunity to plan an outdoor activity, they decided to go rock climbing. To ensure a safe experience, the leader selected a nonhazardous site at a nearby state park. During this trip, the boys, according to Bernadette, were again "chaotic and totally wild." At this point, small successes seemed overshadowed by continuing rowdiness.

They next planned a hike. Trying to bring the group under control, without assuming responsibility for that control, Bernadette turned leadership of the hike over to Adam, who was already serving as spokesman for the group. She moved to the back of the group and put him in charge of reaching their destination. His leadership abilities surfaced, this time in a positive manner, because the group cooperated as he led them through the woods. The cooperation carried over to subsequent meetings and activities "like magic," Bernadette reported. It was at this point that Adam and the other boys began to view "the" group as "our" group.

At the planning sessions the boys began assuming responsibility for such things as proper clothing, equipment, and food. The leader's role was to lend support, be flexible, have a nonjudgmental attitude, and provide consultation for wilderness activities and outings. Another boy, Carl, joined Adam in assuming active leadership. An overnight campout, a caving expedition, and a twenty-five-mile hike all served as practice and preparation for the five-day wilderness trip.

The parents of the boys, at this stage and throughout the program, ranged from very supportive to uninvolved and disinterested. Bernadette thought that it was important to keep the group separate from whatever difficulties were being experienced at home but encouraged limited involvement from parents, such as providing transportation.

Because of the difficulty experienced in bringing this group to a responsible level, Phase I was extended to six months. But in December 1976 they prepared for their five-day wilderness trip.

Phase II—Wilderness Trip

The group journeyed to southern Illinois during an extremely bitter weather period—temperatures reached −22°F. wind chill during the week, and snow covered the ground. The leader described the week as a "real survival situation." The boys slept in sleeping bags either outdoors or in a barn. For added warmth they spread straw on the ground and zippered all the sleeping bags together. When all their water froze, they melted snow, a tedious process. They did their own cooking, at one point eating raw spaghetti because they were having trouble getting a fire started. They finally did manage a fire, and drank hot cocoa to wash down the raw spaghetti. They orienteered through the wilderness with backpacks and climbed rocks. When some of the boys wanted to quit, they were encouraged and led by the others. Bernadette considered it a great compliment when a withdrawn, troubled boy was asked about the trip and he replied, "It was decent."

Completion of this five-day expedition is always an achievement. For these boys, the youngest ever to participate in this program, knowing that they had survived the bitterest weather southern Illinois had seen for years, it was a turning point. The boys boasted of their achievement with justifiable pride.

Phase III—Follow-Up and Involvement in Other Activities

The principal at the boys' school noticed a "dramatic change," saying they had "moved toward positive, dynamic leadership within the school" and spearheaded a school improvement project—landscaping a portion of the school grounds.

Nearly all of the boys became more active, not only in the school, but in community activities. They joined the various sporting teams in school, and two of them signed up for boys' baseball with the village recreation department. Several joined the school choir and several more joined their church youth groups.

Their enthusiasm was utilized to help a new group of boys, most of them a year younger, who were experiencing difficulties, but the original boys were not eager to include other boys.

A group member later said, "First of all, I guess we were a little bit selfish. See, we had straightened out, and we didn't want any other kids in the group, but Anna told us, 'I wanted to give up on you guys when you first came into the group.' She told us to give them a chance. We didn't want to, but we did. After a while, it worked."

Adam explained, with evident pride and self-confidence, "Now we're helping younger kids who are having trouble—we're counselors."

The three-part cycle of the Outdoor Program was repeated with a mixed group of original members and new, younger boys.

Profiles

Of the eight boys we will track, four were in the original group and continued in the ongoing group. Three were referred by the police and one was a self-referral. Another four boys entered two years later—three referred by the school principal and one who joined as a friend of the other boys. All attended one elementary school, lived in the same neighborhood (a predominantly middle-class suburb), and were from upper-middle- to lower-middle-class white families. The only similarity in the boys' positions in their families was the fact that they all had at least one sibling.

Of the eight boys presently in the group, two live with both natural parents. Four live with their mothers because their parents are divorced, one lives with his mother and stepfather (parents are divorced), and one lives with his father and stepmother.

During interviews with us, the parents of three of the boys expressed great appreciation for the work being done with their sons and were enthusiastic and full of praise for the program. The parents of three other boys expressed mild enthusiasm for the program, but had only good and no negative comments. The parents of two of the boys were disinterested or neutral. Their attitude was "As long as the kid doesn't bother me, I don't care what he does."

Although the boys' behavior had escalated from harassing younger children in school to delinquency in the community, the school principal believed that several of the parents were not aware of the seriousness of their sons' behavior. School officials were convinced that by use of peer pressure and intimidation, the boys were requiring illegal activities on the part of prospective members as a sort of initiation.

We were going to burn up the bridge, and we stole the gas, but we got scared, so we just put the gas on fire and ran away. (A group member)

As previously mentioned, their tenured teacher had quit, leaving the principal to handle the class for one week—"holding the fort," in his words—until a new teacher could be found.

The new teacher happened to have experience working in an alternative school setting as well as several years' experience as an Aunt Martha's volunteer, where she had had reality therapy training. With a consistent and sustained approach, the new teacher was able to bring the class under control, and the principal felt that the similar messages the boys were receiving from school and Aunt Martha's were mutually reinforcing and had a high impact on them.

What are the boys and their parents doing today, and what are the changes, if any, in all of their lives since the boys have joined the group?

Adam

Adam, one of the original members of the group, was referred by the police. In his words, "I was the worst one in the bunch."

He was the acknowledged leader of the group, both in the prior activities of the boys as "ringleader" and after referral to Aunt Martha's, where he now refers to himself as a "counselor." His intelligence enabled him to think up more ways to get in trouble and aggravate school authorities than any of the other boys. The school viewed him as the ringleader of all the destructive behavior. He evidently saved all his good behavior for home, but "all hell broke loose" when he walked out of the front door. His parents are, to this day, unaware of the immense changes in his behavior and personality. They view the group as a social activity with little significance in their son's life and his arrests by the police as boyish pranks. They see no connection between his joining our group and the fact that since joining he has not been rearrested.

He admits that he first attended meetings determined to be uncooperative and only "because my mom said I had to." She was aware that the police did not share her view of her son's activities as "boyish pranks" and was eager to show the police that she was doing everything possible to improve her son's behavior.

At school he was extremely disruptive and did poorly in his work. Although likeable, he challenged his teachers in a way that was disturbing, perhaps because, as the principal explained, that although he made them in a rude and disruptive manner, Adam's complaints were often valid.

Adam has probably made the most dramatic changes of any of the boys. He feels that the wilderness trip was the point at which he stopped being delinquent and says, "Now I do regular things. I don't get in trouble, and the other kids have changed, too." Now an excellent student, excelling, too, in athletics, he is also a natural leader who uses that talent in positive and constructive directions spearheading the landscaping project. The principal is impressed with his self-confident manner, maturity, and continuing leadership role. Adam sees himself as an adviser to new boys joining the group and reacts to them with understanding and maturity. He recently told a new boy, "You can't be helped by this group unless you want to be helped." We plan to ask him to go through Aunt Martha's weekend training to become a volunteer counselor.

Benjamin

Benjamin joined the group for social reasons a few months after it started, at the invitation of friends who were already in the group. As far as we know, he had no specific problems, no contact with the police, and no problems at school.

Nevertheless, Benjamin's parents were extremely appreciative of Aunt Martha's work with their son and noticed positive gains, particularly when after the wilderness trip we all noticed great gains in the areas of self-confidence and leadership ability. Benjamin turned out to be very adept at some of the skills needed in the wilderness out to be very adept at some of the skills needed in the wilderness program, and this led to enhancement of his self-concept. His school work improved because his parents could say to him, "Don't tell me you can't write a book report. Any boy who isn't afraid to repel down a big cliff can certainly write a little book report."

The fact that Benjamin's parents were so pleased with his progress while in the group indicates to us that it is not necessarily harmful, and may in fact be very beneficial, to mix children of varying behavior patterns in one group. If properly supervised, the behavior of children can rise to the highest common denominator. Or in other words, "bad kids" are not always a bad influence on "good kids." The "good kids" can, in fact, become "better kids" through the experience of helping others. Benjamin is another boy we are planning to invite to go through training next year to become an Aunt Martha's counselor.

Carl

Carl, more a follower than a leader, was one of the original boys arrested by the police. His whole family seemed to be in crisis, coping with the departure of the father and subsequent divorce proceedings. He was both difficult to live with and having problems at school.

He is still not crazy about school, but makes average grades and is no longer a behavior problem. He has had no further contact with the police, and his mother is very happy about his improvement at home, including a better relationship with his younger brother. He has developed leadership qualities, which first surfaced on the wilderness trip.

David

David joined at his mother's suggestion. He had friends in the group. He had had no contact with police, and we are not aware of any school problems. His mother was in the midst of a bitter divorce, which was evidently having adverse effects on David's behavior at home. Immersed in their own problems, his parents were not able to help him. His involvement in the group helped him to come through this difficult period in his life, and he now appears well adjusted and is continuing to have a good relationship with his mother. The group counseling session provided him with the opportunity to discuss his family problems with other boys who were having, or had had, similar experiences.

Frank

Frank, one of the new boys, was referred to the group by school officials. He is very intelligent and had previously done well in school, but he had become truant, was not completing his work, and resisted authority.

He lives with his mother, father, and two sisters, and the children had been unsupervised much of the time because the parents both worked long hours. His activities had brought him in contact with the police, and Frank was the only boy referred to the group who had further police contact. He was arrested with a different group of boys for burglary. The other boys in the group let him know that they thought he had behaved very foolishly.

Frank had difficulty making friends, and his parents felt he had joined the burglary group in order to feel accepted. After his arrest, though, he stopped associating with the other group. His parents expressed the view that the main reason Frank had the courage to sever his relationship with these boys was the support and encouragement he got from our group. He had new friends to whom he could turn for companionship.

As Frank became active in the group, he became so immersed that his parents felt excluded from his activities. They considered becoming involved with the group, which Frank did not want. They realize that part of the "magic" of the group was that it belonged strictly to the boys.

Frank told his parents that the boys were very critical of each others' behavior, but that the leaders refrained from giving advice. The parents recognized that their son had some real needs, which they had overlooked and which the group was now fulfilling. When they saw how receptive their son was to the attention he was getting, they gave it some thought and decided to revise their life style so they could fulfill more of their childrens' needs. They cut down on their working hours—many of which were by choice and not necessity—and curtailed some of their many social activities. They started to go out once a week as a family, either to dinner or a movie, and spent more evenings at home as a family. The group has indirectly improved the lives of Frank's siblings.

Frank continues to be involved with Aunt Martha's and attends school regularly, receiving good grades.

Gary

Gary was referred by the school principal, who hoped that the group would improve his relations with peers. He is described by the school as hyperactive, which makes it difficult for him to make friends, but he is also intelligent and capable.

He lives with his father and a housekeeper. His natural mother committed suicide a few years before his referral. His father travels a great deal, and although not home often, seems to have very high expectations for his son.

After initial difficulties in accepting him because of his behavior, the group is making progress in getting appropriate responses from Gary. The boys are very open and direct with him. They will say, "Stop talking, Gary, and give someone else a chance," or, "It makes me mad when you do that." This helps him to know specifically which behavior stands in the way of his making friends at school, and he is beginning to show signs of improvement there.

His father has an indifferent attitude toward Gary's involvement with Aunt Martha's, so it is on Gary's initiative that he attends meetings and outings. His father, for example, termed the wilderness trip a "glorified camping trip" and wondered why Gary wanted to go, as he and Gary occasionally go on camping trips.

Harold

Harold, at nine the youngest member of the group, presents possibly the most difficult challenge to the group. He started attending the group with a friend, and not as the result of any recognized problems in school or in the community. He is physically a rugged little boy, having no difficulty keeping up with the older and larger boys, but he has been extremely uncooperative, negative, and angry. He lives with his older brother and his mother. Although protective, his mother does allow him to participate.

Harold is still somewhat detached from the group, but the other boys have a strong commitment to help him and readily include him in conversations and activities, having surprising fondness for him, considering his negativism. He is moving toward a more open attitude, sharing his thoughts honestly. He is gaining self-confidence as he interacts with boys who, although mostly older, are respectful to him.

An added benefit to Harold's introduction to Aunt Martha's was that on one of her visits Priscilla met Harold's fifteen-year-old brother, Bruce. Bruce told Priscilla about some illegal and undesirable activities in which he was involved and indicated to her that he wanted help. Priscilla spent considerable time talking to him, and after altering his life style he went through Aunt Martha's training weekend and is now working as a peer counselor in the drop-in center. He has joined several activities at school, such as the drama club, and is developing a new circle of friends. This training also enables him to be of more help to his little brother.

Edward

Edward was referred by the school after the principal noticed a change in his attitude and behavior. Formerly a good student, he had become apathetic, often truant, and involved with the police. His parents had recently divorced, and he was living with his mother, sister, and two brothers.

Edward was cool, detached, and attempting to live up to the "tough guy" image of his older brothers. His mother was very supportive of his participation with Aunt Martha's.

Edward experienced great difficulty during the wilderness trip, perhaps because, despite his façade of toughness, he had never been away from home before. He had a very negative attitude during the trip—alternately hostile and frightened. The other boys tried hard to reach out to him, but he rejected them. Edward did make it through the five-day period, but didn't participate in all of the activities. On return from the trip, Edward's involvement with the group lessened, and he finally ended his participation.

On the surface, it seemed that Edward got the least benefit from his involvement with the group, but perhaps he actually got the most. His mother reports that he is very involved in sports and other activities now and has had no further illegal activity or police problems. He earned straight As on his latest report card. She thinks his involvement with Aunt Martha's came at an opportune time, and he has regained his old enthusiasm for school and sport. Although he is not continuing with the group, his hostile attitude and defensiveness have changed, perhaps in part because he discovered some of his own limitations and saw that the other boys did not ridicule him.

The principal of the elementary school the boys attended, many in the same grade, was helpful in our attempts to evaluate the impact of the group's experience at Aunt Martha's. Prior to the referral he described them as "a gang." After we started to work with them, they were expected to be responsible for their actions on two fronts, with us and at school, with an underlying assumption that they were capable and competent and were to be held accountable for irresponsibility. The principal felt this consistency had an intensified impact.

Speaking of the outdoor program, he said, "Aunt Martha's opened up an alternative to these boys that the school couldn't offer, an arena that the boys chose." And the results of the group work with the boys "gave them a feeling of their own individual and collective strengths and presented alternative ways of using that strength."

Another difference observed in the boys at school was increased verbalization. The process of thinking, planning, talking, and working things out is a powerful process. Besides interacting with peers, these boys experienced several adults both at school and at Aunt Martha's who listened respectfully and communicated with them. When the boys were asked how Anna and Priscilla were different from other adults, they all answered, "They listen." The principal made a specific connection between the increased verbalization and diminished acting out in a violent or physical manner. For the most part, communicating to solve problems and channel anger replaced former behavior patterns, such as exploding or hitting and shoving.

It is characteristic of youth experiencing difficulty that their thought process is focused in the present and their behavior is geared to immediate gratification. In the group, the boys experienced the success that comes from planning an activity, looking forward to the event, and implementing it at a later date. This is a strengthening process, and one that can carry over to their individual lives. Even the conversation has begun to be future based. At a recent meeting a lengthy discussion revolved around a summer trip to Europe that one boy will take with his father.

Aunt Martha's Structured Outdoor Activities Program utilized pre- and post-tests of internal/external locus of control to measure changes in self-concept. Low scores indicate a belief that external events have a greater impact on situations and people than the individual does.

High scores show that an individual believes that he or she is in control of the events that affect him or her. Pre-tests were administered to the original referral group prior to their participation in the outdoor program and post-tests ninety days after completion. The scores of the boys in the original referral group showed a significant increase, with an average of 31 percent higher in internal control awareness. This is especially remarkable when compared to the average increase of 12 percent, which is also significant, of all the individuals who participated in the outdoor program during that year.

These statistics are important to us in evaluating our contributions, but for our community there was one simple fact that had great impact. None of the boys engaged any longer in illegal activities. And the boys themselves expressed their sentiment best when asked: "How long do you think you'll stay in the group?"

"As long as it lasts."

20

Coming Out of a Corner

A Long-Term Psychotic Man Moves Out of the Back Ward of a Mental Hospital

William B. Tollefson

Henry was thirty-five years old when I met him, and it was immediately obvious why he had spent his last seventeen years in psychiatric hospitals.

His early childhood seemed normal to his family. Henry was the third child in a family of four children. At birth the umbilical cord had been wrapped around his neck, but no complications were reported because of this. He developed normally, and was toilet trained by the age of two and a half. He started school at the age of six and adjusted well, presenting no problems and interacting very well with his teachers. His relationship with his mother was good, but his father was a heavy drinker who was never close to his family, and it was his mother who held the family together.

He experienced the normal childhood illnesses. At the age of ten he fell, striking his head on a two-by-four, but he received no treatment at that time, and no complications were noted. His records contain no other complaints until two years before his first hospitalization.

Henry appeared normal during his adolescence. He was reported as being a good student in high school, one who enjoyed reading, especially in the areas of human behavior and psychology. He and his mother were both active members in a church, and he was highly respected by the other members.

During the last half of his senior year in high school, he began to lose interest in studying, although he did graduate. Following graduation, he got a job in a painting shop and was able to earn enough money to take a two-month vacation in California. About this time, he began having headaches and drinking alcohol excessively, a pattern that continued for a period of two years. He seemed to feel that drinking helped him to think more clearly. However, as far as is known, he never took unprescribed drugs. Even though he drank, his mother described him as always friendly, but a shy and retiring person who related better to older adults than to his peers.

Two months before his first hospitalization, Henry stopped working. He was still drinking at the time, and had begun to use vile and filthy language. He slept all day, waking up around eleven at night, when he would be very hostile toward his family. He fought and antagonized other family members, and even threatened his mother's life. His behavior became more and more aggressive, and he was finally arrested in order to protect the rest of the family.

At the time of this arrest, no charges were pressed, so Henry was transferred to a research hospital. This was his first hospitalization, and it lasted for one year. He was described by the hospital as friendly and cooperative; he participated in sports, was involved in both individual and group therapies, and held a job in the facility. He was allowed to visit his family several times during the year, and the visits were reported as successful.

At the end of the year of treatment, his family took him on a home visit, with discharge being considered as a possibility. However, at the end of six months his family returned him to the hospital, giving no reason for the action. At this time, he was described as extremely delusional and exhibiting bizarre behavior. During this stay at the research hospital, he ran away twice. He continued to regress, became uncontrollable, and was transferred to a long-term institution, where his condition deteriorated rapidly. At this time, his speech was irrelevant and his behavior highly manneristic. He was very aggressive, impulsive, antagonistic, and constantly involved in fights, and he eventually attacked an employee. Because of this combative incident, he was transferred to still another hospital, for more intensive supervision.

Henry showed some slight improvement in this environment, but it was still necessary to isolate him from the rest of the population, due to his continued aggressive behavior. During his isolation, Henry became verbally abusive and refused to cooperate with staff members. He also became untidy. He urinated on the floor or even into his mouth. He also handled fecal matter, and because of this and his incontinence he constantly infected and reinfected himself with staphylococcic bacteria. Henry remained in this institution for five years, receiving intensive treatment, and then was transferred to another long-term facility because his behavior continued to regress.

At the time of this last admission, although continuing on heavy psychiatric medications, he was observed as hostile, suspicious, regressed, autistic, disoriented, untidy and sloppy in appearance, with severely impaired memory and judgment. He would scream as if in pain, apparently because he was experiencing hallucination. Other patients functioning at a higher level began to inflict minor injuries upon him. As a result, he withdrew into a corner of the ward, coming out only to steal coffee or cigarettes. If his attempts were unsuccessful, he would return to his corner to scream and cry. He ceased verbal interaction at this point, and seemed to withdraw even further into himself. If anyone approached his corner, he became extremely agitated and hostile, bellowing loudly until the individual left and was no longer a threat to him.

Finally, Henry was transferred to a "back ward," which was a special treatment area that dealt with those patients of the facility whose behavior was most difficult or who were combative. All the ward doors were locked, and Henry remained in the large main dayroom except when eating or sleeping. Finding himself in an environment where the other patients were even more combative than he, he retreated to a corner of the large, square dayroom and withdrew and regressed further.

I first came in contact with Henry when I was assigned to work on the back ward where he was living. I first saw him curled up in a fetal position, in a pool of urine, his clothes soiled with fecal material. A staff member approached the corner Henry considered his to clean the area, and Henry pressed more tightly into the corner, bellowing and striking out at the employee with his legs. At this point, he was not even able to verbalize his anger or pain in a confrontation like this. I discovered that he had not talked for many years and only expressed his feelings through bellowing or crying.

During my first six months on the ward, Henry perceived me as a new employee. When I opened the locked front door for other patients, Henry would run to the door, push me aside, and run off the ward. At this point, I avoided any involvement with Henry because of my own fears, but several times as I was working I noticed

Henry watching me. I also noticed that he wasn't responding to his assigned therapist, and I reviewed his case with this therapist.

During the six months I had spent on Henry's ward, I had been introduced to reality therapy through an intensive training seminar. I decided to practice the reality therapy principles with a few of the patients who were under my direct supervision, as well as with Henry, even though he would not be under my direct supervision. I thought if he did not view me as his therapist I would have a better chance of becoming involved with him, since I wanted to be able to approach him as a friend and not as his assigned therapist.

My first approach toward involvement with Henry was simply to say "good morning" and "good afternoon" every day while remaining outside his "territory." As the weeks passed, Henry began to perceive my interest in him. As I approached his corner to speak to him, he would sit up. In time, he allowed me to enter his "territory," but he still would not respond to me. If I overstayed my welcome in his corner, he would bellow or make inappropriate facial expressions.

After nine months of effort, I decided to extend the length of time I spent in his "territory," even though I had to stand in his urine and fecal matter in order to facilitate involvement. Sometimes he would drink his own urine, in various ways, and I had to tolerate this as well. Henry would test my involvement by engaging in other bizarre and very inappropriate behavior. Gradually, I began to ask him simple questions, which dealt with the reality of ward life at the present time, like getting a haircut or shower. After a month of this, he started to respond to my questions by shaking his head from side to side or pushing me away.

One morning he did not exhibit these negative responses, so I picked him up off the floor and walked with him across the room to where the barber was shaving the patients and cutting their hair. Henry presented little resistance. I stayed with him while the barber shaved him and cut his hair, then immediately returned with him to his corner. After this incident, I told him that if he would leave his corner once a week with me, I would extend the length of my visits in the corner and also give him a cigarette. He did not respond at that time, but the following week he did leave his corner with me. Slowly, but more and more frequently, he began leaving the corner with me in order to take a shower, change clothes, or play catch with a softball. Occasionally, he would still drink his urine if the time we spent together became too long. I feel that an important element of this initial involvement was my presenting myself as his *friend*, not his assigned therapist.

At the end of my first year on the ward, the entire population was moved to another building. I felt at this point that our involvement was adequate enough that I might attempt to structure Henry's behavior in a more positive direction.

He was already squatting in the corner he had picked out for himself. I approached him and said, "You know the way you've been acting on the ward."

He looked up and stared at me, with a little grin.

I asked, "Is it helping you?"

He put his head between his legs and said, "No." This was the first verbal response Henry had given me.

I said, "Since we have become such good friends, I feel that we should not be meeting here on the floor any more. I think we should meet and talk in my office."

He nodded in agreement.

I continued, "We will meet in my office, and while you are in my office I will not accept your crazy behavior, because you do not act that way with a friend. If you act crazy, you will have to leave my office."

Henry looked me in the eye and said, "Ah, get away."

At this point I felt that the consistent involvement over the last year had made an impression on him. He might be changing his perceptions and even expressing an emotion, which had not happened in the last ten years.

I discussed this breakthrough with his assigned therapist, who said that he and Henry still had no involvement. He could not enter Henry's "territory," and Henry would not respond to him. At this point, as earlier, I felt that as long as I presented myself to Henry as a friend, the possibilities would exist of his changing his perception of himself and of showing improvement.

Two weeks passed, and during this time Henry did not come to my office. However, I continued to speak to him every morning and reminded him that he was free to come to my office to talk with me. A week later, he came into my office and said he wanted to talk. He crawled into the chair, sitting in a fetal position with his arms folded around his knees, and made a face at me. Since he had made this effort toward improvement, I decided to begin work on planning. I asked, "Do you want to make a plan to get better?"

Henry looked up, nodded, and said, "Yeah."
Our conversation follows:

BILL: Do you like pop and cigarettes?

HENRY: [*With a smile on his face*] Uh, yes!

BILL: If I gave you one pop and some cigarettes in the morning
and then another pop and cigarettes in the afternoon, would you
be willing to shower, put on clean clothes, and stay dry all day?

HENRY: [*Smiling and sitting up straight in the chair*] Yes, yes, I
will for pop.

BILL: Now we will discuss the consequences if you do not keep
your part of the plan.

HENRY: What?

BILL: You will not get any pop if you piss or shit on yourself at
any time of the day. If you dirty yourself, then you will have to
take a shower and put on clean clothes before we will talk about
your plan. Do you understand the plan?

HENRY: Yes. [*Then, after a long pause*] I won't do wrong, Mama.
[*At this point, I felt that even in his regressed mental state he
was able to understand and agree to my proposed plan, but I could
not understand why he called me "Mama."*]

BILL: Also, I will not let you talk crazy when you come into my
office. If you do, I will make you leave. Talking crazy will not help
you get better. This will be part of your plan, also. Okay?

HENRY: [*Smiling*] Okay.

For six months, Henry and I worked with our plan. Every morning
I reminded him what was expected of him. Some days he would
follow the plan well. But on other days he would do things like urinate
on himself and then tell me that another patient had pissed on him.
I told him that I would not accept any excuses. His verbalizations
increased daily. He said such things as "Good morning, Mama" . . .
"I'm clean, can I have my pop now?" . . . "I've been a good boy,
could I have a package of cigarettes?" I encouraged these verbalizations by spending extra time talking with him.

In addition, if he did not respond verbally to me as I approached
and said "good morning" or "good afternoon," then I would continue
to walk by until he spoke. I encouraged him to interact more with
me, but also with other residents who were around us at the time.
He started meeting me at the front door when I came in in the
morning so he could show me how clean he was and that he had

taken a shower. He was spending less time in his corner and was even initiating some interaction with other patients. He seemed to be gaining a certain amount of self-esteem by taking responsibility for our plan and his actions.

During this period of adjusting to the plan, he still referred to me as "Mama." He enjoyed the sessions of talking in my office, moved around the ward more independently, and did not exhibit his old behavior patterns. We would discuss how well or poorly he had been doing as far as his plan was concerned. We also discussed whether or not to make a new plan, but he would never agree to this. All during the time I worked with Henry, we stayed with the original plan. I felt that if this plan could help Henry function independently in the ward setting, then it was successful.

Since Henry had a very short attention span, I structured the sessions so they would be as short as possible. Discussion was focused on his daily schedule and what he was going to do next. In many sessions, he would grow tired and then disrupt the session and test my involvement by "talking crazy." My response was to send him out of the office, because this was one of the consequences we had arranged in the initial planning. He did not become upset when I sent him out of the office, but seemed instead to be happy that I still cared enough to maintain a strong structure in our relationship.

Throughout the course of my involvement with Henry, I found that my being consistent was an important determinant of his response to me. Therefore, if I told him I would meet with him or help him at a certain time, I made sure that I was punctual. When I examined his cleanliness, or lack of it, I was very careful to do it at the same time in the morning and the same time in the afternoon every day. If he had accomplished his part of the plan, then I would go to get his cigarettes and pop immediately. I always stated, "Since you complied with your part of the plan, then I'll do my part and go get your cigarettes and pop." He began to follow me to the front door when I went out to get his pop. When I returned, he would be waiting there by the door for me.

One morning, while I was checking his cleanliness, he asked if he could go with me to the vending machine to get his pop. I asked, "If I take you, will you put the quarter in and push the button yourself?" He agreed with a big smile on his face. He had not been off the ward for a long while because one employee alone could not control him if he misbehaved. (He was a large man, six feet five inches tall.) I gave him a chance, and he acted very appropriately. Getting off the ward, and being responsible for controlling his own behavior when off the ward, seemed to improve his perception of himself.

Since frequent off-ward trips to the vending machine had improved his perception of himself, my next step was to involve him in a therapy session. He seemed to have progressed to the point where he could deal with his present fears and possible future goals in a structured therapy session. I felt that the sessions should last no longer than fifteen minutes, due to his short attention span. I also felt that, in order not to let the fact that the sessions were structured drive him away, we should meet only once a week in my office.

I used the first five to seven minutes of the session to deal with present problems. We discussed his appearance, behavior, neatness, problems with other residents and staff, and his responsibility for his plan. At first Henry's responses were very cautious, but soon he felt more comfortable and was able to respond spontaneously. During the remainder of the session, I let Henry talk about anything he wanted to, as long as he did not engage in "crazy talk." He talked about his family and about a previous therapist. He discussed things that he felt had helped him in the past. I feel these sessions helped Henry perceive our relationship as one based on equality. He even began calling me "Bill" instead of "Mama." I felt that he was finally accepting and trusting me.

In the following months, Henry accompanied me off the ward to the commissary, the library, and the gym. He was appropriate in his behavior and in conversations with other people. The ward employees became acquainted with his plan and noticed the change in his behavior. They began to accept him as a person and to feel that he could be responsible for his own life and actions. I viewed this as a supportive structure that helped him progress more rapidly.

It became very rare for Henry to sit in a corner, and the incidents of inappropriate urinating and defecating decreased by 65 percent. He began expressing needs, wants, and feelings to staff members—letting them know, for example, when he needed clean clothes or an extra shower, or telling them when he wanted cigarettes or pop. And he personally stated his likes and dislikes concerning other residents or staff members. During this period, he seemed to be reorganizing his perceptions of himself, others, and his environment. I felt that he was no longer seeing himself as totally worthless and hopeless but was perceiving himself in a new way, one that aided him in taking the risk to improve. He was even able to deal with other patients who provoked him from time to time, by verbally confronting the individual or walking away from the situation. He seemed more sure of his identity and found it easier to relate to other people, regardless of whether they were fellow residents or staff members.

After another six months of treatment, I was in the process of being transferred to another ward. Henry was unhappy about this and reacted to the upcoming move by becoming more independent of me. Sometimes he even asserted himself by pushing his way out the door past the employees, saying, "I want to go out for some sunshine." Before I left the ward, Henry, the ward staff, and I had a meeting. I asked him if he wanted to continue, change, or terminate his plan. He responded by saying that he wanted to stay with the same plan because, as he said, "It helped me." I explained that I would be leaving the ward and he would need another staff member to assist him in continuing his plan. He pointed out a staff member and then left the meeting.

Later, as I left my office, Henry stopped me and said, "Thank you for helping me." Then he smiled and said, "I'll miss you." And he did continue his plan, interacting with other employees to obtain his pop and cigarettes.

At the time I left the ward, Henry was still functioning well, using his plan and continuing to raise his self-esteem and take more responsibility for his own behavior. Later I learned that he had written a letter to his mother. This is especially significant, since he had not contacted her for oven ten years.

21

"When Are You Going to School?"

A Mentally Retarded Boy Learns to Be Responsible

William L. Cottrell, Jr.

Ralph was admitted to the children's unit of a state psychiatric hospital for observation, diagnosis, and treatment of emotional and behavioral problems. He was twelve years old and the middle child of nine. All eleven family members lived in a very small house located on the farm where his father worked as a laborer. His mother and the older children also worked on the farm.

The family had always been very poor. The exact details of the education of the other children in the family were not available, but according to information collected by the staff, all the children had been irregular in school attendance. The attendance officer, who had had to visit the family several times because of the absence of the children from classes, learned that the children skipped school to work. School officials had very low academic expectations for Ralph and his brothers and sisters.

Ralph had been placed in a special education class for the educable mentally retarded. The previous school report showed that he had repeated two grades in school and that he had a speech defect, although no official diagnosis was available regarding this.

Ralph was admitted to the state psychiatric facility by his parents with the help and assistance of school personnel and child welfare officials. Specific complaints that led to Ralph's admission included the statements that he always "seemed to be in a dream world," gave little or no response to direct questions, had wandered off from home and school on occasions, interacted very little with his peers,

and had been observed engaging in public masturbation. School records indicated that Ralph was almost never on time for any activity,
and often personnel had to go look for him when he was reported
missing. Usually Ralph was found wandering aimlessly around near
where he was supposed to be, oblivious to where he should have
been.

Immediately after admission, Ralph began the habit of standing
with his hands clasped behind his head, turning the upper part of
his body slowly from one side to the other. He would usually stand
in the hall near the nurses' station, with his back to the wall. Although
he would appear to be interested in the activities in the nurses' station,
and possibly the traffic up and down the hall, he never asked questions
or volunteered any conversation. When questioned he seldom answered, and when he did his answers were mostly grunts and words
that flowed together in very poor diction. His vocabulary was very
limited. Consistent with the information collected about Ralph at
the time of his admission, he never showed up for classes, counseling
sessions, or any scheduled activity. Various staff members had begun
to escort him to where he was scheduled to be and from one activity
to another. Although this got Ralph to his activities, and usually on
time, the staff began to see that they were the ones acting responsibly
for Ralph and that by doing so it was possible they were reinforcing
his irresponsibility. Several times when he was in his usual position
near the nurses' station, and seemed to be intently watching some
activity, he would masturbate, unaware or unconcerned that anyone
could see him.

The director of the center, Ralph's counselor, two of his teachers,
two unit aides, and a mental retardation specialist met to discuss
Ralph and organize a therapy plan for him. It was decided that he
would receive one-to-one counseling and that the entire staff would
focus on a plan to help him learn to become responsible.

All of the staff members had had in-service training in reality therapy, and some had taken additional workshops. They were familiar
with the discipline portion of the schools-without-failure plan. We
decided to determine first how the staff should act with him. Because
of his noninvolvement with both peers and staff and his lack of verbal
responses, we knew it would be difficult to involve him in the actual
formal planning of his program at this stage.

Basically, the plan formulated by this group committed each staff
member to the following plan of interaction with Ralph:

1. Each member of the group would try to see Ralph several times during the day and talk in a friendly way with him.
2. Each staff member would attempt, in a very friendly manner, to engage him in reality-oriented conversation by using such statements as:

   "Good morning, Ralph."
   "What are you doing?"
   "Where are you supposed to be?"
   "What are you looking at?"
   "Are you going to school?"
   "When are you going to school?"

3. The conversations with Ralph were to be short in time. They were not to be pursued beyond the point where it appeared he was getting frustrated or upset.
4. No staff member was to engage him in conversations regarding how he felt, why he was doing a particular thing, or why he was not doing something.
5. A minimum of three persons of these seven were to come by his residential living unit at approximately five minutes after the other boys left for school in the morning, and the other three were to begin their visits about five minutes after the boys left for school in the afternoon.
6. Each group of three persons in the morning and afternoon were to space their visits to the unit about ten minutes apart. Ralph was to be engaged in conversation directed toward helping him develop a more responsible attitude, a better reality orientation of time and space, and more appropriate verbal interaction with others.

The visits by the groups of three persons to Ralph's living area each morning and afternoon began to have results almost immediately. The visits went something like this:

Each morning at eight-thirty, all the boys left the living unit to go to the school. Ralph never joined this group or went to the school unless he was escorted. It had been decided in the therapy planning meeting that no one would escort him to school any more. He was not to be escorted elsewhere, either, unless it was an emergency. After the other boys left the living area for school, Ralph usually took his position of standing outside the nurses' station, twisting from one side to the other with his hands clasped behind his head.

At approximately eight-thirty-two, the first of the three morning visitors would come by the nurses' station. When this person approached Ralph, he would say, "Good morning, Ralph. What are you doing?" No response followed the first visit in either the morning or afternoon. However, the staff member was very persistent. The questioning would usually continue: "What are you looking at? What are you doing now, Ralph?"

If it appeared that Ralph wasn't going to answer, the first staff member was simply to say at this point, "Bye, Ralph, I'll see you later."

The second staff member was scheduled to come by Ralph's living area at eight-forty-five. By agreement, he began the same friendly conversation.

"Good morning, Ralph."
"What are you doing?"
"What are you looking at?"
"What are you doing now, Ralph?"
"Where are you supposed to be, Ralph?"
"Are you supposed to be here, Ralph?"

The conversation was to be friendly and patient on the part of all the team members. Between each question, each member of the team was to pause briefly and await for Ralph's responses, which might not occur.

If the second staff member received no response from Ralph, he ended his conversation in the same friendly manner as the first. "Bye, Ralph, I'll see you later."

Two principles should be emphasized in working with children like Ralph. Consistency and repetition are very important, and using them appropriately will have a great influence on the results of any plan, particularly one involving the mentally retarded.

For this reason the third member of Ralph's team would approach him at approximately eight-fifty-five and begin the same friendly, even by now boring, conversation.

"Good morning, Ralph."
"What are you doing?"
"What are you looking at?"
"What are you doing now, Ralph?"
"Where are you supposed to be, Ralph?"
"Are you supposed to be here, Ralph?"
"Are you going to school, Ralph?"
"When are you going to school, Ralph?"

Each team member was to attempt to carry the conversation a little further than the previous one. The conversations were not necessarily word for word, as stated above. The goal was to be consistent, and the staff had decided and rehearsed their parts. However, their conversations were to be natural and personal.

During the third conversation on the first morning, Ralph grunted or mumbled something as answers to two or three questions, then, before the third team member had said good-bye, strolled down the hall away from the nurses' station and the staff member. The staff person did not interfere.

That afternoon the boys left the unit for the school at one o'clock. Ralph took his position by the nurses' station and began his now familiar routine of body movements. At approximately five minutes after one o'clock the first team member of the afternoon came into the living area and began the same routine of attempting conversation with Ralph. Ralph, a little irritated, moved down the hall and away from the confrontation after the first or second statement or question had been directed to him. About ten minutes later the second team member came into the unit, walked down the hall to Ralph's new position, and began the same conversation. Ralph again moved further down the hall, while looking at the staff member in sidewise glances. When the third team member came by a few minutes later, he found Ralph and began the conversation with him. Ralph began to mumble some almost unintelligible responses to the questions, in somewhat the following manner:

"Good afternoon, Ralph. What are you doing, Ralph?"

"Nuthin'," replied Ralph in a barely audible voice.

"Sure, you're doing something, Ralph," replied the staff member. "What are you looking at?"

"In 'ere," said Ralph, as he pointed toward the nurses' station.

"Oh," responded the team member. "Where are the other boys, Ralph?"

"I 'on't know," said Ralph.

"Where do the boys go every day?"

"School," replied Ralph.

"School. That's a good place to go. Are you going to school, Ralph?"

"Uh huh," muttered Ralph.

"When are you going to school, Ralph?"

"Now," said Ralph, and he began to move away from the team member. Ralph continued to move toward the main entrance, through which he finally departed out of sight. He never made it to classes that day, but he did enter the school area, which was adjacent to the living unit, and wandered up and down the halls that afternoon. It was reported that on several occasions Ralph took up his familiar standing/twisting position with his back to the wall and looked across the hall into a classroom. Several times that afternoon, the two teachers who were directly part of the plan for Ralph approached him in the hall of the school and began the same friendly conversation he had been hearing. They reported that they either received curious looks and verbal mumbles from Ralph or he moved away from them when he saw them approaching.

The second day of the implementation of this plan, Ralph again took his stand outside the nurses' station as the other boys left the unit for school. When the first team member arrived a few minutes later he engaged Ralph in the same friendly, boring type of conversation as the previous day. This time Ralph looked at him as he asked questions and sometimes responded with grunts and mumbles.

It amused the staff members to hear that when the second staff person arrived as on the previous day, Ralph mumbled, "I'm going," as he approached.

"Where are you going, Ralph?"

"School," replied Ralph.

"That's good," said the team member.

The third team member was notified of Ralph's action, and he located Ralph in the hall of the school. His approach was almost the same as it had been in the living unit with the emphasis, however, on which classroom Ralph was scheduled to attend. His interaction with Ralph started with, "Good morning, Ralph, I'm glad to see you in school. Where is your classroom?"

"I 'on't know," said Ralph.

"Let me check your schedule, Ralph, and I'll tell you." After he had checked through some papers in his hand, he pointed to a room down the hall and informed Ralph that that was his classroom.

When Ralph did not immediately move in the direction of the classroom, the team member asked, "Are you going to that class, Ralph?"

"Uh huh," replied Ralph, but he still did not move.

The staff member asked in the same friendly voice, "When are you going to that class, Ralph?"

"Now," answered Ralph, and he strolled up the hall toward the classroom.

When he arrived at the classroom, the teacher simply gave him some work and asked him to begin. The teacher did not mention that Ralph was late, nor did he make a big deal out of the fact that Ralph had finally made it to the classroom. The teacher simply began to reinforce the personal, friendly relationship he had been trying to establish with Ralph.

When Ralph would sit at his desk and not attempt to do anything, the teacher would begin a conversation: "Where is your work, Ralph?"

"Here," Ralph would usually reply, pointing to where his materials were.

"Do you need some help?" the teacher would ask.

Usually Ralph would say no at first. The teacher would then ask Ralph to show him what he was supposed to do. If Ralph needed help or correction, the teacher would state his instructions again and usually demonstrate to Ralph how the task should be performed. Sometimes this process would have to be repeated four or five times during a forty-five-minute class period. The objectives of the teacher were to remain friendly and continue to show Ralph how to perform the task, particularly the first several days.

After that first day Ralph made it to his classroom, two things of great interest occurred. The first had to do with the staff. At first some of them had been somewhat reluctant about the plan and had expressed misgivings. However, the taste of success experienced by those involved when Ralph actually made it to that first class stirred up a tremendous excitement. Now everybody believed in the plan. However, the director, who had been a part of the plan, warned all of them that the plan was not complete and requested that all of them remain very consistent and observe Ralph over a period of days for any noticeable changes.

The other change was in Ralph. His past history revealed that he had adjusted to being ignored, and being a victim of corporal punishment, by withdrawing from any responsible involvement with other persons, including his family. He seemed puzzled by the new approach, bewildered by the group of friendly adults who always seemed to be asking him the same boring questions. Later it appeared that Ralph had become conditioned to produce the desired response when one of these people appeared without any of the routine questions, as had happened, for example, when the second staff member had approached him on that second morning and he had said, "I'm going," meaning to school, before the staff member had had a chance to approach him.

Someone on the staff theorized that Ralph had decided it was easier to do what was expected than be "hassled to death" by friendly adults who always seemed to be patient, didn't get mad, and who were very concerned about helping.

The plan was not easy. While maintaining consistency on the part of various staff members was perhaps the most difficult task, another problem was to keep the staff on task after a few initial successes with Ralph. He experienced setbacks, sometimes wandering away from assigned tasks, and the staff members had to go through the very beginning approaches again in order to get him to go where he was supposed to be at a specific time.

After a few weeks, Ralph began to respond with more conversation, and it was learned that his speech patterns seemed to be more the result of socio-economic-cultural deprivation than an organic problem. He was excited by the language master and earphones, which seemed to help him in his speech and vocabulary development. However, nothing appeared to be as important as his growing involvement with staff and peers. He was entered in a group counseling program where friendly interaction and positive reinforcement were used for the most part. Also, suggestions were sometimes made to certain of his peers that resulted in his being included in some games and other activities. His progress was slow, but he did improve.

His problem of masturbation was dealt with in the same manner, using the same type of questioning the staff had used in dealing with his other behavior. After a few weeks at the center, he was enrolled in a health class that included sex education for educable slow learners. There were fewer and fewer incidents of public masturbation, and at the time of his discharge none had been reported in several weeks.

Ralph was far behind the grade level achievement for his chronological age group. When he was first assigned to classes at the Child and Adolescent Center, his teachers reported that most of the time he sat apart from the group in an uninvolved way, would often gaze out the window for long periods of time, and usually failed to respond to any effort on the part of others to engage him in conversation.

His educational plan was rather simple, but it dealt specifically with his assessed needs. The plan included the following:

1. Communication skills
   A. Increase his verbal communication skills with staff and peers.
   B. Enlarge his sight word reading vocabulary.

  C. Improve his interest in stories read to him, in movies, television, pictures in books, and other activities available to him at the center or through field trips sponsored by the center.

  D. Become personally involved with him.

 2. Math skills

  A. Improve his basic functional math skills, such as counting by ones, telling time, counting money, and mastering simple addition and subtraction problems.

  B. Learn use of the abacus, simple math games in small groups for recognition and familiarity of numbers, and to develop some knowledge of basic measurements.

  C. Become personally involved with him.

 3. Physical Education

  A. Engage in individual exercise program.

  B. Participate in small group activities, games, and exercises.

  C. Learn to swim.

  D. Improve his speed of movement and his fine and gross motor coordination through a sequentially planned series of activities and exercises.

  E. Involve him with his peers as much as possible.

The reading and math teachers began to work with Ralph on a one-to-one basis during the part of each class period that he was assigned to them. This arrangement was possible because of the small student-teacher ratio and the number of aides available at the center. These two teachers were also a part of the team responsible for the overall implementation of Ralph's reality therapy plan, which was ultimately successful in getting him out of the residential unit and to school on time.

The reading teacher began to read a story to Ralph each day in class. The stories were usually high-interest, low-vocabulary ones that usually portrayed teenagers as the main characters. After the reading of each story, the teacher would tell Ralph a few interesting things about the story. She read to Ralph and talked to him, but for several days she did not ask Ralph any questions that would have required him to respond verbally. The teacher was enthusiastic and would read the story to him in an excited manner, but she purposely at first began to involve herself with him in a way that was designed to get him interested in the story and convince him that she was interested in him personally by devoting this time to him each day. It soon became obvious that Ralph was listening to the stories by his facial expressions, which included looking at the pages in the book as the teacher read, and sometimes a faint smile crossed his face when a funny incident took place in the story. He would also become very still while the story was being read to him. Each time the teacher finished the story, she would leave the book on Ralph's desk. After a very few days he sometimes turned a few of the pages of the book and showed some interest in the contents.

After several days of reading a story to him on a regular basis, the teacher let Ralph come to class one day and made no indication that she was going to start reading a story to him. She spoke to each of the students as he or she entered the classroom, then began to assist them, moving around the room to check on what each one was doing. She made no attempt to ignore Ralph. Instead, she came by his desk several times in the same manner she did the other students. However, she made no effort to start reading to him.

A book had been left on Ralph's desk, and when the class was about half over, he suddenly picked up the book and brought it to the teacher. She said, "Thank you, Ralph. Do you want me to read you a story?"

Ralph looked at her and at the book, but made no verbal response. The teacher told him that there were two stories in the book she thought he would really like and asked, "I wonder which one you would like the best?" The teacher very briefly and simply told Ralph something about each one. "Would you like me to read one of these stories to you, Ralph?"

With his hands clasped behind his head, Ralph nodded in an affirmative manner.

"Good," said the teacher. "Let's sit down, and you show me which one you want me to read to you."

They moved to the seats where they usually sat when the teacher read to Ralph. She showed him the two stories in the book and again mentioned something about each one of them to him.

"Do you want me to read this one, Ralph, or this one?" she asked as she showed him each of the two stories in the book.

Very hesitantly, Ralph pointed to his choice of the two stories. The teacher responded with "Do you want me to read this one?" as she pointed to the one he had indicated as his choice. She was determined to elicit some verbal response from him, but Ralph simply nodded his head yes.

The teacher then asked Ralph if he would tell her something about the story when she finished reading it to him, and to her complete surprise he mumbled, "I 'on't know." Just as it had begun to appear that he was not going to respond, he had.

In a very pleased manner, the teacher replied, "Oh, just tell me if you like the story when I finish reading it to you. Okay?"

"Okay," answered Ralph.

The teacher then read the story to him. After she had finished, she asked, "Did you like the story, Ralph?"

"Uh huh," grunted Ralph, wiggling and twisting in his seat.

"Did you like the boy in the story?"

"Uh huh," answered Ralph.

In the following days, the teacher began to engage Ralph in conversations in which he could respond with one or two words. She talked about the stories she read to him and about other things that were happening in the room. He began to respond to her much more easily as the days went by and began voluntarily to ask her questions about the stories or other things of interest to him. Eventually, the conversations began to involve Ralph in making choices between two things, stories, or activities.

Each day the teacher began to work on sight words with him. She would pronounce each word carefully as she showed it to him, and Ralph would repeat each word after her. His greatest speech problem was leaving the endings off most words, but he responded well to corrective exercises designed to improve his pronunciation. The staff quickly decided that he did not have a specific speech problem but that his language development had simply not included the training he needed. Based on what the staff could determine from his developmental history, both the home and school had decided too early and too soon that Ralph could not talk correctly. Working on the sight words expanded Ralph's vocabulary and improved his speech patterns as well. His conversations with the reading teacher began to increase in frequency and in duration.

The next step in the reading room was to involve Ralph with one of the other students. The teacher began to include another boy, Gregg, when she read to Ralph. Gregg, who was much more vocal in his opinions, was usually pleasant, and he, too, needed friends. The teacher had talked with Gregg in private and enlisted his promise to try to talk and be a friend to Ralph.

After overcoming some initial jealousy because of the time and attention the teacher was giving Gregg, Ralph appeared to accept him. Gregg would ask Ralph questions, and usually Ralph would respond with much more verbalization than had ever been characteristic of his conversations with adults.

It was not long before Ralph and Gregg would respond openly to the teacher's questions after the reading of a story or other activity in which they had been involved. The two boys engaged in word games together, and as a result of these, both of them experienced improvement in their sight vocabularies. They became good friends. At first Ralph did a lot of following and repeating of what Gregg did or said. However, a few disagreements arose between the boys, and in settling these incidents the staff members were on many occasions able to get Ralph as well as Gregg to respond independently. The disagreements also resulted in the boys making plans to solve their differences. These plans seemed to work on most occasions, because the boys continued to associate together in and out of the classroom. The boys got into petty arguments from time to time, but these arguments did not seem to stop them from being partners in most games and activities at the center.

Although Ralph might not have made phenomenal academic progress while at the center as compared to "normal" children his chronological age, his progress and successes were outstanding in light of his very deprived experiential background and his prior school record. He did learn to read simple signs and directions and to master much of the functional type of reading that is a basic requirement for getting along in our society.

The reading and math teachers were responsible for all of Ralph's academic classes at the center. They kept in close contact with each other regarding their work with Ralph, and each attempted to reinforce what the other was doing. Both teachers made every effort to be consistent in their interactions with him. Ralph made significant progress in beginning math. He learned how to count to fifty by ones. His math teacher reported that Ralph was much better at counting objects or things than he was at solving problems on paper, but, he could add and subtract simple problems on paper with the use of the abacus.

The math teacher took a personal interest in Ralph and was successful in developing a responsible involvement with him. Ralph liked both the math and reading classes and was observed standing by the outside door of the residential unit, waiting for the bell to signal the beginning of classes.

The physical education teacher tried to involve Ralph in group games. For one of the games, the teacher assigned the students to run simple, short-distance relays in groups of three while they were holding hands. He always tried to place Ralph in the center between two other students in these relays. The students sometimes objected to this because they complained that Ralph would not run fast, but these efforts did produce some success for Ralph, since a few students were willing to include him as their partner on most occasions.

Ralph liked to bounce a basketball, and when the teacher observed this he allowed him to continue doing it with a partner. The two students were instructed to bounce the ball a certain number of times, and then each was to throw it to his partner. Other exercises were added to this, such as running while they bounced the ball, and eventually three or four students joined in more complicated activities and games with the ball. When the students chose sides and actually attempted to play a game of basketball, Ralph was always on a team. He was not a star player, but he seemed to derive a lot of satisfaction from just being a part of the team. And although he did not learn to swim, he always enjoyed splashing around in the water.

In group staff meetings, the teachers were reinforced in what they were doing in their classes. Their reports to the counselor and other staff members were considered very valuable input to the total treatment plan for Ralph. Each staff member working with Ralph was reminded often that the basic task was to become responsibly involved with Ralph and to help him become involved with his peers. Both individual and group counseling were directed toward getting staff and peers involved with Ralph and him involved with them.

Ralph soon learned that people cared for him at the center. He didn't fail in school, and it soon became apparent that he enjoyed being a part of the school activities. When he did something successfully at school, his pay-off was the positive reinforcement given to him by the staff. When he didn't do his work, some friendly teacher or other staff member always came around to ask him what he was doing, or what he was going to do, or when he was going to do it. When he made mistakes, a friendly person showed him better ways to do whatever it was that he didn't know how to do.

He also soon learned that it was better to respond and do his best than to put up with all the friendly questions from a friendly staff that seemed never to tire of asking them. Some of his reactions were very amusing to the staff. On occasions Ralph would be observed acting very inappropriately. In these instances, if some staff member started toward him Ralph would seem to anticipate the line of questioning by hastily saying, "I know what I did," or "I know what I'm doing." The staff member would sometimes simply smile in reply and say, "What are you going to do now?" or "What are you supposed to be doing, Ralph?" In most cases, Ralph would get back on task immediately.

Ralph was discharged to his family after several months at the center. Follow-up services included visits to his school and home by a counselor, who began to space his visits further and further apart. Ralph's home was characterized by love, ignorance, inadequate food, and not nearly enough of what most people consider the essentials for living, but Ralph did seem to find his place in his family structure and setting. The counselor from the center was able to be of some assistance to the family in helping them to find better ways of dealing with Ralph.

Specifically, the counselor talked with them about the importance of including Ralph in family conversations. The parents made a commitment to talk with Ralph each morning before he left for school and each afternoon following his return home. The parents were instructed to make a special effort to simply say such things to Ralph as "I love you," "Bye, Ralph," "Be good today at school, Ralph," or "Tell me about school today, Ralph." The parent were also counseled about the importance of not accepting Ralph's silence and noninvolvement as excuses not to be included in the household chores. The family had previously found it easier to ignore Ralph than to include him in these chores, as well as in conversations or other activities. Basically, the counselor simply tried to get them to remember to talk to him and include him in performing the work around the house and in the fields where the other members of the family worked.

The special education teacher to whom Ralph was assigned in his regular school also responded positively to help and suggestions from the center regarding Ralph's education and behavior at school. The last reports concerning Ralph from his school indicated that he was making some progress academically and had made a few friends. Although he and his brothers and sisters continued to miss a lot of school, the reports indicated that his behavior continued to be socially acceptable in the school setting.

All cases at the child and adolescent center were certainly not success stories, but from all evidence available Ralph became more responsible when he saw that responsible actions were expected of him by people who cared about him. He left the center able to converse with almost anyone who engaged him in conversation. When he first came to the center he had been almost totally uninvolved, in large part because he was ignored by other persons at home and at school. In his family setting he had simply not been able to get the basic attention he needed in order to grow and develop. His progress was tremendous after staff members at the residential center began to involve themselves responsibly with him and gave him the appropriate attention and concern that he needed.

22

Big Returns on Little Plans

A Principal Helps a Teacher Solve Her Problems

Gerald L. Schmidt

I had just fallen asleep after a late PTA meeting when I was awakened by the telephone. I sleepily yawned, "Hello," and then I heard Frank Benton say, "Jerry, I'm sorry to bother you so late at night, but Linda's been in an automobile accident. She's not badly injured, but the doctor wants to keep her in the hospital overnight. There aren't any broken bones or anything, but he insists she stay there for observation. I'll call you tomorrow to let you know how she's doing, but you'll need a substitute for a few days—I'm pretty sure she'll be back by Monday." Concerned as I was, I went back to sleep almost immediately, little realizing that this was the first of many unfortunate events that were to befall Linda over the next couple of months.

Linda, who was twenty-six, attractive, bright, and full of enthusiasm, had just come to Ventura School that fall. She had taught for three years in Los Angeles, and I felt truly fortunate that her husband, Frank, had been transferred to the San Francisco peninsula. I got a telephone call from her principal, a personal friend for whom I had great professional respect, inquiring about job possibilities for her in this area. Coincidentally, one of the teachers on my staff had just resigned, and I was looking for a replacement. When Joan, Linda's principal, described her, I felt she was just the person I was looking for. And when I interviewed her, I was immediately taken with her, and I hired her on the spot.

As Linda settled into her job with seven-, eight-, and nine-year-olds, everything Joan had said about her was verified. She was involved, positive, made children feel good about themselves, and made a fine contribution to the staff. The kids loved her, the parents were impressed, and the staff thought she was terrific.

The next afternoon Frank called again. He had just brought Linda home and she was okay, although somewhat depressed. He told me what had happened. He had had to work late the night before, and when an old college friend of Linda's who had a two-hour stopover at the San Francisco Airport had phoned Linda, asking her to join her for dinner, Linda had driven to the airport to see her. On her way back to Palo Alto she had collided with another car as she was changing lanes to get on an off-ramp. The driver of the other car was uninjured, but his passenger was in very serious condition with facial cuts and internal injuries. (I later learned from Linda that although she hadn't been cited by the Highway Patrol for drinking, it had been a long cocktail hour in the International Room, something that was at that time unusual for her.)

She returned to work the following Monday, a bit less "bouncy" but otherwise fine. Over the next few weeks she did her work thoroughly, as she had always done, but she seemed to be doing it mechanically, and she seemed both detached and preoccupied as well.

One afternoon, in a planning meeting with her, I mentioned my concern about her "lack of spark" since the accident. Was there anything I could do to help her? Linda said she was worried about the woman who was badly injured in the accident. She appreciated my offer of help, but she was sure she could work it out herself.

A few days later she took two days of personal necessity leave, which is an absence requiring no explanation to the District. When she phoned school to say she wouldn't be to work, Nancy, my secretary, said she could hardly understand her. A week following that, she was absent for several days with a cold. When she returned, she looked terrible. There were dark circles under her eyes, and she was pale. But, more revealingly, her blond hair, which was usually immaculately styled, was showing dark roots; her clothes, which were always impeccably coordinated, were mismatched; and she was chain-smoking on her breaks and lunch hour, something she had never done before.

Phone calls started coming in from parents:

"Jerry, I hate to talk to you about Linda, she's been so sensitive to Eric's needs, but last week . . ."

"Wendy was so excited about her teacher this year, but for the past week I literally have had to drag her to school."

"Alan came home from school today in tears! Mrs. Benton tore up his writing paper in front of the entire class. I want to talk to you about changing teachers!"

My observations in her classroom, which had always been welcomed by Linda and exhilarating for me, were now really painful to endure. She was sarcastic and short with the children, and the atmosphere, which had been relaxed, warm, and informal, was now tense, impersonal, and rigid.

Linda had worked through problems and plans with children so skillfully before her accident, but afterwards, this changed. One day she sent a boy home at lunchtime for the rest of the day, stating flatly that he had misbehaved all morning and she just wouldn't tolerate that kind of behavior in her class. The day before that she had "benched" her entire class during the morning recess because they had been so noisy. Then, a few days later, I learned that she had canceled a field trip to the Baylands that the children had been looking forward to for several weeks, telling the class that the reason the trip was canceled was because they had been so poorly behaved the past few weeks, and she couldn't trust them.

I scheduled a conference with her to discuss my observations on her change in behavior, the change in her classroom climate, and the parent concerns that were being called to my attention. I tried to be nonjudgmental and still communicate my concern and offer my willingness to help. She responded by accusing me of being nonsupportive and siding with parents who didn't know or understand what she was trying to do. She left the conference very upset and angry.

The following morning the District Personnel Office called school to let me know that Linda had called for a substitute again. She was ill.

About midmorning I decided to telephone her to see how she was feeling.

I said, "Linda, I'm sorry you're ill. I'm concerned about you and would like to help you if you are willing. Is there anything I can do?"

She responded angrily. "You woke me up! *No!* There is nothing you can do! I don't need any help!" And she slammed the receiver down. Her voice had been slurred and she had sounded drugged. If I hadn't known better, I would have thought she was drunk, but I attributed her speech and anger to her being awakened.

Then I thought about Nancy's comment on her call from Linda some time before. "Jerry, I could hardly understand her."

Even though I was very concerned about her, there was really nothing I could do without her cooperation. Talented as Linda was, the stress she was enduring, for whatever reasons, was greatly affecting her job performance and her personal life. I felt we were involved with each other, but I couldn't help her unless she was willing to be helped.

She was not at work the following day either. Late in the afternoon, however, she phoned me.

"Jerry, I need to talk to you. Have Nancy and the teachers gone? I can come over right away."

She sounded both terribly anxious and relieved when I told her, "Yes, I would like to talk with you, Linda. Nancy and the teachers have all left for the day."

She came in about half an hour later. She looked troubled and tired, and she chain-smoked throughout our entire meeting. She opened our conference by saying, "Jerry, I've got to take a leave for the rest of the year—or quit!" Then, bursting into tears, she sobbed, "I've just got to get out! Away!"

I let her talk, and with a great deal of hesitancy she told me about Frank's being involved with a woman in his division at work and having told her he was leaving her, about her having just received papers that meant she was being sued as a result of her accident, and about the financial difficulties that would come about if she and Frank separated—and he had made up his mind that they would.

Finally, with her voice barely audible, she said, "And with all these problems I've been having trouble sleeping at night, so I've been taking a few drinks to forget and put myself to sleep. . . . No! That's not right! The truth is, I've drunk so much every night, at least lately, that I practically pass out when I go to bed.

"I love kids and teaching, but I just don't have the energy to cope with all my problems and do a good job."

In her judgment, there were no solutions. When I pressed her, she said that right now there was nothing in her life that was giving her satisfaction, nor was there anything that she could see to do to exercise some control over her life. She was miserable and desperate. She did say, however, that the one thing she enjoyed was working with children, even though "I'm messing that up, too."

I responded to this statement by saying, "Linda, I can't solve your problems for you, only you can ease the pain by dealing with your stress, but I can help you if you are willing. If, as you say, working with kids is the one thing that you get satisfaction from even though you feel you're 'messing that up, too,' then what can you do to make it better, to make it good?"

She was very thoughtful, then she said firmly, "I hate myself when I'm unreasonable with the kids. If I could only end the day feeling that I had been fair, I'd feel much better."

"Can you think of anything you can do to end tomorrow 'feeling better'?"

"Oh, I just can't think of anything right now! I can't think of anything, period! . . . Yes! Tomorrow morning I could start the day reminding the kids that I was in an accident, have been out of sorts with myself, and have been hard on them because I have been upset with myself. I can tell them I don't like it when I'm short with them because it's my fault, not theirs. I could ask them to help me by telling me when and if they think I'm not being fair with them. We could probably work out a signal or something."

"Do you think you could do it?"

With relief and a first glimmer of a smile, she said, very firmly, "Yes!"

I stated again that I wanted to help her very much. Would she be willing to talk with me tomorrow at the end of the day? We could review how things went and make further plans.

She said she'd really appreciate that, thanked me for my support, and said, "Jerry, I think I'm going to make it!" That was about 6:00 P.M.

About nine that evening Linda called me. She had obviously been drinking, but her speech, though somewhat slurred, was very coherent.

"Jerry, I'm not coming in tomorrow. I can't come in. I got home. Frank's packed his things and left! I want to, but I just can't, I don't think."

"I don't think." That was a plea from her saying, "Help me! I want to make it!"

I said, very firmly, "Linda, you made a commitment today. You can make it. It's still early. Rest. Go to sleep. Come to work tomorrow. You can do it."

In a very faint voice, she said, "I'll try, Jerry, I really will," and hung up the phone.

I worried that night about whether she would remember her plan, our conference, or the phone call.

The next morning she did come in, although she was shaky. Did I have a few minutes to talk? I did. She sat down in my office and said, "I'm sorry about last night. I almost lost my courage. Thanks. Uh . . . could you tell I had been drinking? Oh, Jerry, I need to have a good day, and I feel awful! Can we still meet after school?"

"I want you to make it, Linda, I know you can do it. After talking to you last night I was worried about your not coming in today, but you did it! You can do it. Sure, we'll still meet this afternoon after the kids have gone home."

After school she came into my office, perspiration on her brow. "I did it! It was a good day! I talked to my class this morning about our plan and again, at the end of the day, about how it went. The kids said, 'Good!' "

"It really is a good feeling when you make a commitment to yourself and fulfill it, isn't it, Linda? You're perspiring, tired, but I'm sure you must feel good about today. Do you want to go on as you planned today? For tomorrow? Or do you need to make a new plan?"

"No, I think I can live with my plan for school for the rest of the week. Since the kids are involved with it, I know I can make it but . . ."

"Is there something else?"

"I've got to do something about tonight. Every night! I feel like having a drink to celebrate my having a good day. Isn't that ridiculous? Meeting a commitment and them compounding the problem by having a drink!"

I said, "Linda, you *should* feel good about today. With good reason. You said so yourself. You made a commitment to deal with your class, you came in, you dealt with it. Is there anything you can do to deal with tonight? Not every night for now, just tonight?"

After thinking for a moment or two, she said, "You know, I only drink before dinner. If I have dinner at all! It's my sister's birthday next week, and I need to send her a present. If I went shopping for her present and had dinner out while shopping, I might be able to do it—but I can't shop and eat out every night."

"Are you saying it's not a good plan? That it won't work?"

"No, I think it will work tonight, but I just can't do it every night."

"Linda, we're not talking about every night. Do you think it will work tonight?"

"I think so."

"Remember, you're not making a commitment for every night, Linda, you're talking about tonight. Surely there are other plans for the future than this one. Do you think it's a good plan for tonight?"

"I think so. Yes. Yes, I do."

"Will you do it?"

"Yes!"

"I have a meeting after school tomorrow, but I think we should meet some time, if you are willing. What about lunchtime? Would you be willing to meet then? Remember, your plan is only for tonight."

"Yes. We need to do it. . . . Jerry?"

"Yes?"

"Would you call me about nine tonight?"

"Do you think that would better help you to meet your commitment?"

"Yes."

"I'll call you at nine o'clock sharp!"

I called her at exactly nine. When she said, "Hello," her voice was clear—even cheerful. She was fine. She had bought her sister's birthday present and had dinner and added that although she would still like to meet tomorrow, she had already come up with a plan for tomorrow night as well.

I had a conference before school the next morning, so I didn't see Linda when she came to work. I was surprised at lunchtime when she came into my office. The dark roots were blond again, and she looked as rested and stylish as she had in her first interview with me.

"You look terrific!" I exclaimed. "Like the first time I met you."

"Oh, thanks, Jerry, I needed that. Last night wasn't as easy as I thought it would be. Knowing that you would call, that you could tell by my voice, helped me to not have a drink. But this morning! For the first time in a long time I felt I was in control. I got home from shopping and dinner and wasn't at all sleepy. A little nervous and uptight, though, so I did my hair, pressed my clothes, and took a long, hot bath. I did sleep. I feel good today."

"You said you had a plan for tonight."

"Yes. Actually it was just for tonight, but it led me to think about what I could do about other nights—and make plans for work, too, which I'm kind of excited about."

"Great! It sounds like you're really dealing with it. Tell me about it."

"Well, I called Kathy after I got home. She and I have been wanting to work on designing a good individualized spelling program, so I asked her over for an early dinner and to work on it tonight. She said, 'Yes,' and after talking with her I felt good. Then I felt depressed. There's a plan for tomorrow night, I thought to myself, but what about Thursday? I said to myself, 'Linda, do you have the energy to come up with something creative every night?' It seems like I'm playing a a game with myself. But then I thought, Frank's gone, although he hasn't been home all that much in the evening for months anyway. My life style is changing. Making a plan every day for a while is a good investment. It won't be forever. I've just got to repattern my life until I break some habits and then I've got it licked! My plan is this: Every night for the next two weeks I'm going to plan for the next night and I'm also going to include something in my plan that is special the next day for my class. I think if I can do this for two weeks the pattern will be broken. If not, then I'll come up with another plan. You're right, Jerry, there is more than just one plan for dealing with a problem."

"It's a good plan, Linda, but a big one. Two weeks is a long commitment. Are you sure you can do it?"

"I've got to do it. I know I can! It would help, though—that is, if you are willing—to meet with me several times in the next two weeks. Oh, by the way! You're welcome to come into my class to observe any time."

The next two weeks were critical for Linda, and certainly more difficult than she thought they would be. We did not meet the next day, but we did meet on Friday. Planning for the entire weekend was agonizing for her. To ensure success, virtually every minute of the entire weekend was planned out. As much time as possible was spent with a friend, but it was also important to leave some time for herself. Doing laundry. Tennis with Peggy. A hair appointment. Checking out a field trip to the Exploratorium in San Francisco. Inviting a friend for dinner on Saturday night. Promising Kathy that her portion of the individualized spelling program would be ready by

Monday morning. Baking some cookies to share with her class. The list was written down.

Since she had overplanned, she then made priorities. For example, finishing the spelling program was toward the top of her list. She had made that commitment to Kathy. Baking cookies was toward the bottom, since that was to be a surprise for the class and they were not expecting it. The trip to the Exploratorium was toward the top of the list. The class knew about the field trip, and the date had already been set. Besides, that would take a good portion of the day on Sunday. Doing the laundry was toward the bottom. If she overcommitted, that could wait till one evening during the week. She thought it out very well. She did make it.

It took only a few days to realize that the plans did not need to be complicated, grandiose, or special. Cutting a pattern for a skirt, planning an art project, enrolling in a ceramics class, attending a lecture or a free concert at Stanford were all simple plans, but they used Linda's time in a constructive way, and frequently there was a product of tangible evidence that she had succeeded. A seemingly very small plan had a big pay-off for her one day. The plan was simply to give herself a manicure that evening. The compliments she received the following day from a couple of teachers in the staff lounge made her feel very special.

Each night that she met her commitment provided tremendous reinforcement for meeting it the following day. Planning something special for her students each day most certainly helped the climate in her classroom, which in turn helped her to feel like a worthwhile person. There were a few "slipbacks," too, but they were minor ones, and only one concerned alcohol. The first time she did not live up to her plan was after eight consecutive days of having met her commitment successfully. She was traumatized!

We decided to chart the days on paper, to check off each day when a plan was successful. It was a simple contract, just like the one she used with the boys and girls in her class. That visual check provided additional reinforcement for her, enabled her to see that she had done it. Could do it. It helped her to see that she had met many commitments successfully, and there was always the opportunity to make a new plan. There was always today, tonight, tomorrow. What happened yesterday was history. It was no longer important.

Linda and I met on a regularly scheduled basis for several months. With the one exception of her classroom, where she was able to get things back in order rather quickly, none of her problems have gone away. As far as I know, the lawsuit resulting from her automobile accident still has not been settled, and she and Frank reconciled very shortly but are again separated, although not divorced. Things are still difficult financially for her. However, she has learned to cope, to deal with her problems, not to look back, to plan in small increments and stick to them. The feelings of worthwhileness she has been able to engender within herself, as a result of successfully meeting commitments, has enabled her to function as a highly responsible person. The problems are still there, but the pain has gone away.

23

Banking on Your Interest

A Counselor Helps a High School Student to Stop Using Drugs

William J. Abbott

In my second year of being a counselor for Fairfax County, Virginia, the job of drug counselor for one of our high schools became available. Our school district had always placed a great emphasis on drug prevention and counseling, and a major part of the program was for one counselor in each high school to take specialized training in the counseling and psychology of substance abuse. I had just completed my first week of reality therapy training in Los Angeles and was eager to use some of my newly learned techniques. When I volunteered for the drug counseling appointment, I was not surprised when I received it—no one else wanted it.

Shortly after my in-service training, I was approached by another counselor in the school and asked if I would be willing to take one of her counselees. The counselee, Janet, was heavily involved in all kinds of drugs, to the point of selling them in school, had become truant and suicidal, and had a terminally ill father and a mother with problems of her own.

I was more than just a little leery. The referring counselor had her doctorate in counseling and was known as one of the best. If this was an example of the cases I would receive from the seven other counselors, I may have bitten off more than I cared to. Nevertheless, I accepted.

My first impression was confusing. A tall, lithe, attractive sixteen-year-old girl with long chestnut hair, turned-up nose, and pale complexion entered my office. Her dark eyes expressed loneliness and insecurity, yet contained a contrasting sparkle of intelligence. When I invited her to sit down, she slumped into a chair and almost immediately started to talk about her problems. My confusion grew as I learned more and more in depth of the failures in her life, all told using a vocabulary that expressed intelligence and with an openness that showed insight.

She started our conversation with "My name is Janet, and I understand you are a counselor who works with people on drugs." She told me she had experimented with marijuana, LSD, and mescaline and had considered trying heroin, and as she did she used words like "profound," "vicarious," and "inept," which I rarely had heard while counseling tenth-graders. I was perceiving a perplexing mixture of shyness and openness, as though her intelligence was striving to combat her insecurity. I observed her biting her nails and scratching nervously on her arm. She alternately spoke candidly about events in her life and withdrew into simple one- or two-word answers, as if she was suddenly not sure that she wanted to talk on that subject. My goal for our first few meetings was to get to know her and let her know what I thought we could accomplish. I hoped that I would be able to like her.

I quickly became genuinely interested in her, and I told her so. As Carl Rogers has said, "If you have a strong persistent feeling, express it."[1] Rogers' "reflective technique" and Gordon's "active listening"[2] are good ways, in my opinion, of building the friendly relationship of trust, listening, and caring so important to lonely teenagers. I used such phrases as "I care about you," "You are important to me," "I find you an interesting person," and "I feel confident that we can work this out." I cannot stress enough the importance of honesty and sincerity at this point. Just saying "I care" or "I believe in you" is not sufficient. You must really mean it. I was not born with a good poker face, and I doubt that Janet or any other student would be fooled if I did not sincerely mean what I said. Phoniness can break the involvement very rapidly, but honesty, even to the point of saying, "I don't trust you that far, but you will always know where I stand," builds trust in the relationship.

Janet said later that the way I set the tone of the relationship was very important. I stated, "I am going to believe in you and trust

[1] Carl Rogers, *A Discussion on Encounter Group Therapy* (San Diego: University of California, 1973).
[2] Thomas Gordon, *Teacher Effectiveness Training* (New York: Wyden Press, 1974).

you no matter what you do or say. Whatever becomes of our relationship is up to you." Talking to her today reveals that this important first step caused her to start evaluating her situation and think about what help she could obtain from counseling.

She had been playing a number of deceiving "games" with her previous counselor and the guidance director prior to our meeting. She would make up stories and events just to see what kind of reaction she could get from them. She once told our guidance director that she had completely given up all drugs and had not smoked pot for two weeks—and she was high when she told him this. I suspected at first that she was not totally honest with me either, but I decided to take whatever she said at face value. Even if I did not believe a "story," I would respond with "Okay, let's take a look at that, how are you going to handle it?" The emphasis was never on her use of drugs but on faulty decision making and her responsibility for dealing with situations so that her life would be more successful. If she told me a lie, she would then either have to choose to preserve the façade, make a plan to deal with a fictitious situation, or decide to move on to something else she really had to cope with.

One day Janet stomped into my office angrily and announced that she was going to drop a class because that ———— Mrs. Jones was picking on her and putting her down in front of the class and she didn't need all that extra ———— in her life.

I suspected that something else was involved, since I knew Mrs. Jones was quite sensitive to her students' feelings and did not use put-down techniques. But all I said was, "Okay, what are you going to do now, will dropping the class help? What about graduation requirements?"

There was a long pause as she evaluated the outcome of pursuing this theme and then answered, "Maybe if I asked her to help me after school, I would understand more and wouldn't ask such dumb questions." She returned to the class, got help after school, and passed her geometry course. I had showed her no sympathy and had kept the ball of responsibility in her court. Having to make a choice, Janet opted to face the real problem. She realized she had no reason to lie—it would not help her. This helped to show her that the responsibility for the outcome and success of our relationship was hers.

Her behavior continued to be erratic. One day she would seem happy and enthusiastic about school and make an A in every class.

The next day she would be down in the dumps, skip half of her classes, and get high. Sometimes the fluctuation occurred in one day. I learned quickly that the helping process is not a steady upward climb but more like a roller coaster, with ups and downs and curves moving onward with varying speed. My patience often waned during those cycles, but we were making progress toward more serious planning for change.

One incident really tested my acceptance of her. It was a cold fall day, and Janet appeared in my office, quite distraught, with the familiar statement, "I've got to see you." When she removed her coat, I saw that her attire consisted of blue jeans and a tight red see-through body shirt with no undergarments. Now the Fairfax County dress code states that dress is inappropriate if it is distracting. According to my perception, she was clearly in violation. I sensed that she didn't need a lecture on dress at that time, so I bit my tongue and tried to look into her eyes and pay attention to what she was saying. I also considered the possibility that she may have been trying to determine whether my interest in her was professional or otherwise.

Later, when she left, Bob, a fellow counselor with a room near mine, came in and asked, "Did you see that?"

"See what?" I replied with a wink. "I was too busy listening intently."

This "testing behavior," as I called it, seemed to indicate that Janet was clinging to old behaviors out of fear of letting them go. She was saying, "I don't feel very good about myself, so I'll see if I can at least get some attention with my body." It also tested our relationship, to see if it was strong enough for me to stay with her, keep calm on a steady course, and not give up.

I invited Janet to join a group of ninth- through twelfth-graders with varying degrees of academic success. My goal for this group was to help them understand that they had a lot in common; I hoped that students at both ends of the spectrum would grow stronger from the experience. Honor-roll students need to find out that they are not alone facing the ordeals in their lives and can benefit from learning more about people who don't cope as well as they do. Unsuccessful students can benefit from learning that the "winners" in the school don't always have it so easy, that they suffer, too, in dealing with life's challenges. Both can learn new, more successful ways.

Janet was quiet at first, participating only in the warm-up exercises, but as the group progressed into its second and third meetings, she began to reveal more of her problems. She started to make friends with some of the group's honor-roll students, finding she could converse at their level. We met once a week for about thirty to forty minutes, starting with a warm-up exercise and then discussing topics such as friendship, loneliness, and coping mechanisms. The group frequently picked the topics for our next meeting. We talked about how we perceived ourselves and how others perceived us, and we always concluded with a feedback session by writing down on each person's 3 x 5 card what we had learned about that person that day. Usually the last five to ten minutes were spent reading those cards and asking for clarification from other members.

Janet said she wanted to graduate and made sporadic efforts in that direction, but truancy remained a problem. She was showing improvement, but she was still cutting classes and sometimes missing an entire day, especially if she had been up late partying. After one weekend her mother phoned to say she had not come home at all. I could only reassure her mother that there was nothing either of us could do until she came home.

After a couple of days she phoned for permission to return home. She said she had been staying with friends, and we set up a conference immediately to help her reevaluate her behavior and make a new plan. I asked her to examine what she was doing and to make a value judgment. "Are you happy with the way your life is going now? What is happening as a result of your behavior, and will it help you accomplish your goals in life?"

But Janet disappeared again, this time for five days, and she returned looking very tired. When we talked about what she did while she was a runaway, she revealed that she spent most of her time in Washington, D.C., staying with people who bought and sold drugs. She had helped them in exchange for her room and board. These friends, I learned, carried weapons and talked about "contracts" on people who had "narced" (informed the authorities) on them. I was worried for her and said so. "There must be other things you could be doing that would be better for you. You can get arrested or killed living with these people. Do you want that kind of life?"

After her third time as a runaway, she was charged with incorrigibility and placed in a detention center for delinquent youths, a fairly modern barracks-type center with a high barbed-wire fence and security guards. I was feeling defeated and wanted to give up on her, but I knew I could not let her know that.

Salvaging what little was left of my optimism, I went to see her. Very few visitors were allowed, and I had to plead to see her, saying I was her link with school. During my one-hour visit we spent a few minutes getting reacquainted—I brought news from school and messages from her friends. The remainder of our time was spent evaluating. "Do you like it here?" I would ask.

At first she answered with statements like "The people are okay" or "The food is good." She was reluctant to admit that she did not like being where her actions had put her. I kept pressing her to talk more about her life in the "pen," and she admitted that there had been a few fights—some of the girls carried knives—and what she really wanted most was her freedom.

When I asked her what she would do with her freedom, she said she would like to return to school if the school would allow her back. "What kind of a plan can you make to convince the authorities to let you out and to convince the school to readmit you?" She didn't know and wouldn't blame the school for not taking her back but really wanted one more chance. I made the suggestion that perhaps if she did her schoolwork while being detained, it would help.

Our first plan started with my bringing her books and assignments to the center. She was to let me know through her mother when she had completed them and I would then speak on her behalf to the principal. She returned to school after five days of completed work and my hopes rose again. Janet later told me that I was the only school person to make a visit to the center while she was there. This cemented her belief that I really did care and would not give up. When she returned to school, she managed to complete the tenth grade.

During the summer my travels to California for further reality therapy training would break our contact for a month, and I worried about this. I was relieved when Janet made a plan to get a summer job and then got one. This gave her something to look forward to, and it also got her out of the house and away from frequent confrontations with her parents.

Although I knew that money was scarce in the household, I encouraged her mother to allow Janet to spend her money on clothes or whatever she wanted, and told her mother to take a positive interest in the worthwhile things Janet bought. When I learned upon my return that Janet, on her own, had given up a little of her pay each week to help with the bills, I felt this was a positive step toward responsibility.

Janet was now expressing a need for freedom and a full-time job, so at the end of summer we started working on a plan to help her accelerate into the twelfth grade. She seemed to need stronger goals to work toward. This meant obtaining permission to double up on courses and taking a heavy schedule.

Things went smoothly on this schedule for about three months, and then she ran away again. This time the court decided to place her temporarily in a foster home away from our community. Still struggling not to give up, I visited her and gave her my home phone number to call if she needed to talk. I encouraged her to continue her studies while attending a different school.

Janet became depressed and suicidal. She would call at two in the morning, sobbing and threatening to end her life. After the first call I panicked and could not sleep. But she did keep her commitment to call me the next day. Groping, I used a technique I had picked up in one of my seminars but that had sounded very cold to me. When she next threatened to end her life, I bit my lip and ventured, "If you do that, I won't be able to help you any more, and that will make me very sad." It seemed like a risky, dumb thing to say to someone over the phone, and I would usually add, "Why don't we think of something else?"

The results were surprisingly positive. "I guess you're right, Okay, I'll hang in there another week."

It's important to note here that the personal involvement is the key to the entire process. If you have nothing left at a given point, the involvement you have built up may be enough to see you through. Like an emotional savings account, the involvement (friendship, strength) of the process can be saved and spent later when the need arises. Janet and I had enough in our "account" to see her through the difficult times. She told me, "The steadiness of our friendship meant the most to me."

After two weeks in the foster home, Janet returned to her home and school. Although we had never completely lost touch, I felt it was necessary to reestablish our relationship before moving on to more serious planning. I deliberately steered her into making plans small enough to make success probable.

One of the first plans we worked out was to reestablish her commitment to graduation. She was now a senior, and I thought she needed to plan to achieve the necessary credits to graduate. Since her past two years had been academically disastrous, and she had passed only on her high ability, a lot of work was necessary to achieve the plan. Nevertheless, due to her intelligence, I thought it wise for her to continue, and she agreed.

After establishing that truancy would only hurt her grades and would make the teachers less willing to help her, I decided not to focus on drugs at all but only on her success in school. I believed that she must take it one step at a time and focus her efforts on one segment of her life. Arriving at class on time and alert were necessary if she were to learn as much as possible. One of the first planning questions I asked was "Can you make it to all of your classes today?" Now I know this seems like a very simple plan for a high school senior, but I had to be fairly certain the plan would succeed, and there were periods in her life when she didn't make it to classes for one complete day.

She wanted to make the plan bigger. "Oh sure," she said, "I can make it through a whole year or at least a semester."

I countered with "Let's just see how today goes, we can always expand the plan later." When one day was successful, and she came back to tell me, I smiled and told her I was glad and asked if she could do the same the next day. I related her behavior to her feelings, asking, "How did it feel to do well in school for a day?" Her smile was my answer.

From this small step we went to two days, one week, two weeks, one month, and during the last nine weeks she was mostly on her own. There were very few slides back. When she did cut a class, I would ask, "Did it do anything for you? Do you still want to graduate?" Remembering never to accept excuses or ask why wasn't it hard for me. I knew that the minute I came across as not expecting her to be responsible, she would be in trouble again. The few times she did slide back needed only a fifteen to twenty minute session, making an evaluation and a new plan and commitment. She would check with me daily at first, then weekly, for feedback. I was genuinely very pleased when she had a successful week and showed it. I even risked giving her a hug. This feedback gave her more strength to keep trying.

At this point she was working on fulfilling her plans mainly to please me. She made the mistake of telling this to one of her friends in the drug culture by saying, "I can't cut class with you because it would disappoint Mr. Abbott." The teasing and suspicious looks she received for this information made her realize that others who didn't have the same relationship couldn't understand that she wasn't a "narc" or brainwashed by the administration (I was now an administrative intern). She felt isolated—not trusted by her former peers or accepted by the most successful students and needed me to lean on.

She was again attending the group, and they helped her to handle this. The others told her they hadn't told their friends about the group for fear of being teased, and they shared with her the lonely periods of their lives. I accepted her loneliness as temporary, and with the group, I encouraged her to find new friends. Our relationship provided essential stability in her life. "You're always the same," she said. "I can count on you not to change, and to be there no matter what mood I'm in." She decided to enter a drug rehabilitation program at a community center, just to check out what others could offer. Unfortunately, her home life was further complicated at this time by her belief that her mother was having an affair with a community drug counselor.

A stable relationship now became even more important for her to have the strength to carry out her day-to-day plans to graduate. In spite of everything else, I kept steadfastly focusing on graduation. We marked the days left on the calendar and talked about what she would do with her diploma. On one particularly bad day I even handed her a "mock diploma" to perk her up and remind her of her goal.

One day I thought I should give her some additional responsibility to further show my trust and lift her spirits. I sensed that she needed a jolt of confidence. Janet had stopped in to let me know how her classwork was going and was waiting for a pass to return to class. She asked for a few minutes extra on the pass to use the restroom and go to her locker, and an idea struck me. I gave her the pass with the date and signature but with no time written on it. "You forgot to put the time on it," she said.

My hopes soared. "I trust you. When you're finished with what you have to do, put down the time and go to class—that way you won't have to return here." Janet tells me today that she wrestled hard with the temptation to take a "free afternoon off" with my blank pass, but actually hurried to get to class so as not to let me down. The point—to get a student to take responsibility, you have to give responsibility, even if it means taking a risk.

As often happens in life, just as Janet started to make real progress in school, she had an unfortunate setback. She became physically ill and could not attend school for almost one month. Although most of the faculty and students thought that was the end of her plans to graduate, and she would not return to school, I made sure she had her assignments and phoned her to ask how she was doing. I encouraged teachers to stay with her and provide alternate assignments that she could do at home. Understandably, the teachers were reluctant to spend the extra time and paperwork providing assignments for work they did not believe would be done. Two teachers, however, Mrs. Jones and Mr. Smith, remained most cooperative. One of them even visited her at home and helped her with homework. With their help, she was able to graduate with her class. Neither of us could have done it without them.

At her graduation, Janet expressed her joy in a way I will always remember. I was seated on stage behind and to the left of the principal. After receiving her diploma, Janet walked over to me and said, "Thank you, Mr. Abbott, for all of your help," and kissed me in front of all those parents. My face was the color of a well-done lobster, but a happy one.

Then Janet decided that if she could handle that tough senior year, she could handle college courses, and she enrolled in George Mason College, working to help pay her tuition. Around that time I left Jefferson and lost track of her for four years. While writing this, I contacted her to discuss the important aspects of our relationship as she saw them and to find out how she was doing. Currently, she is maintaining a 4.0 average while studying biochemistry and has obtained a traineeship in one of the university laboratories. She also works part time in a hospital. Her friendships with university students have grown. She smokes pot only occasionally. That and social drinking are the extent of her drug use. She no longer needs drugs to get through the day.

Janet's intelligence is continuing to earn her more responsibility, and she uses it wisely. Her work in the biochemistry lab so impressed her professor that he gave her access to the lab for special projects. This entailed giving her a set of keys so she could work after normal hours. She told me frankly that the lab contained chemicals that could easily be used to make street drugs such as PCP, but that she was not once tempted to take them. She was even asked by other students to lend the keys to them so they could steal the chemicals, and they promised her a share of the profits. Janet told me proudly that those keys never left her possession and that she would quickly report anyone who ever tried to break into "her lab."

24

What Good Are the Rules If No One Obeys?

A Principal Steps In, a Student Learns Discipline

Bill Borgers

The new school had open classrooms—no walls—and the equipment, furniture, and principal were all new as well. I was the principal. I came in loaded with a hundred new ideas on curriculum revision and methods of teaching—and one month after school started I had discarded all of them and was looking for one good idea on discipline. It was difficult in an open school to hide our many serious problems, which included racial tension. Punishment and strict rules had not worked—it doesn't do much good if a school has strict, tough rules and no one obeys them. I've heard many principals tell me about their absolute rules as though that meant they had a well-run school. Usually, the opposite is true, unless they have some means of working with students to develop the self-discipline necessary for most students to obey these rules. It's like General Custer saying, "I'm tough on Indians—show me one and I'll prove it." Well, the problem was they showed him three thousand, and that was more than he could handle with force.

When force did not work, we decided to try Glasser's Ten-Step Discipline System. These are procedures used in counseling students demonstrating irresponsible behavior. We use questions to bring out the present behavior and try to get a value judgment concerning that behavior. The therapist then works with the student to develop a plan and a commitment to follow the plan for a set period of time. No punishment or force is used and no excuses are accepted for breaking a commitment. The Ten-Step Discipline System allows for certain logical consequences to take place if the student does not adhere to the plan.[1]

In our school, we isolate the student so we can have a one-to-one conference. The last step is the supervised optional study class, or SOS, as the students call it. This is a holding area for students who have not solved their problem in the classroom and have been referred to the administration. The whole process is built around helping the student develop and make better decisions concerning his behavior in school.

This system is not a miracle worker but takes involvement, persistence, and toughness to make it work. Through the use of the Ten-Step System, Jersey Village High School decreased its dropout rate from 18 to 5 percent and behavior problem repeaters by 80 percent. More noticeable was the reduction in the degree of problems we were dealing with. It is easier on one's peace of mind to take time with problems of tardiness rather than with fights.

One of the students who tested us and our system that first year was Howard. He had one amazing characteristic. In spite of overwhelming evidence to the contrary, he was *never* at fault. No matter what the incident, he would claim outside forces had caused it. The school, his teachers, classmates, and parents were to blame, never Howard.

He first came to the attention of the deans when he was disrespectful to two teachers who would not let him go to his car during school hours. Asked what the problem was, Howard told the teachers he didn't have one, they did. The teachers tried to bring out his present behavior, and when they could not, they recommended Howard to SOS. SOS is supervised by an aide, who maintains order and keeps the students working on their classroom assignments. When the students in SOS are ready for a reentry conference, the aide contacts a counselor or principal.

In conference, Howard admitted being disrespectful to the two teachers and stated that he could have gotten permission to go to his car from a principal. He was permitted to return to his classes, but before the day was over he cut his world history class. He was back in SOS. After two days he met with a counselor and a commitment was made for Howard to attend world history.

[1] For further information on the Ten-Step Discipline Program, write to Educator Training Center, 100 East Ocean Boulevard, Long Beach, CA 90802.

For nine days he kept his commitment. Every day the counselor attempted to reinforce Howard's responsible behavior. He would see him in the morning or at noon and ask how world history was coming. Surprisingly at this time, Howard made it nine days without an incident, but on the tenth day he skipped a class and altered the roll to show that he was present. Referred to the dean of students, he promptly told her to take a flying leap. He was reassigned to SOS.

As I had known Howard for several years, I decided to meet with him when he indicated he was ready for a conference again. I sensed that he was playing a game. He had all the "pat" answers, yet he wanted to make bargains. He told me it wasn't his fault that teachers picked on him. You'd skip, too, he said, if the classes were as boring as his classes. "If the teacher will do a better job of teaching, then I'll go to classes and behave." When I asked him how he would like to be taught, he told me he wanted to be treated like an adult. I asked him what an adult would do if he thought he had been mistreated. He responded sensibly. I asked whether in real life everyone is treated as they want to be treated. He seemed to realize that teachers would not change their attitudes toward him until he changed. The conference ended with my role-playing with Howard several incidents that could arise in class. He showed me that he knew how to react responsibly to each incident. He then made a new commitment to meet his classes for one day.

I saw Howard for the next five days to reinforce his commitment, each time asking him if he could do it for one more day. I thought the battle was over, but a month later he was back in SOS for three tardies to class. This time he would not make a value judgment, insisting it was his parents' fault that he was late. He walked out of the SOS class three days later.

In the meantime, Howard had been fired from three jobs, all because of a "mean boss."

We called Howard at home each day to ask him how it was going. He would say, "Fine," and hang up. One day, he called and said he wanted to see me. We had a conference and I told him that he could no longer be in the half-day work program for upperclassmen. He stomped out.

The following day, I called him and asked him if he wanted to go to school. He said yes, but *we* would have to change his behavior. The next day he came in for another conference. Did he enjoy what he was doing? He told me that he was ready to come back—he was bored at home. I asked what he could do differently at school to make it. We went through the steps, and his plan was excellent.

But Howard was still making excuses, and if I did one thing right, it was that I never accepted any of them. I always asked him if what he did was responsible.

Howard was fairly responsible until December, when he was caught cutting classes again. He was sent to SOS. After an unsuccessful meeting with a counselor, during which he could not make a value judgment, he asked to see me, but since his last commitment had been to a counselor, I told him he would have to work out his problem with the counselor. Howard remained in SOS ten more days, refusing to have a conference. About once a day I would drop by and discuss everything but his problem. Finally he said, "Let's talk."

Howard and I had become friends and it had been a long time since he had seen the counselor. I decided to change my plan and take advantage of his eagerness to show responsibility. We developed another plan, but this time he was put back in only one class. The agreement was that if he made it in that class for a period of time, we'd put him into another class. By Christmas he was attending all classes.

Howard had managed to keep his grades in the 70s by doing his work in SOS. Each of his teachers had held a conference with Howard at one time or another. Each stayed involved with him and would not allow him to excuse his irresponsible conduct.

I have to admit that Christmas vacation was a relief from Howard. We may never give up, but teachers and administrators need a rest every now and then from all of the Howards. After the rest, we are willing to try, try, and try again.

Howard made it until January 27. He had been skipping homeroom, and on this day he was discovered in the parking lot. During his conference with the dean, he was again asked if what he was doing was helping him. Like most habitually irresponsible students, Howard resented the implication that his behavior was his responsibility.

He said, "Punish me, but don't give me that 'responsibility' bit."

The dean said calmly, "I care too much about you to allow you to be irresponsible. You have too much potential as a future citizen." Howard walked out of the office. The dean found him in the Commons area and gave him an option—go home, or let's talk. Howard went home.

At this point it would have been easy to give up on Howard. The time we were spending with him was valuable. However, what better way could we have spent the time?

In a conference with his parents, we asked that they put him to work around the house. They were asked not to bring up the subject of school and were very cooperative. Three days later, the dean called Howard. When the word "responsible" was mentioned, Howard cursed the dean. The dean said calmly, "Let us know when you are ready to work this out," and hung up.

It was February 26 when Howard finally came to see the dean for a conference. On the way to the office, he encountered his homeroom teacher and blamed everything on her. When I met him later, I had already heard about this.

Howard started to tell me how he had changed. I interrupted, and told him that he was playing games that I did not want to play. He asked me what I meant.

"Howard," I said, "what did you do when you met your homeroom teacher?"

He started to walk away, but I caught his arm and told him to go to the dean's office. The dean, after learning of his behavior, asked him to go back home. He was not ready to be responsible.

At this point, Howard asked, "What do you want out of me?"

The dean said, "I want you to be a responsible student. Stop making excuses. I don't want to hear them."

Howard asked for another chance. The dean asked him to return the next day.

Howard must really have thought everything over during those twenty-four hours. He wanted to get mad at someone, but everyone had treated him with respect, which he had not reciprocated. He knew that the school would not give in, or give up.

Howard did come back. He said he would be responsible, and a plan was worked up, with the emphasis on his schoolwork. He even smiled for the first time in a long while.

Was it all worth all our efforts? Well, anyone who saw Howard's face when he made the honor roll at the end of the six weeks grading period knew the answer.

Howard showed everyone his report card. It was to the credit of his teachers that they allowed him to make up his work and even reinforced him when he completed his assignments.

It was a happy night when Howard, all smiles, graduated. He made a point to come by and see everyone who had dealt with him. He didn't say much, just "Thanks," but at that time I had no doubt that Howard would make a good, useful citizen.

There are many Howards in our schools. They continually test us to see if we care. With patience, we can pass these tests.

25

"I Want You to Keep Me"

A Caring High School Counselor Helps to Turn a Life Around

Suzy Hallock-Butterworth

Out of the general confusion that always marks the opening day of a new school year, I heard someone ask: "Who is the new counselor for kids whose last names start with G through O?" I looked up and saw a girl standing there, bent over, carrying a huge load of books and papers and with a couple of satchels slung over one shoulder. Her shoulder-length brown hair was dirty, and one ear was double pierced. A plump, untidy girl, Stephanie presented herself in an unattractive way.

"Are you Ms. Hallock?"

I nodded assent. "Who are you?"

"I'm Stephanie Newell, and I guess you're stuck with me. The morning notices said to see you if we were interested in working at the Children's Center. What would I have to do?"

Stephanie and I discussed the program, which releases students from school one day a week so they may help brain-damaged children learn to walk, eat, or even play. Our students are trained by staff at the center so they understand the patterning for each child. Their performance is evaluated by the center's staff and by me. They are asked to read selected writings and keep a journal of their experiences, and they are awarded academic credit for their volunteer work. But I hastened to tell Stephanie, "It involves time and responsibility— in short, a real commitment to the children. They become accustomed to certain people and learn to rely on them. If you do have to miss a day because you have a cold or anything else, you'll have to arrange a substitute to go in your place. When you go, you have to be on time. If you go over there, it has to be more than just getting out of school for a day. How does it sound?"

"It sounds okay. I think I can do it."

"Stephanie, what do you think you might do next year? You say you're a senior. Do you ever think of studying special education? I mean, you seem to have an interest in it."

"I don't know. I try not to think about next year. I have to get my stuff together."

"All right. Let's meet and talk about getting your stuff together." Stephanie made an appointment to see me and we began our long relationship, which has now spanned three years. She was in therapy for about eight months.

In an early session, she appeared to blank out. She stared off into space or at the floor. Long pauses would ensue, but these didn't cause me any special discomfort. During those times, I would tidy my desk or glance at my mail. I guessed these lapses weren't real. I suspected she was trying to manipulate me. If she wanted to test my involvement, she would have to put it to a real test and not manufacture one.

Finally, one day she said, "You know, I have times when I blank out."

"Really?" I said. "Tell me about them, Stepha."

She told me that she didn't have definite memories of those times, but that other people had observed her and told her she was sometimes violent and sometimes placid. Stepha expressed a conviction that she was a witch whose soul "tripped out." I asked her whether she had taken drugs before having such experiences. She responded by telling me she "dropped acid a couple times a month and smoked pot several times a day, but this tripping out is different. When I smoke grass, I *remember* it. These other times people just tell me about."

"People like who?"

"Like my mother and sister. Mostly the two of them. Sometimes they see it, but I think there must be other times when they don't see it."

"What do they tell you about those times?"

"They tell me I'm a little crazy. It's like I'm having a bad dream."

"When was the last time this happened?"

"I don't remember. Maybe a year ago, maybe only six months. It doesn't happen very much."

I continued to question her about her activities, diet, and behavior. She didn't eat well and she smoked tobacco constantly. She was eager to discuss the reasons for her symptomatic behavior and negative addictions. She liked telling me about her adventures, which she called "partying," but I didn't show much interest, choosing instead opportunities to validate her when she performed well in class or at the center.

Once I remarked, "Do you think these party adventures are helping you get your stuff together? What are they doing for you?"

"Well, getting high is something I can always do. I mean, I can do it alone or with other people. Before my father committed suicide, I remember always being alone. I still feel lonely. Everything I do, I fuck up. I don't think I could ever pull anything off and make it work." Then came the test for involvement: "Are you going to refer me, too? Last year Mr. _____ referred me to a social worker."

I told her I hadn't planned on making a referral and that I usually didn't make referrals unless the counselee felt comfortable about it, too. I asked, "Are you asking me to refer you or keep you?"

"I want you to keep me," she said. We grinned at each other. Our friendship was cemented.

Teachers and ex-counselors told me Stepha was the kind of person who just "freaked out." Her personality was inconsistent and her academic performance minimal. She had no motivation, very few friends, and a lot of problems. She constantly cut class, was suspended, smoked marijuana in the parking lot and lavatories, and came to school "stoned."

It was in this frame of reference that I abruptly asked her for a plan for the following year. She seemed absolutely shocked. What nerve I had, asking for a plan for next year when she could hardly make it through a single day! She said she wanted to move out of her house because she hated her mother.

We examined several options. If she left, where would she go? She told me about the two times she had tried to move out. Once she lived with a woman who expected her to do housework and care for her dogs. The house was gloomy, and Stepha didn't like the dogs. The other time she arranged a legal guardian for herself, but when the guardian got involved in several escapades, Stepha decided the guardian was crazier than Stepha was herself. Stepha decided that going somewhere else was a good idea, but that it hadn't worked out. We role-played new scripts she could try out with her mother. We talked about getting the strength to stay for this one last year and to leave when leaving is natural for both parents and children.

We talked about the things you cannot change—such as who your parents are, when you were born, and the relative wealth or poverty of your family. I said, "If you could have things the way you'd like them, how would they be?"

She laughed. "I'd like to start over from day one." I noticed about this time (November) that she had started to laugh frequently and that she was developing a genuine sense of humor. She had also begun to wash her hair almost every day.

I continued to be concerned about her weight and her lapses. Now that our relationship was on very solid footing, I asked Stepha to have a complete medical examination, including an appointment with a neurologist, at a nearby clinic.

Results of the testing were significant. The doctor called me, as she did not want Stepha to learn them either on the telephone or when she was alone. We decided I would have to give her the bad news, as we did not think Stepha's mother would be especially helpful. Stepha was epileptic.

Telling Stepha was carefully planned. I wanted the school nurse to join me and bring information for Stepha to take with her and read. We would meet after school so we had unlimited time.

When I told Stepha, I held onto her. "Why me?" she kept saying over and over. "Everything happens to me. Life isn't fair." I agreed.

The nurse and I talked in a positive way, reassuring her that while there was, from time to time, a disturbance in the rhythm of her brain, her intelligence and emotions do not have to be impaired. We said the cause was unknown. We told her she wasn't insane, that epileptics are not necessarily inferior or superior, although many famous people had epilepsy, including Julius Caesar, Peter the Great, and Dostoevski. We told her about psychomotor seizures, which accounted for her inability to remember. The nurse described the electroencephalogram and the medication Stepha would be taking. We emphasized the helpfulness of a well-balanced diet, and we talked with her about abusing her body. I told her that since she would have to take a drug on a daily basis to control the epilepsy and prevent seizures, it made sense to stop taking other, nonessential drugs. "I haven't had any acid since you started working with me," she said.

This session was followed by a period of calm. Stepha was relieved to *know* about her situation. She had, after all, spent hours trying to figure out what was so different about herself.

Shortly after our session with the nurse, Stepha appeared with a medic alert ID bracelet on. "Stepha," I commented, "I am really pleased with the responsible way you're handling your situation. I hope you're pleased about it, too."

"Yeah, it's okay."

We continued to work on a plan for the following year. During the first semester, Stepha had decided college would be the most ideal, but (1) she wasn't sure she would be accepted, and (2) there were no funds to pay for college. Her second plan was to get a job. Her third plan was to run away and become one of the lost children. When she said that, I told her to send me a post card.

One day she announced she was going to kill herself. "When?"

"When I'm twenty-one," she said firmly.

"What are you going to do in the next four years?" We continued to talk about possibilities for college and tried to narrow her interest areas. She was performing well at the center, a positive sign. She was able to make relationships with the children there and keep her commitment to them. Perhaps a career in special education? Toward the end of the meeting, she said, "Do you think I have inherited the destiny to kill myself because my father killed himself?"

"This fall you asked me if you were a witch, and now you're asking me if you'll kill yourself because it's in the stars," I responded. "Stepha, the only star I see for sure is in your right ear. We could spend a lot of time pondering the imponderables. Let's do that after you get those ten letters to colleges in the mail."

She sent inquiries, visited campuses, and talked about the pros and cons. She applied and was "conditionally accepted," since her grades were so uneven.

Then we began the long search for money. She filled out applications, at first with great dependency but later with increased autonomy. At first she was eager to have me do this for her. I refused, but I did offer to help "demystify" the process for her. We went over the first form together and she realized she really could do it herself. We put together a financial plan, which included Social Security, veteran's benefits, summer earning projections, a job on campus, and a basic education opportunity grant.

We had a big plan, and it was feasible. It appeared that Stepha was really going to leave home under honorable circumstances. It was likely the money for college could be found. Her grades were better. She looked better. At this vulnerable point, Stepha made a gesture to resume her failure identity: she "ran away" with one other student.

She called me long distance. Instead of worrying and saying, "Oh dear, where are you?" I said, "When are you coming back?"

"Tuesday."

"Good," I said. "You're due at the center Wednesday." I knew she was acting out again, and this time she would gain the recognition of her peers.

School was buzzing with gossip about Stepha's escapade. One student said, "Stepha has pulled off something we all think about doing. None of us has guts enough, that's all." I remained unimpressed. Later, as she reflected on this episode as well as other parties, Stepha remarked that while she *seemed* to have fun during those times, the fun hadn't lasted. And while Stepha had gained some recognition in the eyes of her peers, it wasn't the same kind of worth that has lasting value.

"Tell me which has greater value in your life, Stepha, the center or running away? Booze? Grass? Your move toward independence or your escapades?" Apart from this mention of her escapades, I showed no interest in them and never invited her to talk about them.

She lost her open campus privileges at school (not having to account for time during free periods), and while I was not a part of that, I did not interfere with it. In fact, I thought it was appropriate, and when she wailed her predicament, I simply said, "When you do this kind of thing—run away, cut classes—this is what happens to you." The whole notion of losing responsibilities she could not handle was new to her.

She discovered she could prepare excellent meals in her home economics class. We talked about cooking with woks, and I bought her a bottle of tamari. She made stir-fried chicken and mushrooms with white rice. She invited a new friend of hers, the school nurse, and me to the meal. We ate with chopsticks and drank black Chinese tea. Stepha served the meal in a small private dining room off the home economics classroom. We talked about movies and books. Stepha brought us together, was the organizer and creator of our time together, and it was delightful.

She tried to drop a class and I suggested it was a bad idea. She had a commitment to the class and to the teacher. She said she didn't like one student, who "bugged" her. On a particularly busy day when I could not see her, she wrote the following note:

Last night I asked Mom if I could use the car—all was great. When I got up in the morning and got ready to go, my sister got pissed cuz I was taking the car and she wanted a soda. I could stay and wait for the store to open. I would have been late for my appointment. Then she started giving my mom a hard time about not having the car. In turn Mom got on my case about several things besides the car. And Fran was shitty when I got home in the evening. I didn't even feel welcome and I do live there.

Friday I told Mom I got on Honors so the insurance rates for me on the car would go down. She says good. She says let me see the report card. So I show her the report card and she gets on my case about being tardy 13 times.

I remember the night I got out of the hospital when I went for those tests. I figure it would make her happy if I cleaned the kitchen and put the dishes away and wash the dirty ones. What did she do? Bitch because I didn't make her dinner.

It doesn't matter what I do—it's not right or good enough. There has to be a way out.

I guess I would like to stay in Mr. Holden's class for the half year and receive the credit. I know you'll help me find something for the other half, and something has to work out as far as that _____ kid.

Since we had had many talks about what Stepha could do to enhance her home situation, my response to Stepha was to commend her on her decision to remain in the course. I noticed that her writing was clever, well organized. So when Stepha called one Saturday, in a typical swing, saying she was shaky, depressed, and scared, I asked her to write it all down and see me Monday morning. The account read:

Nothing was really as it appeared to be, nothing at all. The sun was so bright and gave a feeling of warmth which made the sky sort of smile, but this was not real, and it was cold out. The mountain seemed dead in that gray and white coat, but I knew it was very much alive.

The feeling of coldness outside gave the people a look of coldness, but they were very warm indeed with the Christmas spirit in them. I visited

some friends and I laughed and joked with them, but inside I felt very sad
and angry with myself.

On the way home the sun became a fiery orange and gave the mountains
a fiery red effect, and as I went over the mountain, I was to be deceived
again as the mountains went back to their dead gray color. I was home,
and nothing was really as it appeared to be, nothing at all.

We talked about the quality of her writing, the nature of perception,
and the use of symbolism. I told Stepha I had been an English teacher
and a feature writer for a newspaper, and I thought her writing was
good enough to help someone else.

I asked the learning specialist at school whether Stepha could tutor
a younger student in English composition or spelling. The specialist
arranged it and matched Stepha with a junior high student who was
experiencing difficulty in English. Stepha was asked to keep a written
journal describing her work with the student. Gradually the specialist
began using Stepha as an assistant in a spelling class. My folder on
Stepha contains the following note from the specialist:

> Stepha is terrific. I couldn't manage a double spelling session without her.
> . . . She's a great asset to me.

Stepha was beginning to have some real successes. The specialist
told Stepha she had earned academic credit as a tutor.

In her session with me, I tried to help Stepha open up her world
more and more. I read the course list for her science fiction class
so that we could discuss *Childhood's End* and other futuristic novels.
She still wanted to talk about suicide, and we discussed the concept
of a soul. I told her about Kubler-Ross's works *On Death and Dying*
and *Death: The Final Stage of Growth.*[1] She brought in a copy of
Journey to the Other Side[2] and I lent her my copy of *Life After
Life.*[3]

Early in spring, a college student whom she knew committed suicide by slitting his throat. Stepha was depressed. When she told me
about it, I told her I knew it was difficult, but it was his choice and
an irreversible one.

Despite this setback, several of her teachers commented about the
improvement in Stepha. An ex-counselor told me Stepha appeared
"almost pretty." But while she was walking more confidently and

---

[1] Elizabeth Kubler-Ross, *On Death and Dying* (New York: Macmillan, 1969); *Death:
The Final Stage of Growth* (Englewood Cliffs, N.J.: Prentice-Hall, 1975).

[2] David R. Wheeler, *Journey to the Other Side* (New York: Ace Books, 1977).

[3] Raymond A. Moody, Jr., *Life After Life* (New York: Bantam, 1976).

holding herself erect, she hadn't lost much weight. I still considered her a high-risk counselee.

In May Stepha tried out and got a part in the senior play. She literally brought the house down and stole the show. She had finally earned the right kind of recognition from a very large group of people. Her home ec dinners were admirable and touched a few people, her tutoring was excellent and reached a few more people, and now the play had reached hundreds of people. The successes had a snowball effect. Stepha built a puppet theater complete with red velvet curtains and handmade puppets as extra credit for an art appreciation project. In June, she received notification that she had qualified for a grant of $850.

Third-quarter teacher comments include:

I feel that Stepha has grown up considerably in the last year. She follows through meticulously with assignments. She contributes ideas for projects to the class and then helps to carry them through. She communicates well, is friendly and thoughtful of others. She has a sense of humor and is developing a philosophy I enjoy! [Home economics teacher]

She is warm and sympathetic and enjoys other people. She does take responsibility now, but still doesn't shoulder too much. She seems extra mature now. [Art teacher]

Stepha has improved to the point one is tempted to believe that the age of miracles is not over. There is plenty of room for improvement—but she has taken giant steps! My hat is off to her! She has become much more thoughtful of others, careful about herself, is essentially friendly, and trying to be positive. [Art appreciation teacher]

One morning a greeting card appeared in my mailbox. It read:

> You listen to so much more
> Than I can say.
> You hear consciousness.
> You go with me where the words
> I say can't carry you.
> —Kahlil Gibran

Inside it simply said, "Love, Stepha."

Stepha's therapy program was one that encouraged her to deal with the reality of her life. I hoped to help her open up her world so she could make a commitment to stay in it and make a place where other people would be drawn to her and comfortable with her for long periods of time. I hoped she would develop self-discipline, and she now has some, but not a great deal. I know that she became able to form durable, satisfying relationships, that she was able to have fun that was not dependent on drugs or alcohol, and that I watched her grow to be a person worthy of recognition. She still has moments in which she suffers, as we all do, but her life is considerably more positive. She is stronger.

She's in college now, and I still hear from her. In one recent conversation she dropped a little comment. "By the way," she said, "I've stopped smoking. Thought you'd like to know." She also said that things were good with her mother. "And oh yeah, I wanted to tell you that we went to English class the other day and the professor said to write in a free way, whatever came to mind, for an hour. At first it was hard and then it was easy. Today he read my composition to the class. Can you believe that?"

I believe it.

26

"I Hate School"[1]

All the Things a Teacher Can Do

Jean M. Medick

Al, a fourth-grader, was usually soberfaced—in fact, he rarely smiled. He interacted with peers infrequently. He sat by himself or with one long-time friend, Burt, and played only with him at recess. Burt was the only one Al ever spoke to. Al gave the impression that he had given up on school. He was withdrawn, spoke little, and lacked the usual spontaneity of a nine-year-old. His inscrutable face and lack of involvement in the classroom caused me immediate concern. I also suspected that he was suppressing a lot of anger. He chose to sit in the corner farthest from my desk—sometimes with his friend and sometimes alone. It seemed to me that he just wanted to fade into the wall.

Interaction with me at first was zero. Al rarely participated in class-room activities. He never asked me questions, volunteered informa-tion, or spoke in discussions or classroom meetings. When I made a point of speaking to him, he answered softly, "Yes," "No," or "I don't know." In classroom meetings when I would ask him if he would like to share his thoughts or opinion, he always said, "No," emphati-cally, revealing a bit of hostility. He avoided eye contact with me and avoided all interaction with any adults in school.

At recess Al and Burt giggled, whispered, or talked softly with one another, and then bugged their classmates by snatching hats

[1] This chapter, with a few changes, is from *Effective Classroom Strategies for Hostile-Aggressive, Passive-Aggressive and Withdrawn Failure-Image Children*, Occasional Paper no. 30, Institute for Research on Teaching, Michigan State University, East Lansing, 1979.

and running off, picking up a ball that came near them and kicking or throwing it away from the others, kicking down a snowman or a fort that kids were building, or by teasing and taunting. Often Al and Burt would go in the bushes and come dashing out to do something foolish and then run away. Students frequently complained about their behavior.

Occasionally, a fight erupted at recess or in the halls when I wasn't around. I would hear about it from another teacher if kids in my room were involved. If Al was implicated, his face registered fear. I do not think he ever got into a fistfight in school. He was careful and not overly aggressive but was often part of the fringe group around two kids who were fighting. He would chant, along with the others, "Fight! Fight! Fight!" If the "group" fighting and the surrounding fringe element were sent to the office and Al was included, he nearly went to pieces. Thinking his parents might be called and told that he was misbehaving, he was terrified.

At first there was no way for me to interact with Al. The distinct message I was getting from his body language was "Leave me alone— go away." I said hello to Al every morning as he came in the room, but for at least a month he gave no indication that he heard me. After a while he'd look at me but say nothing and go to his seat. Eventually he began to show recognition that he had been greeted, and perhaps two months into the year he finally said, "Hi." I made a point of talking to him briefly every day during class—commenting on what he was doing—especially writing or drawing, reinforcing anything done well, no matter how small. These were very conscious acts. I was trying to develop a friendly relationship with Al and to initiate conversation hoping he would respond.

Academically he did little and didn't seem to care. He worked slowly and carefully, but gave up quickly. During the first two months of fourth grade he rarely completed any work and just kept saying, "I can't do it," or, "I don't have anything to write about." He took out books but never talked about what he read. In math he seemed confused and almost paralyzed. His hopeless, resigned attitude was scary. I think he said a lot about himself in the way he wrote his name. Although other words were written normal size, his name was always in tiny letters.

Early in the fourth grade I gave the kids a questionnaire to fill out for the purpose of getting to know them better. It contained approximately fifteen open-ended statements to complete. Some were, "I like to _____," "I don't like _____," "My favorite color is _____," "One thing I'm afraid of is _____." Al left most of the questions blank and answered some with, "I don't know." The question he did answer was "One thing I don't like is _____." In the space that followed he wrote in large capital letters, I HATE SCHOOL. This gave me the first opening for meaningful interaction with Al.

I said, "Al, I noticed that you wrote 'I hate school' in really big letters. You must feel strongly about this."

"Yes, I hate school," he replied with strong feeling. I asked him why. Giggling and glancing sideways at Burt, he said, "It is dumb and boring." This was a beginning.

I thought a lot about Al's "I hate school" statement. I asked myself, "What must it be like to have to go to a place you hate every weekday from nine to three-thirty? What would you *feel*?" From what I had observed, and knowing Al's feelings about school, it seemed to me that he must see himself as a nonentity or a failure. School was a painful experience. Something had gotten badly out of whack. I wanted Al to be able to say out loud, right there in the classroom, "I hate school," and have that recognized and accepted as a statement of reality. I made no attempt to pass over it, change his mind, or talk him out of it.

Sometime later I spoke privately with Al. "Al, I feel bad that school is a terrible experience for you. Maybe together we can make a plan so that things will get better for you. I'd like to know what I can do to make school more fun for you."

He just nodded his head but didn't say anything. I didn't give up.

An important step in my plan for Al was to identify his strengths. His handwriting (printing and cursive) was absolutely beautiful. I would say, "Al, your handwriting is beautiful," and casually show a paper to a group of kids who were near. Others would hear my comments and come over to have a look. I made my comments brief and didn't make a big deal over it. Al was more responsive and showed pleasure—a little smile, brief eye contact with me—after this simple recognition.

It didn't take long to discover that Al had a flair for drawing and all art activities. His drawings were original, highly imaginative, and done with authority. I would ask Al to tell me about his drawings, mentioning specific details, compositions, or color schemes that I liked for this or that reason, and I encouraged him to draw. Drawing excited Al. He didn't like to write, so I said, "Draw what you have to say."

I gave him much time to draw, even during reading and math. I wanted to see what would happen. Drawing was the way I felt I could establish a relationship with Al. He talked freely about his drawing and began looking me in the eye as he spoke, and our conversations provided many opportunities to laugh together. I had fun and so did Al. The group became as interested in Al's drawing as I was, and he obtained much support from his peers. It was the beginning of interaction with his peers on a larger scale.

You may wonder if the other children resented the fact that Al had so much time to draw. Occasionally a child did ask why Al got to draw so much. I would say, as friend to friend, "I think Al needs to draw a lot," or, "It makes him feel good about being in school. He's starting to smile more." By using the principles of reality therapy in the classroom, I am able to work simultaneously with each child so that he or she is recognized individually and feels special. Regular classroom meetings enable the children to become aware of one another, to understand that each one of them has special needs. In a schools-without-failure classroom, children quickly learn to care about their classmates' problems. Feeling cared about themselves and knowing that I want each of them to succeed, they become quite generous in helping each other. Caring and awareness from their peers is what helps children to change their behavior. No teacher, no matter how much he or she cares, and no matter how exhaustive his or her efforts, can bring about this change alone.

It was easy for all of us to admire Al's artwork. It was good. The art teacher often selected Al's work for special exhibits. But I found something else particularly interesting—the theme. It was all violence—torture chambers with an infinite variety of torture devices; war, complete with planes, bombs, cannons, machine guns, rifles, and wounded and dead soldiers; and car accidents or junk yards filled with wrecked cars. The war theme is a favorite for fourth- and fifth-grade boys, but most use a variety of themes in their free-time art work. Not Al. He portrayed only violence, gleefully.

The war and violence theme again appeared consistently when Al started to write. He was very interested in the Mafia and wrote a composition about a gang slaying. When I read it I found it confusing—incomplete sentences, little punctuation—so I asked him to explain it to me. He did so, with considerable enthusiasm and giggling. He thought it was funny, and so did the other boys. I think Al thought I was going to preach to him about the theme. I ignored the giggling and Al's obvious embarrassment and proceeded to review the structure of the writing and his choice of words. I asked him if he could think of a more specific word here and there that would provide sharpness or add color to the writing. One sentence I remember. "There was a pool of blood on the floor." I asked Al if he could describe that more vividly for the reader. He added "red" in front of blood, and after more questions from me the sentence expanded to "Bright red blood oozed from the hole the bullet had made as it shattered his face, making a big puddle on the wood floor." He really got into that sentence, and he walked around reading it!

I asked him, "Al, are you interested in the gang-slaying kind of thing?" He said yes—that he had read something about Al Capone. I suggested we talk with our librarian and see if she could locate some books about the Al Capone era and organized crime during the 1920s and 1930s.

Al was delighted and intrigued when the librarian located several books he liked. He would bring these books to my desk and show me pictures of various outstanding criminals, telling me what they had done and what had happened to them, giggling at first, but more seriously as time went on. I was saying, "It's okay to be interested in gangsters and their activities," and by encouraging this interest getting him to do more reading and writing. He was also talking to me more and more and coming close to me (physical distance).

Initially, his writing didn't make a lot of sense. With each composition I asked him to explain it to me a little more, and as he talked I'd say, "Oh, let's put that in," and I'd squeeze his spoken word in between the lines. Gradually his interest grew in making his writing clear to the reader and selecting just the right details. He began asking me to help him find the right word and check out a paragraph to see if it made sense before continuing. Other kids loved his gangster stories, and Al's interaction with the boys increased.

I asked Al if he would be willing to take charge of the handwriting program. Three times a week we watch a three-minute cassette that has no sound but shows a hand tracing the letters to be practiced. Following each cassette, the children complete a practice sheet. Al was eager to take charge of this project, and he did a fine job. To increase involvement in classroom life I asked Al to deliver messages, get supplies from the office—lots of little things to help him feel that he was contributing.

Al and his friend, Burt, were in charge of cleaning erasers once a week for the third floor. They'd collect all the erasers, clean them, and then bring them back to the individual rooms. This activity increased Al's involvement and verbal interaction with other adults in the school in a responsible way.

Within the classroom I arranged for Al to work with small groups of different children in various science, social studies, and language arts activities, sometimes with his friend and sometimes not.

Classroom meetings provide a wonderful way to involve children, like Al, who are withdrawn or isolated. Although he rarely said anything, there were opportunities to recognize him in different ways. At least once during each classroom meeting I would say something like, "Al, is there anything you'd like to share with us?" or, "Al, I notice that you've been listening very carefully to the discussion. I'd be interested in hearing what you think."

He usually said no, with or without giggles, but he had been recognized. Later on in the year he would occasionally say something, prefacing his remarks with, "This is dumb, but . . ." or, "Well, I don't know if I should say this because it's probably stupid . . ." with giggles, and I would encourage him to share his thoughts.

During fourth grade I talked openly with Al and Burt about their immature behavior at recess. I told them what I saw them doing and asked them if it was helping them. They'd say, "No-o-o," in a goofy kind of way and start giggling, but it wasn't until Al was a fifth-grader that I was able to make a lot of headway in this area.

Al's mother attended the first parent conference alone. I mentioned his strengths and a few concerns, then outlined my plan for work with Al. I wanted Al's father to hear my concerns firsthand, and I wanted to assess the way he responded to the school situation, to me, and to my strategies for helping Al overcome his failure image. I requested that both parents attend the next conference, and they did. Again, I mentioned Al's strengths first—talent in art and a beautiful handwriting. The reading test indicated grade-level achievement. I showed them the progress he had made in writing, talked about the positive change in his attitude toward school, and told them that I thought Al was very bright.

Then I proceeded to talk about what needed our concern. I showed them the "I hate school" statement, talked about the withdrawal, inscrutable face, lack of verbalization, and immature behavior at recess. Considerable progress had been made, but we had a long way to go. In math there was still a mental block. I suspected that Al had a lot of bottled-up feelings, which accounted for the fact that his face rarely showed much emotion. Bottled-up feelings come out in some way sometime, usually in inappropriate behaviors. If this problem were not attended to, it would continue to grow and most likely erupt in some kind of explosion in middle school or in increased withdrawal.

I made three recommendations to Al's parents:

1. I told them to encourage Al to talk a lot at home without evaluating or judging—just listen, as much as possible.
2. I told both parents that I thought Al needed touching. Al had made it very clear in the beginning of the year that he wanted to keep a large distance between himself and me. When I came close, he moved away. This is a concern with children of this age. Normally they do not mind a teacher coming within two or three feet of them. When a child consistently moves away from the teacher, this is a problem that needs attention.
3. I encouraged his father, in particular, to spend a small amount of time daily just with Al, doing fun things together, encouraging him to express himself verbally and listening to the feelings behind the words, wrestling with him, putting his arm around him, laughing together.

All through the conference I encouraged the parents to share their thoughts and ideas with me. Neither said very much, but both expressed appreciation for the progress that Al had made already. All in all, it was a pleasant experience and, I think, a profitable one. The parents approved of the strategies I was using and requested that I be Al's teacher for fifth grade.

As the fourth-grade year came to a close, an event took place that I believe was of great significance in Al's school life. Several children had requested a classroom meeting to discuss rearranging the room, particularly the location of the "quiet reading platform." The latter was about seven feet long and four feet wide, stood about a foot and a half off the floor, and was adorned with an old ratty rug and three pillows. One of the children served as moderator of the meeting, and I sat out of the circle and observed. Usually we sit in a circle on the floor for classroom meetings, but for this one the children sat in chairs. Al listened to the discussion for a considerable length of time in silence, as he usually did. After twenty minutes he raised his hand and made a suggestion about where to put the platform. When he made his suggestion he stood up. No giggling, no self-consciousness. He was serious and calm, and he supported his suggestion by summarizing the pros and cons of how this arrangement would allow for maximum choices for desks, audio-center, and other furniture in the room. This kid had not only been listening well, but thinking through how his and other suggestions would affect the entire room setup. It was an excellent plan and received much support from his peers. The discussion continued, and Al contributed three or four more ideas as the children worked through the entire process of rearranging the room. Al was asserting himself with confidence and logic. And what had struck me most was the fact that he stood up to offer his plan. This action said, "I have confidence."

Fifth grade brought other significant changes. I had Al only for reading, writing, and social studies, as he studied math and science with my co-teacher. His artistic talent blossomed. Everything he did in art class was put on exhibit somewhere in the district. The art teacher talked with him at length about his work and encouraged him to take as much art as possible in middle school and high school. This was reinforced by his peers. The kids considered him "their artist." Whenever someone needed a drawing for his/her "student of the week" poster, a book they were putting together for Young Authors' Day,[1] or an illustration for a story, he or she went to Al. He was very obliging. Recognition and the value his peers placed on his talent did much to build Al's self-confidence and sense of self-worth.

Al was talking more often and became totally involved in classroom discussions. He was eager to develop social skills and make new friends. I remember clearly a remark he made that was particularly insightful. We were talking about fighting—why people fight, feelings they experience, alternative ways to work out bad feelings that arise between people. I had asked the question, "How do you feel when you hit or kick or say hurtful things to another person?" Several children spoke, and then Al raised his hand. "I feel okay right afterwards, but later on when I'm lying in bed in the dark, I feel real bad and I wish I hadn't done it."

Socially Al began to branch out. He began making new friends and entering the football and kickball games at recess. It was very clear that Al wanted to be an active and accepted part of the fifth-

[1] Sometime in April, all fourth- and fifth-graders in the East Lansing Public Schools gather to hear a noted author of children's books speak and to share, in small groups, books they have made.

grade boys' group. This caused Burt much anguish, and he tried to prevent Al from accomplishing the social expansion he wanted. Burt put a lot of pressure on Al not to join in the games at recess. Then the two of them would proceed to cause trouble at recess through their immature, annoying behavior.

This problem was my first priority with Al and Burt in fifth grade. I talked with both of them privately about it, first telling them what I saw them doing and how it affected their classmates. Then I asked them to evaluate the behavior. "Is it helping you?" At first they'd laugh and say, "It's fun." I'd respond with something like, "It's fun when the other kids think you act like babies and that the stuff you do is dumb?"

As Al and Burt and I continued to discuss their immature behavior, both let go of "It's fun" and "We think it's funny" and began to say things like, "Well, so and so does this and that to me all the time," so I enlarged the discussion to include the kids they named. A lot of grievances (from as far back as three years) were aired and worked through. Once the past history was cleared out of the way, the boys were able to move forward and deal more effectively with the present. Al and Burt's behavior did improve, but Al was still very torn about what to do at recess. He would have liked to join the other boys at games, but Burt was putting a lot of pressure on him not to.

One day after Burt had persuaded Al not to play football and other kids were complaining about Al and Burt's disruptive behavior, I called the two boys over. I spoke directly to Al, saying, "I feel sad, really sad."

We had a good relationship by this time, and Al looked at me very seriously as he asked, "Why?"

"Well, you've been doing such terrific things this year—behaving maturely, working so hard and well at your studies, and expanding yourself so beautifully—and now you're back to this nonsense. If Burt chooses to do this, that is his decision—but I just hope that you are not going to let Burt or anyone else decide for you how you are going to behave. I know that Burt is your good friend, but maybe the time has come for you to say, 'I don't want to do this stuff any more. I want to play football.' " Burt turned and walked away while I was saying this to Al. When I finished, Al just stood there hesitantly for a moment, without speaking, and then he walked over and joined

Burt again. The point of this was simply to encourage Al to reflect upon his progress and think about the fact that maybe Burt was making some poor decisions for him.

I was very aware of Burt's problems and at other times was trying to help him. By this time we had developed good understanding. Burt had always been the leader in his relationship with Al, and was normally self-assured and not intimidated by adults. When he walked away without saying anything before I could finish speaking, I knew I had gotten through to him in a way I had never been able to previously. He knew I was not putting him down—we had talked before about his using leadership qualities in positive ways— and he understood that I felt he was trying to persuade Al to join him in foolish behavior and that I was trying to help Al understand this. Truth is sometimes painful, but there comes a time when it is the means through which a child is helped to change his or her behavior.

Not long after this incident I discovered that Burt had "crowd phobia." He was afraid that if he played football, he would be tackled and the kids might pile up on him. During a classroom meeting on the subject of fears, the kids became aware of this and encouraged Burt to play, offering to give him more space. As Burt became more willing to enter the games, one of Al's major problems decreased.

Al's writing steadily improved in fifth grade, and so did his attitude. He began to enjoy writing and voluntarily spent more and more time putting his thoughts and stories on paper. The violence theme gradually disappeared and was replaced by imaginative stories and well-thought-out pieces based on personal experiences. He wrote a beautiful free-verse poem entitled "What a Friend Is," and I had it published in the school newsletter to parents. Gradually he internalized the rules for our written language and began to "care" about correct spelling. The book he made for Young Authors' Day, complete with beautiful, hand-drawn original illustrations, was terrific. Al's mother made a special trip to school to tell me personally that she and her husband were amazed and thrilled by the writing Al brought home and by the book he had put together.

Being able to verbalize feelings had become very important to Al. One thing he told me he liked about school was the freedom to sit wherever and with whom he liked. He thought this was neat. Frequently Al and Burt sat together, and in the beginning they socialized about 99 percent of the time. I told them they had the responsibility to get their work done. "We have rules about getting work done, and you're not following them. Either you work it out or *we* will work it out." I was pretty patient with both of them, since I knew they would not stop socializing and do serious work all at once, but gradually I got tougher.

Once in a while, feeling they had had ample opportunity to work out the problem of excessive socializing and little work, I'd walk over and quietly say, "Separate your desks, boys," nothing more. Burt would be angry verbally. Al would show that he was angry with a red face and set jaw, by shoving the desk and chair and looking like he was going to cry, but he said nothing. He swallowed his anger. I would then say in a friendly way, "When you can show me you're getting your work done, we'll talk about a plan so you can sit together and follow the rules about work."

Gradually, in fifth grade, Al was able to verbalize his angry feelings, and then we were able to make progress in working out mutually agreeable plans for work and socializing. The angry feelings had to be aired, and once we dealt with them, Al was free to approach confrontations more rationally.

I did not know toward what the anger was directed. Part of it was directed toward school, where he teased and annoyed peers, but I suspected there was more to it than that. Afraid of acting out in school, Al released anger through drawing and writing—for a long time. He vicariously enjoyed reading about gangster activities and killings. I never felt any anger directed toward me personally—just a general anger, expressed through an avoidance of responding to authority figures. I think suppressed anger was Al's major problem and the failure image secondary. Al and I never discussed his anger. The strategies I used to get him talking—accepting his feelings about school and letting him know that I wanted to work with him to make school a better, happier place to be, valuing and praising his strengths, and encouraging him to express violent themes in drawing and writing—worked. The need to explore the anger never really presented itself.

Burt, too, after much patient work, learned to recognize and talk about his angry feelings, which helped him move forward. His leadership eventually turned in positive directions and his academic work improved significantly, but that is another story.

During fifth grade, Al continued to be interested in gangsters, but his focus of interest shifted to FBI men. Having two brothers who are FBI agents, I talked to him about my brothers' work. He began reading everything we could get hold of on the FBI. Even after Al went to middle school, if I read an article in the paper about FBI activities, I often phoned him to alert him, and he always showed appreciation and interest. I wouldn't be at all surprised if Al joins a law enforcement group when he gets older—possibly the FBI.

Al and I developed a fine relationship during his fifth-grade year. He talked with me freely and spontaneously, approached me frequently for help or to show me what he was doing, and he returned my hello each morning with a "hi" and a smile. He didn't mind my coming close, and when he came to my desk, he stood very close to me. I could put my hand on his shoulder when we were talking or around his waist when explaining something to him at my desk. He smiled a lot and was always eager to tell me about interesting things he was doing outside of school. We were good friends. Frequently, he hung around after school to talk or continue working.

It was during Al's fifth-grade year that I discovered his ability to organize and manage. He set up, stocked, and managed the art center. Periodically all of us cleaned up and reorganized the classroom. Al volunteered to take charge of these large-group work details, and he was terrific at it. He worked beautifully with his classmates, enlisting their suggestions, working out the plan of action with them, and then dividing up the tasks. He was a smooth, intelligent, and diplomatic manager.

I learned about another side of Al through a classroom meeting in which power was discussed. In his chosen peer group of "athletes," Al was recognized as the comedian—the one who made them laugh. This was a role he fulfilled out of my hearing and sight.

During a period of two years Al changed from a silent, withdrawn failure-image student who hated school to a verbal, involved, successful student and socially accepted and admired member of his chosen peer group. On the Stanford Achievement Test, administered at the end of the fifth grade, he scored at grade level 8.2 in reading comprehension. But what was equally important to both of us was that for Al, school had become a comfortable and happy place to be.

List of Contributors

William J. Abbott
Assistant Principal, Stonewall Jackson
  High School
Manassas, Virginia

Gary Applegate, Ph.D.
Private practice
Faculty, Institute for Reality Therapy
West Los Angeles, California

Pat Baldauf
Private practice
Associate, Educator Training Center
Altamont, New York

Bart P. Billings, Ph.D.
Private practice in marriage, family,
  and child counseling
Clinical Psychologist, University of
  California Davis Medical Center
Sacramento, California

D. Barnes Boffey, Ed.D.
Private practice, Norwich, Vermont
Director, Teacher Education,
  Dartmouth College
Hanover, New Hampshire

Bill Borgers
Consultant, Educator Training
  Center
Austin, Texas

William L. Cottrell, Jr.
Director of Patient Education
  Programs, Austin State Hospital
Austin, Texas

Edward E. Ford
Private practice
Faculty, Institute for Reality Therapy
Scottsdale, Arizona

Gerald B. Fuller, Ph.D.
Professor, Psychology Department,
  Central Michigan University
Mt. Pleasant, Michigan

William Glasser, M.D.
President, Institute for Reality
  Therapy
West Los Angeles, California

Melvin L. Goard
Director, Oklahoma County Juvenile
  Bureau
Oklahoma City, Oklahoma

E. Perry Good
Private practice and consultant
New York, New York

Suzy Hallock-Butterworth
Private practice, Norwich, Vermont
Counselor, Woodstock Union High
  School
Woodstock, Vermont

Ronald C. Harshman
Certified clinical psychologist in
  private practice
Edmonton, Alberta, Canada

309

Richard Hawes, Ed.D.
Private practice
Vice-President, Institute for Reality
  Therapy
West Los Angeles, California

Ann Lutter
Private practice
New England Faculty, Institute for
  Reality Therapy
Norwich, Vermont

Jean M. Medick
Teacher, East Lansing Public Schools
East Lansing, Michigan

Kathleen Kahn Miner
Administrator, Aunt Martha's Youth
  Service Center
Park Forest, Illinois

Judith Jones Nugaris
Reality Therapy Associates of
  Colorado
Denver, Colorado

Gerald L. Schmidt
Principal, Creekside Elementary
  School
Palo Alto, California

Lee M. Silverstein
Private practice, Columbia,
  Connecticut
Director of Human Services,
  Rockville General Hospital
Rockville, Connecticut

William B. Tollefson
Psychologist, Manteno Mental Health
  Center
Manteno, Illinois

Douglas D. Walker
Chaplain, United Ministry at
  University of Southern California
Faculty, Institute for Reality Therapy
West Los Angeles, California

Phyllis Mitlin Warren, J.D.
Private practice, Olympia Fields,
  Illinois
Program Coordinator, Aunt Martha's
  Youth Service Center
Park Forest, Illinois

Robert E. Wubbolding, Ed.D.
Director of Tri-State Center for
  Reality Therapy
Professor, Department of Guidance
  and Counseling, Xavier University
Cincinnati, Ohio

For additional information on reality therapy, contact one of the above people or write the Institute for Reality Therapy, 11633 San Vicente Boulevard, West Los Angeles, California 90049.

Books by Contributors

BORGERS, BILL. *Return to Discipline*. Austin, Tex: Privately printed, 1979.

FORD, EDWARD E. *Why Marriage: A Reality Therapist Looks at Married Life*. Niles, Ill.: Argus Communications, 1974.

FORD, EDWARD E., and ZORN, ROBERT. *Why Be Lonely?* Niles, Ill.: Argus Communications, 1975.

FORD, EDWARD E., and ENGLUND, STEPHEN. *For the Love of Children*. New York: Doubleday & Co., 1977.

———. *Permanent Love*. Minneapolis: Winston Press, 1979.

GLASSER, WILLIAM, M.D. *Mental Health or Mental Illness?* New York: Harper & Row, 1961.

———. *Reality Therapy*. New York: Harper & Row, 1965.

———. *Schools Without Failure*. New York: Harper & Row, 1969.

———. *The Identity Society*. New York: Harper & Row, 1972.

———. *Positive Addiction*. New York: Harper & Row, 1972.

KARRASS, DR. CHESTER, and GLASSER, WILLIAM, M.D. *Both-Win Management*. New York: Lippincott, 1980.

MEDICK, JEAN M. *Effective Classroom Strategies for Hostile-Aggressive, Passive-Aggressive and Withdrawn Failure-Image Children*, published as Occasional Paper no. 30, Institute for Research on Teaching, Michigan State University, East Lansing, 1979.

SILVERSTEIN, LEE M., BRETT, JON; and ROBERTS, LINDA. *Consider the Alternative*. Minneapolis: Comp-Care Publications, 1977.

NOTES

NOTES

NOTES

NOTES

NOTES

NOTES